MW00988435

Interpreting Matthew

WATCHMAN NEE

Christian Fellowship Publishers, Inc.
New York

ISBN 0-935008-71-3 Cloth
ISBN 0-935008-72-1 Paper

Available from the Publishers at:

11515 Allecingie Parkway
Richmond, Virginia 23235

Printed in the United States of America

TRANSLATOR'S PREFACE

In the providence of God, the Gospel of Matthew heads the twenty-seven books of the New Testament. It serves the same purpose as Genesis does to the thirty-nine books of the Old Testament. It is the seed plot of the entire New Testament, and it introduces the rest of the books therein. For this reason, it is imperative that God's people have a good understanding of this book. It is the book of the King and of His kingdom. This is the gospel that "shall be preached in the whole world for a testimony unto all nations; and then the end shall come" (Matt. 24.14). Satan knows the significance of this gospel, so he tries every means to keep it unknown or misunderstood throughout the Church age. Now we are living at the end of the last days. The message of the King and His kingdom is not just relevant to our days, it is also urgent to our understanding so that we as God's children will be better prepared for the manifestation of the kingdom of the heavens as well as be effectively used as instruments to usher in His kingdom.

Throughout his ministry Watchman Nee gave several studies on the Gospel according to Matthew. Early on, in the mid-1920s, from 1924 to 1926, he prepared some notes on Matthew chapters 1 and 2 only and had them published in the *Morning Star* magazine by the Morning Star Publishers, Chefoo, China. Then, in his early ministry in Shanghai, from 1927 to early 1935, he held a protracted study with the saints on Matthew, the longhand notes of which are published in English as: *The King and the Kingdom of Heaven.** Finally, he gave another study on Matthew in

---

*Available in English under the title, *The King and the Kingdom of Heaven* (New York: Christian Fellowship Publishers, 1978). Translated from the Chinese.
—*Translator*

Shanghai between 1950 and 1952. Full notes were taken, but the manuscript was never finished nor published. All this indicates how important it was to Watchman Nee that the message of the King and the kingdom be proclaimed and understood.

This present volume includes both the author's last study on Matthew (1950–52) as well as his earliest notes on this Gospel (1924–26). Part One gives his matured view, while Part Two presents his earliest study. These two studies have been put together purposely in order to illustrate the progress our brother made — from knowing the letter of the word to entering into the spirit of the word while still keeping to the letter. This ought to be true in the study of any of the sacred letters.

May God, who mercifully preserved these manuscripts, use this book to bless His children.

CONTENTS

PART ONE

THE LAST STUDY ON MATTHEW*

---

*Part One contains the notes taken from the study on Matthew given by the
author in Shanghai from 1950 to 1952, up to the time of his arrest.† He had
actually finished chapter 17, but unfortunately the notes which the present
publishers have obtained cover only to the beginning of chapter 12, but are
nonetheless complete. The manuscript had been copied by many hands, and,
thank God, it was preserved at great risk through the period of the Cultural
Revolution of the Chinese Communist regime and only recently came to the
publishers' hands. The study is invaluable. It represents the matured view
of the author, and constitutes the very last of all the many Bible studies he
had held with the saints.—*Translator*

---

†For more information on the author's arrest, trial, imprisonment, and even-
tual death in 1972, see Watchman Nee, *Gleanings in the Fields of Boaz* (New
York: Christian Fellowship Publishers, 1987), particularly pages 135–6.—*Translator*

Introduction

How to Interpret the Bible

There is a special something behind God's word. To rend the veil and open it so that what lies behind is seen — such is called revelation. It can also be called interpretation. Without the latter, neither you nor I will receive much benefit. To study the Bible, interpretation is absolutely necessary. We cannot be lazy; we must seek the inner thoughts.

Reading the Bible with an idle mind does not require much time. Brethren like that probably number about half of God's people. And the nearly total of the other half possess a wild mind. Both kinds of brethren are unable to truly study the Bible. For the word of God is fine and delicate. It will be damaged when handled by such a rough approach.

Young brothers and sisters must learn to be diligent in studying the Bible. Let us ask God to deliver us from our wild and rough thinking. Let our thought be neither overmuch nor too limited but just the right amount. For the kind of Bible which is read depends upon the kind of person who approaches it.

Now the Gospel of Matthew is the most difficult portion to study among the entire contents of the New Testament. It is ten times more difficult than the Book of Revelation. Yet, there is a special purpose in taking up Matthew for study. It helps us to learn how to think and how to ask questions. To fail to ask what *needs* to be asked reveals ignorance; and to ask what should *not* be asked undermines the Bible. We must understand the principles of interpreting God's word.

The Gospels

The four Gospels were written by the Evangelists whose Gospels bear their names. Matthew was an evangelist, and hence the Gospel according to Matthew was the particular gospel he preached. These four Evangelists presented all the things concerning the Lord without any reservation or consideration. What, especially, Matthew, Mark and Luke wrote is more or less the same. Why, then, were there these three Gospels instead of just one? For it would appear as though there is much repetition in these three books. Yet, with John's Gospel, we have four separate Gospel narratives. And what John recorded in his narrative turns out to be quite different from the others.

Although the first three Gospel accounts might record the same historical facts, God has nonetheless ordained to have all three. It is therefore clear that God's decision was not based on historical facts but on something else. Many, in studying these three Gospels, pay attention to the similarities and dissimilarities among them. Yet this is going about it in the wrong way, for the purpose of these three accounts is not grounded upon history.

The history in them may be the same, the story may be alike, but God still desired to have all three. If the reason lies not in history, it probably rests in the Lord himself. For the history— the story— is the Lord's. Therefore, it will be wise to pay attention to the Lord, to turn our thought towards Him. The Lord Jesus is not a simple person: He is a multi-faceted Man: consequently, it requires a multi-faceted Gospel presentation to understand this special One. And hence, these three Gospel narratives present different facets of this Man's personality. Each book has its own special emphasis.

All four Gospels speak of the life of the Lord Jesus. God's life has two essential qualities: one is light, the other is love. So that the life of the Lord Jesus likewise has these two fundamental essences. We may therefore say that the Gospel according to John exhibits the life of the Lord as love, while Matthew, Mark and Luke disclose His life as light. In John, the Lord declares God himself, who is love. In Matthew, Mark and Luke, He exposes all things, since "everything that is made manifest is light" (Eph. 5.13b).

In addition, it needs to be pointed out that Matthew reveals the Lord as king; Mark, as servant or bondslave; Luke, as man or priest before God; and John, as deity. These four aspects are the main presentation of the Lord on earth. At the very threshold of the New Testament we see the four Gospels as four pillars. The lack of any one of the four considerably reduces our knowledge of Him. The glorious King, the lowly Servant, the perfect Man and the perfect God are the four aspects of Him that we must comprehend. We are told in Ezekiel that the cherubim have four faces. We note in Revelation that there are four living creatures with faces, respectively, of a lion, a calf, a man and a flying eagle. Three are on earth, and one is in heaven. A lion is the king of the beasts. A calf is a most serving of animals. Man bears a heavy burden from year in to year out. And an eagle flies high, symbolic of God.

In Leviticus we find that there are five offerings: four are blood-shedding in nature; but one of them, the oblation, is non-blood-shedding. Ignoring for the moment the oblation, the other four offerings can be designated as the burnt offering, the peace offering, the sin offering, and the trespass offering. These four have their representations in the four Gospels. For example, the characteristic of the burnt offering is to obtain full acceptance of God: it is an offering of consecration: and hence, the Gospel according to John addresses the Lord as the beloved Son who satisfies God's heart. The Gospel according to Luke features the Lord as a Man who is in perfect harmony with God, and it stands therefore as the representation of the peace offering. Mark presents Christ as the sin offering, whereas Matthew depicts Him as the trespass offering. In Mark, Christ's death is primarily for the sake of atoning for sin. But in Matthew, His death is to satisfy the righteous demand of God. In their accounts, both Matthew and Mark record the word: "My God, my God, why hast thou forsaken me?" (27.46b, 15.34c), since these two books are for dealing with the matter of atonement. Luke and John, on the other hand, do not include this word, since they are not principally concerned with atonement. According to Leviticus the offerings were divided into two different kinds: sweet savor and non-sweet savor. Both the sin offering and the trespass offering are non-sweet savor in character. Matthew is different from Mark in that its emphasis is on "debt"—such, for example, as: "forgive us our debts, as we also have forgiven our debtors" (6.12). In the same so-called Lord's Prayer, Luke uses the word "sins" instead of "debt" (see 11.4). In Matthew there are many parables on debt, because sins in this Gospel are viewed as trespasses. The sins people commit offend God, and hence there is a need for trespass offering. The death of the Lord as viewed in Matthew is to satisfy God's sense of having been offended. In the trespass offering, therefore, not only forgiveness is asked for but also restitution is made: our Lord as presented in Matthew died to repay our debts.

From all this, then, we can see that the history may be quite similar in these three or four narratives, yet the historical Person is multi-faceted.

1 | Division One 1.1–2.23

First Section 1.1–17

The Gospel according to Matthew, as noted earlier, presents the Lord as King.

1.1 "The book of the generation of Jesus Christ, the son of David, the son of Abraham."—There are only two genealogies given in the New Testament. Matthew presents the one which numbers forty-two generations, commencing with Abraham. Its emphasis is on Abraham and king David. Why? Because Matthew speaks of the Lord as a king, and kings have genealogies. Luke gives a genealogy, but it begins with Adam, for there the Lord is presented as a man, and human beings have genealogies which all commence with Adam, not with a monkey. On the other hand, Mark has no genealogy included in his Gospel because there the Lord is shown as the lowly bondslave who has no genealogy to be spoken about. In John, the Lord is introduced as God, and deity, of course, has no genealogy at all.

In the Old Testament, prophecies concerning the sufferings of the Christ (Messiah) form one line; and prophecies about His glory, another line. Each has over one hundred prophecies. For the first time Matthew combines the suffering and the glory in one Christ, one entity. The Old Testament teaches for sure that the Lord is the Messiah of the children of Israel, but it also tells us that He is the Savior of the whole world. As the Savior of the whole world, He could not be restricted to Israel. These two concepts seem to be conflicting, and these two lines of prophecy appear to be irreconcilable. Yet Matthew shows us that the Jewish Messiah has become the Savior of the entire Gentile world. By reading Matthew we come to see how the Lord who is the Messiah to the Jews turns out to be the Savior of the whole world as well, from the King of Israel to the King of the kingdom of the heavens. This is the course of study we must follow. For Messiah in Matthew is—though admittedly very important— only a point in the line.

Futhermore, David is entitled "David the king" in the first chapter (v.6a), thus suggesting that the Lord is truly the Messiah. But the name Abraham is added, and Abraham is for the whole world. If Abraham alone had been mentioned, how could the promise of a Messiah be fulfilled? or if only David the king had been given, the nations would be finished with respect to the matter of salvation. Yet neither the Jewish nation nor the nations at large can be eliminated from view. The "son of David" phrase intimates the purpose of His coming to reign. The "son of Abraham" phrase denotes His coming to die for us who are in the world that we might be justified by faith. For Abraham— called "the father of faith" for the nations—was justified on account of faith, thus signifying the place which justification by faith would have among the Gentiles. So that God wants us to be saved and to submit ourselves under the lordship of Christ who brings to us not only the authority of David but also the redemption of Abraham. The purport of this list of forty-two generations is to be found in *both* Abraham and David. The Lord comes to be the Savior of the whole world as well as to be the King. He is the King of the Jews, but He is also the King of the kingdom of the heavens.

This genealogy, consisting of forty-two generations, God divides into three periods: the first period is from Abraham to David; the second, from David to Jechoniah; and the third, from Jechoniah to Christ. We see election, reign and captivity. Here we are given fourteen generations three times. As a matter of fact, though, in one place three generations have been eliminated, and in another place the nephew succeeds the uncle. Even so, God purposely divided the genealogy of our Lord into fourteen generations thrice over. This indicates to us that He regards the number "14" as quite meaningful.

I personally pay little attention to most numbers, for although some of them are meaningful, others are not. The number 14, however, cannot be treated as having no meaning. 14 is the product of 2 and 7. 2 is the number of testimony in the Scriptures, and 7 is the number of the perfection of God. So that 2 times 7 is God's perfect testimony. 10 is a number of testing. The two hands have five fingers each. There are five wise and five foolish virgins. 4 is the number of creation, for it comes out of 3. The four living creatures represent the created beings, among whom man is the most important. Hence, 4 is the number of man. 10 plus 4 means the created man is being tested.

I prefer to look upon 14 as 10 plus 4, because in Hebrew, as in Chinese, that is how 14 is arrived at. In other words, the generations from Abraham to David are being tested, but in the process there is not to be found among them "the seed of the woman" (see Gen. 3.15). The next fourteen generations are also tested; once again, there is not to be found "the seed of the woman" among them either. But when the third of the fourteen generations is tested, a woman at last gives birth to a Son. One can find in Genesis 3 the first reason why the names of women should be included in this list of generations. This is because God is seeking for "the seed of the woman." One after another passed away till with the last one the Seed was finally found. The created ones were being tested, and all were proven to be sinners. Not a single person was worthy to be Savior. But at the very last, there comes "the seed of the woman" who is not a sinner, but the Savior. He alone can be the Savior of the world.

As intimated a moment ago, three generations — those after Joram — were omitted, for God would be "visiting the iniquity of the fathers upon the children, upon the third and upon the fourth generation" (Ex. 20.5). He had not visited the iniquity to the full measure of the law. The three generations missing between Joram and Jotham are Ahaziah, Joash and Amaziah. This is due to the fact that the wife of Joram (Jehoram) was the daughter of Ahab's wife, Jezebel (see 1 Chron. 3.1-12; 2 Chron. 21.6).

Shealtiel and Zerubbabel succeed each other. The "begat" here does not refer to the birth of a son to the father; rather, it denotes a succession.

We would now study briefly the four women except Mary listed in the book of generations. They are Tamar, Rahab, Ruth, and the wife of Uriah. These four women represent the created human beings who are all sinners. Their histories are not very good. In grouping these women together we must not put Mary with them, for she does not at all belong in that group. These four women are all tested by God. The differences between them and Mary are manifold. All of the four are re-married women, but Mary is a virgin. Of the four, all except Ruth are blatant sinners. Spiritually speaking, to remarry speaks, in the Scriptures, of the believer being joined to Another, who is Jesus Christ (see Rom. 7.14). In that sense all of us believers have remarried. Now the result of the remarriage of these four women brought in Christ. And hence it can be said that these four women represent all who have been tested and have received grace. They signify how people will turn to Christ.

Tamar is the worst of the four women, for she initiated the crime that is associated with her. She, therefore, stands for sin. (In Chinese, incidentally, the word "sin" is made up of "four lawlessnesses"). The first condition for a person to receive God's grace is to acknowledge sin. He who is not sick needs no physician. Tamar sinned and yet she justified herself. This fully exhibits the sin of the world (that of sinning and justifying it by means of clever maneuvering). Rahab stands for faith (see Heb. 11.31; James 2.24,25). Ruth stands for redemption, especially that aspect of it concerning inheritance. Hence, she also represents grace and its fruit, which is inheritance. The wife of Uriah stands for eternal security. Bathsheba was not returned to Uriah after she came to David. We may begin as the wife of Uriah, but we are not to be Uriah's wife for life. After we come to the house of David, we never ever depart from it. For God never sends a redeemed sinner away.

These four, therefore, present the four cardinal points of the gospel. "Who shall lay anything to the charge of God's elect? It is God that justifieth" (Rom. 8.33). What God has given us is eternal life. We condemn ourselves, but God declares His sheep shall never perish. The story of Bathsheba demonstrates how God not only does not cast us out but even purifies and perfects us in His fire after we have repented of our sins.

These four women are all Gentiles. This, incidentally, is a good answer to those who insist that the Gospel according to Matthew is for the Jews alone. These four "grandmothers" are all Gentiles. Though without doubt there is a Jewish line here, nevertheless, God's grace also comes upon the Gentiles. The Gentiles have their special place in God.

We notice that Mary is a virgin. The record does not say Joseph begat Jesus. In the genealogy now before us we see that one generation follows another generation up to Joseph. Then the grammatical structure in the record changes: it reads, "Mary of whom was born Jesus." Clearly paternity is set aside here and a new maternity is brought in. The four re-married women represent sinners because their condition changes from one of badness to goodness as a consequence of their remarriage. This is how their names came to be listed in the book of generations. Only through the virgin, however, is the child born who fulfills "the seed of the woman" promised in Genesis 3.15. In the ordinary way of recording, it is the father, not the mother, who begets the son. But here God causes woman to bring forth the Son. Otherwise, there will continue to be only the seed of men, there will never be "the seed of the woman."

Individually speaking, woman sinned first. Representively speaking, man represents sinners, while woman represents mankind. Had our Lord been the seed of man, He would automatically have become a sinner. Yet being "the seed of the woman," He is a man but not a sinful man.

The prophecy God gave to Jeconiah (Coniah) was this: "no more shall a man of his seed prosper, sitting upon the throne of David, and ruling in Judah" (Jer. 22.30). Joseph is a descendant of Jeconiah. Had Jesus been born of Joseph, He could not have sat on the throne and ruled. For this reason, the Lord Jesus could not have been born of Joseph, but must be born of Mary. He is the only Savior, the One born of God. This is the One whom we serve and worship.

1.1–17 How is this section related to the Lord Jesus as King? How is it connected with the theme of this book? In studying the Scriptures, we need first to find out the theme and then connect every section to the theme. What is the relationship between the list of the generations and Jesus as King? (Jesus is not only the King of the Jews but also the King of the Gentiles. He is to redeem as well as to rule.) In the list of the generations given, it especially makes a point of mentioning "David the king," thus indicating that the seed of David is to be King. Though in chapter 2 we see Herod as king in Jerusalem, the wise men nonetheless asked those at Jerusalem, "Where is he that is born King of the Jews?" (v.2) For the list of the generations already tells us how Jesus is the descendant of the royal family. The Son of David is to be praised.

Second Section 1.18–25

This second section speaks of the birth of the Lord Jesus. We will take up a few points first and then look at their meaning in this section collectively.

"Jesus Christ" is the name used in the Gospels. In the Epistles the name is often "Christ Jesus." These names are distinctive. For the Gospels show us that this Jesus in the flesh is the Christ whom God will establish in the future. So that when we think of the life of the Lord on earth, we use "Jesus Christ." But when we think of His being raised in the Holy Spirit, we use "Christ Jesus." For this Christ is formerly Jesus. One name looks forward while the other one looks backward. We learn in Acts 2 that after the ascension of the Lord, the Holy Spirit came down. What did Peter say to the multitude? The coming down of the Holy Spirit is not primarily for us to be filled with the Holy Spirit; His coming is for the purpose of proving that Jesus is the Christ of God. In other words, the Holy Spirit is poured forth for the sake of Christ, not for our sake. At His ascension, the Lord was made Christ. Then the Scriptures begin to call Him "Christ Jesus." Before His resurrection and ascension, it is never "Christ Jesus" but is always "Jesus Christ." But after resurrection it uses both "Christ Jesus" and "Jesus Christ." The latter refers to His days before resurrection. For this reason, we do not find the phrase "in Jesus Christ" in the Scriptures, only the phrase "in Christ Jesus." This is because the subjective experience of every Christian comes from union with the risen Lord.

In Genesis, there is only marriage; in Matthew there is also engagement. Matthew 1.19 says that Joseph is a righteous man. (Let us here pause to note that Matthew uses especially such words as "king," "kingdom" and "righteousness." Of the four Gospels, Matthew employs the word "righteousness" the most. In the Epistles, Romans uses the word "righteousness" a great deal. But whereas Romans emphasizes "the righteousness of God" Matthew emphasizes the righteousness of man.) Now being a righteous man, Joseph should have stoned Mary to death, but he did not do it. He was thinking of putting her away secretly. Such an attitude is both righteous and merciful. God loves mercy more than judgment. God calls a person with such compassion righteous. He who bears and forbears and is merciful is reckoned a righteous man by God. Yet this kind of forbearance and mercy is not without restriction. For sin must be dealt with, though the extent of such dealing is always tempered, never extreme.

1.20 "When he thought on these things." Let us not be afraid to think. Error comes from not thinking, it never comes from thinking before God. A person who speaks hastily is a fool. The less a person learns, the quicker is he to judge and be critical of others. One of the greatest signs of humility is the fear of being wrong. He who is afraid of being incorrect will naturally think and consider before God. Hence, in deciding many matters, one must spend time in considering before God. How easy it would have been for Joseph to have made a mistake here. We may say that the error was right inside him. But one thing kept him from making a mistake, which was, that he considered before God. Followers of the Lord must be "slow to wrath, for the wrath of man worketh not the righteousness of God" (James 1.19–20). A righteous man not only has forbearance and patience, he also is one who lives before God: he questions his own judgment and feeling before the Lord. Have you been delivered to such a degree as to doubt your own self?

Because the commencement of the New Testament period was not very distant from the conclusion of the Old Testament time, the angel appeared to Joseph here in a dream. In the case of Mary, however, the angel appeared directly to her (see Luke 1.26,28). God used an angel to communicate with man, and even that in the form of a dream. It shows the distance that still existed at that time between God and man. But when the New Testament had progressed to its zenith, someone could say: "I have no commandment of the Lord: but I give my judgment, as one that hath obtained mercy of the Lord to be trustworthy. . . . and I think that I also have the Spirit of God" (1 Cor. 7.25,40). So that we see that the two ends of the New Testament are vastly different from each other. There is progression. To dream is good, but that is only a beginning stage, one that was akin to the Old Testament procedure. The height of the New Testament is reached when a person has been so wrought upon by God that he not only has the Holy Spirit in him but he has also been transformed to be one with the Holy Spirit.

Why does revelation come to Joseph, a righteous man, by the distant way of an angel speaking in a dream? This is to show that revelation comes step by step. It progresses from the extreme outside to the deep inside. This is also because God is giving us a great revelation: "Immanuel; . . . God with us" (1.23). This constitutes the salient point of this section. How did the revelation of "God with us" come? It came through an angel speaking in a dream. "God with us" is the consummation of salvation. God revealed the most intimate message from a distance. The two ends of Christianity are both found in this first chapter of Matthew. On the one side is an angel speaking to man in a dream; on the other side is the reality of "God with us." The starting point of New Testament revelation lies in an angel speaking in a dream, but the end result is to enable all to touch the reality of "God with us." A shallow beginning leads on to the deepest touch. "God with us"—that is the essence of Christianity.

1.21 As indicated earlier it does not say Joesph shall beget a son, but "she shall bring forth a son; and thou shalt call his name Jesus." "Jesus" is Greek; the Hebrew for the same term is "Joshua," which means "Jehovah Savior" or "Jehovah delivers." Here we are shown that this Jesus is indeed "the seed of the woman," who was long awaited for four thousand years. Genesis 3 tells us concerning "the seed of the woman," but it does not inform us at all as to what kind of person "the seed" is to be. It awaits Matthew 1 to show us what kind of man He is.

Let us notice some of the pertinent prophecies of the Old Testament. Genesis 3 prophesies about "the seed of the woman"; Isaiah 7.14 foretells the virgin birth; and Isaiah 53 predicts Jehovah our Savior. Matthew 1 sums up these three prophecies. If the seed of the woman is only a man, he has the possibility of failure. So, Isaiah 7.14 shows us that this seed of the woman is Immanuel (God with us), which means that in Him God and men met. The Lord Jesus is God as well as man, the One in whom God and man are joined in one. His very essence is Immanuel. If only we are in this God-Man, we are saved and eternally secured. Immanuel is the ground of our eternal salvation.

1.22–23 These verses explain verse 21. How is it that Jesus can be Savior? It is because He is "Immanuel." Immanuel is not a corporate entity; Immanuel is a Person. Only Jesus Christ is Immanuel, for in Him alone God and man become one. In Christ, God is with us. In Christ all the saved ones become "Immanuel," that is, God with us. For this reason, salvation is eternally secured. Salvation is God with us. We are saved to such a degree that even as God is, so we shall be like Him. This is called "Immanuel." This is salvation. Henceforth, God's glory is our glory: His destiny becomes our destiny: His security becomes our security. The Lord Jesus came to this world as Immanuel. This makes Him Jesus who shall save His people from their sins: the Seed of the woman—Immanuel—Jesus.

This King is different from all the kings of the earth in that He shall save His people from their sins. Hence, He is called Jesus before He is called Christ. This section tells us what kind of king He is when He came. Unlike earthly kings, He is not to extend his territory but is to save His people from their sins. The word to note in the first section was "king"; in this second section it is the word, "people." The problem with the people is not Roman oppression. Their problem is that they need a Savior King. We thus see the connection of this section with the theme of the Gospel according to Matthew. Jesus is Savior because He is Immanuel. God and man are both in Him. There can be no salvation without Immanuel. For otherwise, how can man ever touch God? In the Lord Jesus, man and God are at last joined in one. The aim of salvation is not in saving man to be innocent and perfect without also establishing a life relationship with God. The point of union between God and man is Jesus. This is called

Immanuel. In Christ, God and man are reconciled. Outside of Christ, God is *not* Immanuel. But in Christ, He *is* Immanuel. Outside of Christ, man is God's enemy. In Christ, he is Immanuel. In Christ both God and man become Immanuel, for God is with us. Anything more or less than this is not salvation.

1.24 After one receives revelation from God, he should no longer doubt or consider. If he does, he will be led into darkness. This is doubting the word of God.

1.25 Christianity is not an ascetic religion. This verse is proof against such a concept. Had God's word lacked this verse, the sexual instinct would have been viewed as unclean.

Third Section 2.1–12

2.1-2 As soon as the Lord is born, His relationship with men begins. How do men react to this King?

This section points out that Jesus came to be King of the Jews, and yet He was unlike all Jewish kings; otherwise, the Jews would not have treated Him in such a manner. Hence, the emphasis is on His being King, not on His being King of the Jews.

In the first verse there is mentioned a king called Herod, an Idumean, a rebellious man who reigned under the Roman Empire. There was therefore already another king in Jerusalem. The Lord came to be King, and yet there was another one who opposed Him. Here came some wise men. In the Old Testament period, aside from the prophets in Judah and Israel, God had also raised up Gentiles as prophets — Balaam, for example. These people feared God, and some even knew God. How did these wise men know that Jesus was born? They saw a star. Balaam of the Old Testament also made mention of a star (see Num. 24.17). God had people in the nations who knew Him, though their knowledge was quite limited. Now as these wise men saw this star, God must have revealed to them that the King of the

Jews was born. As yet no Jews had confessed Jesus as their King, but some Gentiles did. These Gentile wise men of the East declared that the King of the Jews was already born. Thus we see that Matthew persistently indicates to us that the Gentiles also have a part in the Lord Jesus.

Where should the King of the Jews be born, thought the wise men. Human thinking came in. They thought they could not be wrong by seeking Him in the capital. But the direction of the star had not been pointing towards the captial, yet they followed their reasoning. Upon their arrival at Jerusalem, these wise men saw that things were quite peaceful there, and Herod was sitting on the throne. They discovered they had taken the wrong way, so they began to inquire. Later, after they had left Jerusalem, the wise men again saw the star before them, thus indicating that for a period of time they had not seen the star. Whenever we follow reason and mind, God's guidance disappears. Only along the pathway of the guidance of God is there light. The moment we depart from God's appointed way, we fall into darkness. His guidance needs no help from our thought, anxiety or discussion. He will naturally lead us to the place of appointment.

It was the pure mercy of God that these wise men, given Herod's wrath, were able to come out of Jerusalem unscathed and travel to Bethlehem. Note that their guidance was still external. They had not touched the guidance of God's word nor the guidance of the Holy Spirit. There are two different kinds of guidance: the external kind and the kind gained from God's word. It is easy to make a mistake if there is only external guidance. We must therefore learn to be led by God's word as well as by environment. One is not adequate; we need both. Far better, too, if the leading of the Holy Spirit is added to the mix as well.

In verse 2 we learn that the wise men had seen the star and yet inquired of men. This betokened failure. "Where" was not the word to be used by those who had seen the star. However, the people in Jerusalem failed much more since they took no action at all. When Herod the king heard the news, he was troubled, and all Jerusalem with him. Neither Herod nor the people of Jerusalem were willing to receive the Lord Jesus.

2.5 "They" denotes a corporate body, not one individual. They were so familiar with the Scriptures that they could give the answer right away. They knew the verse by heart; yet to study the Scriptures is one thing, to love the Lord of the Scriptures is quite another. These Jews were so acquainted with the Old Testament Scriptures that they instantly recited the pertinent portion from memory: "Bethlehem." Nevertheless, they made no move. From this we can see that there is a great difference between preaching on prophecy and waiting for the Lord's coming. Those who only make research concerning prophecy are at best like these scribes. It is profitable for only a little. It is far better, however, if we can be both the wise men and the scribes. Yet if we can be but one, let us be the wise men rather than the scribes. For at least the wise men went to worship Jesus, but these scribes did not even care to see the Lord, for they had no love for Him. May we cultivate our love towards the Lord.

2.7 Herod was very cautious. He dared not question openly lest it stir up some faith and love in others. How strange that aside from the wise men, none other went.

2.8 Herod told a big lie. This is no surprise, for politicians usually indulge in such conduct.

2.9 How happy the wise men were after they rediscovered the star which they had lost sight of.

2.11 "Into the house" is a different description from those of "the manger" and "the inn" in Luke. For here in Matthew we see that the Lord was the King who received the worship of the wise men from the East. This account in Matthew will not fit in with the record of Luke. Then, too, the phrase "the young child" here in Matthew is also different from that of "the babe" in Luke. Hence, the event of the wise men occurred subsequent to the events of Jesus' birth recorded in Luke's narrative.

These wise men worshipped the young child, not the mother. Let the Roman Catholics beware. Though these wise men from the East had not read the Scriptures, they nonetheless had greater understanding than many Catholics.

"Gold" signifies the glory of God; "frankincense," a fragrant life; and "myrrh," a symbol for burial. This King had three characteristics: (1) He had the glory of being God; (2) He lived a perfect life on earth; and (3) He died a victorious death. In offering these gifts the wise men might not have understood their significance.

2.12 As a consequence of their seeing the Lord, the guidance the wise men now received was much improved. If a person depends on but one way of guidance all the time, it is evident he has not learned much before the Lord. But the more he learns, the more his guidance improves. "Another way"— that is to say, not having to pass through Jerusalem again. It would be a serious mistake to pass that way again. That mistake should not be repeated. After they saw the Lord, worshipped and offered, they received God's guidance to go another route, never again to travel the old path. May God deliver us, too, from making the same mistake twice in our own lives.

Prior to this third section the territory always in view was limited to the land of Israel, but at various points in the narrative we shall see the Gospel according to Matthew breaking out of the Jewish boundary. This third section is a case in point; for it was the Gentiles and not any of the Jews who came to worship the King. Thus this is a breaking out by Matthew of the Jewish boundary. Later on in this same Gospel, we shall see how the Lord is the King of the kingdom of the heavens as well as the King of the Jews.

Fourth Section 2.13–23

This section concerns the flight to Egypt.

2.13 Still once more an angel appeared to Joseph in a dream. For the way of the New Testament is progress from afar to close by. This was the first incident in our Lord's life on earth. In this first recorded incident, God notified Joseph by an angel to take the young child to Egypt. This case was rather special. For God's notification was indeed special, although His way of protection was common. Herod had decided to slay all the male children from two years of age and under. The Lord shared the same place as these two-year-olds. God did not send an angel to protect Him, but told Him to flee. There was therefore nothing special in God's protection. God did not place His Son on earth in a special position. Even as Immanuel, He shared the common experiences of all human beings — including that of fleeing to save one's life. How humble and lowly was His coming to earth! This should draw out our adoration.

The most meaningful thought in the third section was that of "another way," while the most meaningful to be found in the fourth section is that of "be thou there until I tell thee." Each time after receiving the Lord's instruction one must stay to where he has come (the "there") until he is told again. The first move was taken by Joseph after he had been told by the Lord. So would be his second move.

"And he arose and took the young child and his mother by night." Possibly it was the very night on which Joseph had received the divine instruction to flee. Such immediate obedience is most precious.

2.15 "And was *there* until . . ." This was Joseph's obedience to God's order given to him earlier: "be thou *there* until . . ."

2.16 Herod was "exceeding wroth." Man's wrath is of two kinds: one is righteous; the other is selfish, because his objective is not attained. Of ten thousand people, nine thousand nine hundred and ninety-nine become angry for their own selfish reasons. When we get angry, let us ask ourselves if we are trying to save ourselves. Herod's temper burst forth upon finding that his scheme had failed. And as a result, he hardened his heart to slay many people—even all the male children of two years old and under.

2.17 "Then was fulfilled . . ." This fulfillment concurred in spiritual thought to what the prophet had said, though it was not the exact objective of that prophecy. Rachel ought to be comforted, for the Lord was not slain.

2.19 An angel of the Lord appeared again in a dream.

2.20 "Arise and take the young child and his mother, and go into the land of Israel." Verse 15 says: "that it might be fulfilled which was spoken by the Lord through the prophet, saying, Out of Egypt did I call my son." However, Hosea 11.1 alluded to here does not seem to speak of Christ. The primary characteristic of section four is to be found right here. Hosea had spoken of Israel, but Matthew said this event from the past referred to the Lord Jesus. Hosea directed attention to the nation of Israel, but Matthew pointed to the personal Lord Jesus. How is this to be explained? Hosea had said that God so loved the children of Israel—who were nonetheless rebellious and unfaithful—that He called them out of Egypt. In their history, they always failed, being ever rebellious and even inclining towards returning to Egypt. So that on this *one* point of history ("called my son out of Egypt") and not the *entire* history of Israel, reference is made to Christ: it had reference to His personal escape from death. Not the entire history of Israel, but only this one point of their history is Christ's. Such an interpretation of Hosea 11.1 is the only feasible one, and Matthew is right in adopting it.

Do we have any trustworthy evidence elsewhere in Scripture

to confirm this kind of interpretation? Let us look at Peter's
Pentecost message in Acts 2.24–28, where David is quoted from
the Psalms as having said, "I beheld the Lord always before my
face." The "I" was undoubtedly David. But what did Peter say?
David, the apostle noted, was dead and was not resurrected. Then
to whom did this passage refer? In verse 31, we find Peter's interpretation: "he [David] foreseeing this . . ." All the experiences
throughout David's life were his own, yet this one particular experience pointed to Christ, that is to say, to the resurrection of
Christ. Why, then, did David use "I" instead of "He"? Because
in the Old Testament time Christ had appeared many times in
men by His Spirit. So that when David spoke, he did not use
"He" but "I." For at that moment the Spirit of the Lord was in
David speaking.

There are many types in the Scriptures, but some so-called
types are not types at all but are instead the manifestation of
the Spirit of the Lord himself. The coming out of Egypt of the
children of Israel is not a type; it is Christ leaving Egypt among
them. Even though many of David's psalms speak of himself, at
least in this passage the "I" is not David, but Christ. In other
words, the personal history of the Lord had been manifested
through many fragments in the Old Testament; and now, in the
last days, He has made His complete manifestation.

Look at Isaiah 49. The subject is the servant of God. In verse
3, the servant is identified as Israel. In verse 5, we are told that
the servant is the One to bring Jacob again to God and gather
Israel to Him. So that the servant is not Israel, but Christ (as
a matter of fact, verses 2 and 4 can only refer to Christ). One
servant becomes two, and two become one servant. During the
time Israel is the servant of God, Christ is God's Servant in a
portion of it. The Bible says that "salvation is from the Jews"
(John 4.22). In actuality, it is from Christ. Consequently, many
so-called types do not typify Christ; they are instead the very
manifestations of Christ.

Look also at 1 Peter 1.10–11: "the Spirit of Christ which was in them." In the Old Testament period the Spirit of Christ had already touched the prophets. And hence, when the prophets used "I," it was the Spirit of Christ speaking. In the period of the Gospels we see the once and continuous full manifestation of Christ, but in the Old Testament period we see only His many fragmentary manifestations. The coming out of Egypt of the children of Israel was done by the Spirit of Christ, so God said, "Out of Egypt did I call my son."

Consider Genesis 1.26–27. Verse 26 reads "in our image," but verse 27 reads "in his own image." Grammatically speaking, the latter should be "in their own image." Yet the first phrase is plural, the second, singular in number. Is this not surprising? For at the council of the Father and the Son and the Holy Spirit before creation, the word used is "our"; but at the time of actual creation, man was created according to the image of the Son, who alone in the triune God has an image. So that Adam was created in the image of Christ. Christ was not born according to the image of Adam; rather, Adam was created in the image of Christ.

When, as recorded in Psalm 22, David had cried out, "My God, my God, why hast thou forsaken me?", it was the speaking of Christ in him, not the speaking of David himself. Such a thing happened not only in the time of the Scriptures, it happens even today: many times Christ manifests himself in the Church.

"For they are dead that sought the young child's life." Man may be ferocious within a limited period, but time is on God's side. He who dares to resist God shall find his life far too fleeting. History confirms that the Church has always prevailed over those who persecute her.

2.21 The land of Israel has already been mentioned once in verse 20.

2.22 In returning to the land of Israel, Joseph was warned of God in a dream to withdraw into the region of Galilee because Herod's son, Archelaus, was reigning in Judea over the Jews.

The mention of "Galilee" in the Scriptures was often followed by the descriptive phrase, "of the Gentiles" (Matt. 4.15). For it was not only inhabited by the Jews but also by people of the nations.

2.23 "Nazareth" means "sprout." In the entire Old Testament there is not a single place where the Messiah is called the Nazarene. Yet Matthew said: "that it might be fullfilled which was spoken through the prophets . . ." Since Nazareth means a sprout, which is an entity that is exceedingly small, it fits with what Nathanael was to say later about Nazareth, as recorded in John's Gospel, to the effect that the town was greatly depised. The people of that day looked down upon Nazareth, they saying, "Can any good thing come out of Nazareth?" (John 1.46) It was a despised and rejected place, and hence, by extension, the Lord, too, was despised. In the Old Testament there are many prophecies about the shame and reproach which the Messiah would suffer; so in the New Testament period the Lord Jesus was contemptuously called the Nazarene. What the prophets had prophesied about the Messiah being despised and rejected found their fulfillment in His being called a Nazarene by those of the New Testament period. Many passages like Matthew 2.23 have to be understood according to their contemporary circumstances.

The four sections just now discussed constitute the first division of Matthew's Gospel, the primary subject of which was the birth of the King. There then follows a gap of thirty years between chapter 2 and chapter 3. And hence we have placed the third chapter within the second division of the book.

First Section 3.1–12

This section speaks of the preaching of John the Baptist. It is the first section in the second division, but is also the fifth section of the entire book of Matthew.

3.1-2 Concerning John, the first three Gospels call him John the Baptist. Only the writer of the fourth Gospel does not use the title of "the Baptist." The difference is because the writers of the first three Gospels are not John the writer of the fourth Gospel; and hence, in their eyes there are two Johns who need to be distinguished. The father of John the Baptist was a priest, but the son did not function as a priest. The father served in Jerusalem while the son dwelt elsewhere. According to rule, priests ought to be in the temple, yet John was in the wilderness. He preached along the line of the Old Testament prophets, not following the way of the priests. When the nation of Israel was in a normal state, one could witness the priests serving in the temple. But when the nation was abnormal in its condition and therefore unacceptable to God, there would be prophets in the wilderness. This was the situation, for example, with Elijah. It was the way the Lord looked at the prophets, among whom He considered John to be the greatest. John could have been a priest among the people and at the temple, yet he became a prophet in the wilderness instead. Such was what the Lord meant by commanding Hosea to name his newborn son Lo-ammi (Hebrew for Not my people), saying: "ye are not my people, and I will not be your God" (Hosea 1.9). The nation of Israel was thus rejected by God.

The message John preached was as follows: "Repent ye; for the kingdom of the heavens is at hand" (original). Here, the word for "heaven" in the Greek is plural in number. This is therefore the kingdom of the heavens. This kingdom is wholly of God, and all the heavens participate in this kingdom. In the Gospel according to Matthew, this term "the kingdom of the heavens" is used thirty-three times. In the Old Testament, it is never used; nor is it used in other books of the New Testament, though there are similar ideas being conveyed. Consequently, this term "the kingdom of the heavens" occupies a special place here in Matthew.

What does "the kingdom of the heavens" mean? In Genesis 1.1 we read that "God created the heavens and the earth." The heavens and the earth belong to God. This is worthy of all attention. The heavens (in plural number) and the earth are God's. In Genesis 14.19–22 we read that God is the "possessor of heavens and earth" (Hebrew original). From Genesis to Chronicles, God's title is either "the Lord of the heavens and earth" or "the God of the heavens and earth." It was a title which men used at that time to address God. Why? Because up through the time of 2 Chronicles, God had a kingdom upon the earth (though never perfect). God had His chosen people. Hence He was not only the God of the heavens but also the God of the earth. But by the time of Ezra 1.2, His title was changed to "the God of heaven" because the nation of Israel had been destroyed and God had no habitation on earth any longer. He had no kingdom and no people on earth. So that He was thereafter called simply "the God of heaven." This was a noticeable change. It was ever afterwards used continuously by the prophets in exile (for example, see also Neh. 2.4,20). This was a Biblical fact.

In the New Testament we find that the term, "the kingdom of the heavens," suddenly makes its appearance. It cannot be found in the Old Testament, yet this is a continuation of the authority of the heavens spoken about in the Old Testament. Its scope is broader than the nation of Israel, and its nature is more heavenly and more of God. Daniel 2.44 is the only place in the Old Testament where the kingdom established by the God of the heavens is mentioned. It is a prophecy concerning this kingdom of the heavens. In the so-called Lord's Prayer, heavens and earth are mentioned together ("Thy kingdom come. Thy will be done, as in heaven, so on earth"—Matt. 6.10). This means God will regain the control of the earth. The kingdom of the heavens will come upon this earth, and the will of God shall prevail over it. At present God's will is done in the heavens, but it is hindered upon the earth.

The kingdom of the heavens means only one thing: the authority of the heavens shall be manifested on the earth. Do not view the kingdom of the heavens as mere history. For the fundamental aim of God is to gain this earth as He has gained in the heavens. Thus, disobedience becomes the greatest sin. In the Old Testament period, obedience was viewed as the most beautiful virtue. It far surpassed sacrifice (see 1 Sam. 15.22). It alone could bring the kingdom of God down to earth. Regardless how much you labor and toil, you are still a great failure if you do not obey in your heart. For the authority of the heavens is seen in our obedience, not in our works or sufferings or sacrifice. Man's rebellion may be manifested in disobeying God as well as in sinning. Wherever the authority of God is not, there the kingdom of God is absent.

Now John the Baptist came and proclaimed that "the kingdom of the heavens is at hand." This would clearly imply that God had not had His kingdom of the heavens during the Old Testament period. The Baptist declared it was near because in his words that were to follow, he also affirmed that the King was here. What did John the Baptist preach? And how should people get prepared for the kingdom of the heavens? There was nothing profound about it. It was simply to "repent." "Repent" means a change of mind. In the Greek the word speaks not of action but of an altogether different matter. This repentance is related to the baptism of John (the baptism of repentance is different from the baptism unto Christ). What does the baptism of repentance mean? John baptized in the river Jordan which signified death. In John's baptism, therefore, the children of Israel were put to death in Jordan.

Repentance is not linked to Christ, nor does the baptism of repentance join us to Christ. It merely indicates a change in our opinion concerning ourselves. The baptism is unto death. It declares that men ought to die. In receiving baptism, men confess their sins and acknowledge that the wages of sin is death. So that when the people came to John, they in essence confessed that they deserved death. If a person has not changed his thought and opinion about himself, he has not repented. Only by voluntarily taking the place of death and burial is repentance proven.

The kingdom of the heavens begins with John. Its first lesson — that of repentance — must be learned. May we learn the deeper lesson of the cross. May we by the grace of God review this lesson of repentance that we may have a new assessment of ourselves, reckoning ourselves as sinful and dead.

3.3 This was a very good preparation to make ready the way of the Lord. Unless people knew themselves, they would not accept the baptism of John. Thus they would not accept Christ, nor have any relationship with Him.

3.4 This was not the manner of a priest, but the manner of a prophet.

3.5 All those who had changed their evaluation of themselves went forward to receive the baptism of repentance.

3.6 In baptism they stood before God on the right ground of sinners. They abdicated the false position of the righteous —

considering themselves unworthy to be called the children of Abraham — and recognized that they were totally unfit to see God's face. Accordingly, they should not remain on earth to be seen by God but be forever buried in water from the sight of God. Such was the sentiment of the people who received the baptism of John. "No excuse for oneself." You hate yourself to such a degree that you hope you will never be seen again. This proves you have repented. But if you entertain the slightest thought of retaining the good while rejecting the bad, you still have not repented. "Repentance" is not washing hands and feet; it is burying the whole body in water. And if you commence to touch the spirit of repentance in that way, then the kingdom of the heavens is indeed at hand.

In 3.2, to repent is noted as a kind of preparation. As intimated in 3.3, it is making straight the way. Repentance itself is not the kingdom of the heavens; it only helps people to touch that kingdom. Repentance is the foundation of becoming a Christian. The closest word in the Old Testament to expressing the kingdom of the heavens was spoken by Daniel to King Nebuchadnezzar, wherein the prophet said: "thou shalt be driven from men, and thy dwelling shall be with the beasts of the field, and thou shalt be made to eat grass as oxen, and shalt be wet with the dew of heaven, and seven times shall pass over thee; till thou know that the Most High ruleth in the kingdom of men . . . after that thou shalt have known that the heavens do rule" (Dan. 4.25,26). This authority needs to be manifested in our speech, thought, temperament, judgment, inclination and action. The kingdom of the heavens must come to earth and be demonstrated there. Every Christian brother or sister ought to be clear what repentance is. It is a drastic and absolute new judgment on oneself. Otherwise, the heavens will not be able to rule over the Church on earth.

For four hundred years God had no prophet, and there was no word. Now, God spoke for the first time through His prophet John; and the first word was: "the kingdom of the heavens is at hand." The heavens shall rule. What a thunderous voice and message is this! All who love the Lord shall leap for joy at hearing this word. Instantly, there comes a subjective demand: you must repent. What, then, is repentance? Not a change of conduct, but a change of mind. Yet wherein does the mind change? It is a change in self-estimation.

Those who repented confessed their sins and were baptized. The Scripture here puts baptism and repentance together, since the baptism of John *is* a baptism of repentance. The Christian baptism that we know of is a being baptized unto Christ, whereas John's baptism was a baptism of repentance. We have earlier mentioned that to be baptized is to stand in the place of death, thus having no position before God.

3.7–9 "I say unto you." Whenever the prophet used this word, he was speaking with authority. "God is able of these stones to raise up children unto Abraham." Along the river Jordan there were many stones lying about. On the one hand, God brought John to prepare the way of the Lord; on the other hand, He guarded against the misunderstanding of the Jews that because the kingdom of the heavens was at hand the Jewish nation would soon be revived. In the first chapter Abraham was mentioned, and in this chapter he was again mentioned. But here he was mentioned in connection with stones, not with the Jews. By this John indicated that the kingdom of the heavens now being mentioned was not to be viewed as the revival of the Jewish nation. Flesh and blood had nothing to do with Abraham. Those who were born of Abraham might not be his children, whereas those who were *not* born of him could be his children. John injected faith here. For only those of faith could become Abraham's true children.

"Ye offspring of vipers" (v.7). The natural children of Abraham became the offspring of vipers. This was seeing self under a great light. Such a description was not too brutal. How different had the prophet seen the natural here. He who lacks such insight as this cannot be a good Christian. A cup that receives water must be placed under the kettle spout. For the grace of God to come upon him, the receiver of grace must prostrate himself in dust while the Giver of grace sits on the throne. Do not follow people into baptism while your heart says something else. What matters is not what you do outwardly, but what you think inwardly. Do not think you are better than other people!

3.10 This is a most serious and yet exceedingly plain word.

3.11 John baptized with water for the purpose of repentance. He merely called them to repent. Even after a person has the right estimate of himself, he is not yet saved. For the water does not have any mysterious power. Repentance only corrects one's own assessment, but it does prepare him to receive the salvation of Christ. Man must repent before he can receive mercy. Hence faith is positive, while repentance is negative. Repentance causes me to lose myself, but faith enables me to gain Christ. A century ago, a Christian brother once said, Repentance is the impression while faith is the expression. When repentance faces self, one's faith faces Christ.

John said, "He that cometh after me is mightier than I," because that Mightier One was able to raise up children to Abraham out of these stones. Repentance alone is not enough since it only causes us to remember our failure just as we formerly always boasted of our good. Repentance is not the final end; it is but a way that leads us to Christ. It is therefore right for us to consider repentance as the way to Christ, but not right to think of it as an end. John was quite clear on this point. Though multitudes followed him, he understood that his work was but to baptize with water. He had a correct rating of himself: according to Jewish custom, the slaves were to unloose the shoes of the masters. Hence, John was not trying to be humble; he merely had a right estimation of himself. Humility is not maintained by memory. Does a humpback need to remember his hump?

"He shall baptize you in the Holy Spirit and in fire." Here is the difference between the work of John and that of Christ. What is the baptism in the Holy Spirit? And what is the baptism in fire? When the Lord came, He would not only give new life to men, He would also baptize them in Spirit just as John baptized them in water. All this proved that the Lord was mightier than John.

What is the baptism in the Holy Spirit? A basic principle in interpreting the Scriptures is to first find out fact before attempting a conclusion or an interpretation. If there are several explanations, try to harmonize them into one interpretation in explaining the fact. Such is the principle of interpreting Scripture. Now since there is but one Bibilical explanation to the baptism in the Holy Spirit, there is no need for harmonization or reconciliation here. The one interpretation is found in 1 Corinthians 12.13: "in one Spirit were we all baptized into one body, whether Jews or Greeks, whether bond or free, and were all made to drink of one Spirit." It eliminates all that we were naturally and joins us into one body. This is the only place in the entire New Testament where the interpretation of the baptism in the Holy Spirit is given. Each individual Christian is born of the Holy Spirit, and all Christians have been baptized in the Holy Spirit into the body of Christ.

What is meant by the baptism in fire? In other places, the matter of being baptized in the Holy Spirit is the only thing mentioned, but here we have both "baptize . . . in the Holy Spirit and [baptize] in fire." Thus we know that the baptism in the Holy Spirit is one thing, and the baptism in fire is another. The conjunction "and" is a coordinate term; accordingly, just as the Spirit is real Spirit, so the fire is also real fire. The latter cannot be taken to be the "tongues. . . like as of fire" mentioned later in Acts 2.2. *Both* must be interpreted either literally or figuratively. So that if Spirit is real here, so must fire be real here too.

What, then, is the fire? Scripture needs to be read within

its context. In this section "fire" is mentioned three times. In the first and third instances, it is employed to denote actual fire (vv.10,12). And hence, in the second instance, it cannot be viewed as denoting "zeal." This second instance of fire must also be actual fire, and hence it is the unquenchable fire of hell. Many people were in the presence of John. Some were truly repentant, but some others were the offspring of vipers. Accordingly, some would be baptized in the Spirit, but some others would be baptized in fire; for the One who came after John had the authority to judge sinners as well as to build the Church.

3.12 explains verse 11 as to how people are to be baptized in the Holy Spirit and how they are to be baptized in fire. There are two kinds of people presented here: one kind is as wheat, the other kind is as chaff. The wheat will be gathered into the garner, but the chaff will be burnt up with unquenchable fire. The work of the Lord is to separate the wheat from the chaff. He will thoroughly cleanse His threshing-floor. For God would not have those who believe in Him to permanently remain in the world. One day the believers and the unbelievers will be eternally separated. On the one hand, the Lord will baptize the believers in the Holy Spirit so that they become one body, and He will seal them with the Holy Spirit. On the other hand, He will burn up the chaff with unquenchable fire. The fire spoken of in verse 11, just as the fire mentioned in verse 12, is against the chaff. The chaff is on the wheat and looks like wheat. Outwardly speaking, then, it resembles a repentant person; but inwardly, it is without self-judgment or true repentance — because repentance is an inward change of mind or a change of judgment.

To what does this repentance point? Some say it points to sins, others say it points to past things of the world. It may possibly include both. Yet it is more than confession of sins, for it requires the entire being to be immersed in water. The Scripture calls it the baptism of repentance. And hence, the objective of repentance is not just inclusive of sins and the past, it is inclusive of

the person himself. This "I" is the most horrible thing. The scope
of repentance is therefore this person "I" and not limited to other
matters such as sins and the wordly matters of the past. This
serves as a prelude to the kingdom of the heavens. Although I
cannot say I am a member of the Church, I have to admit as
well that I have not changed my view of myself. To repent means
that there must be a basic, inward, constitutional, absolute change
of mind: no longer looking at self according to my own opinion,
but looking at myself from the viewpoint of God.

This thus ends the first section of Division Two of the Gospel
of Matthew—the proclamation of the kingdom of the heavens.
Only one kind of people can touch the kingdom of the heavens;
they are the repentant ones.

Second Section 3.13–17

This forms another section, though it is still related to baptism. It is the Lord Jesus himself coming to be baptized.

This book of Matthew—as we have several times noted—
presents the Lord Jesus as King. Step by step it shows Him forth
as King. Hereafter the Lord is to be manifested in public.

God takes special notice of the birth of the Lord, but He keeps
silent on the thirty years of His life on earth. During those thirty
years, our Lord has neither preached nor performed any miracle.
He comes to be *Savior* first, then to be King. This is His way.
He *will* be King, for He is the Son of David. But to be Savior,
He must himself be without sin and be the delight of God. And
hence, those thirty years are the period during which the Lord
lives before His Father. The state and condition of those years
is summed up for Him by God at the hour of His baptism: "This
is my beloved Son, in whom I am well pleased." These thirty years
have determined if He qualified to be Savior. And the verdict
is: He is the well-pleasing Son of God; and so, He is indeed
qualified to be Savior.

As the paschal Lamb, He is tested by God from the first day

to the tenth day of the first month, and He is watched by men from the tenth to the fourteenth day (see Ex. 12.1-14, especially vv.2,3,5,6,11). During His first thirty years, he is tested by God (3 x 10); and then for four years He is scrutinized by men. His public ministry spans three and a half years till He is crucified.

3.13 "From Galilee to the Jordan." The Lord did not come from Judea, from Jerusalem; instead, He came from Galilee of the Gentiles. Grace is thus not just for the Jews, it reaches even to the whole world.

Why should the Lord come to be baptized? Neither you nor I — nor even John — can understand. The Lord, however, did understand why. John tried to hinder Jesus, for he considered himself as the one who should be baptized. All would agree that under ordinary circumstances, the baptizer is always higher than the baptized. And John is quite clear on this point and attempts to dissuade Jesus. Yet the Lord responds with: "Suffer it now: for thus it becometh us to fulfil all righteousness."

What, then, is the meaning of the Lord's baptism? This word "righteousness" is very important. In its root meaning in the Greek it is used six times as a noun in the Gospel of Matthew, and twelve times as an adjective. Here is the first instance of it used as a noun. The Lord comes to be baptized, yet not to confess sin but to fulfill righteousness — that is to say, this is the right thing to do. It is right for a sinner to confess his sins before God and be baptized. It is unrighteous for a sinner to say in his heart that he is a son of Abraham. But for a sinner to stand in the right place as a sinner before God, now that *is* righteousness. For a sinner to confess himself a sinner, this is righteousness. So why did the Lord say He must fulfill all righteousness? He stood in the place of the sinner and received baptism. This was righteous.

Now if it was right for the sinless Saviour to stand in the sinner's place and be baptized, it must certainly be right — and even more so — for us sinners also to be baptized. The Gospel according to John declares: "Behold, the Lamb of God, that taketh away the sin of the world" (1.29). The Lord stood indeed in the sinner's place and was baptized. If we should ever entertain the idea that we are good and right, such a thought is unrighteous. For the more we say we are right, the worse we sin. The more we reckon ourselves as clean, the more unrighteous we become. "Righteous" in the Scriptures means "right" or "yea." Those who do not judge themselves according to the light of God are unrighteous. "For thus it becometh us to fulfil all righteousness."

3.16 "Went up straightway from the water." (Please note that this is not to be interpreted as a pastor's hand, as it were, coming up out of the waters of baptism.) And the heavens suddenly were opened "unto him."

3.17 Once again God declared Jesus to be the Son of God. Such a declaration happened four times: (1) at the birth of Christ (Luke 1.35); (2) at His baptism (here in Matt. 3.17); (3) on the Mount of Transfiguration (Matt. 17.5); and (4) at His resurrection (Rom. 1.4; Heb. 1.5). These were the four times when a formal declaration was made by God.

The Lord came to the world to be the Son of God. This term was applied to the Lord Jesus as He became a man. It is not an appellation used for pure Godhead, for as to the latter, the descriptive name "the only begotton Son" is used. On each of these four occasions when the Lord Jesus is said to be the Son of God, it signifies that He has both deity and humanity in Him. The first and second of these four instances are joined together, while the third and fourth are also grouped as one.

"Thou art my Son; this day have I begotten thee" (Ps. 2.7). This is explained in Acts 13.33 as, "he raised up Jesus." The Authorized Version reads: "he hath raised up Jesus again." But in the original Greek, the word "again" is not there. Hence, according to the original, here as well as in Acts 3.22, 7.37, Romans 15.12 ("he that ariseth") and Hebrews 7.11 ("that ariseth") and 15 ("there ariseth"), the phrase used should in all cases be translated as "raised up." Paul, in explaining to the Jews in Antioch of Pisidia concerning the gospel which had been preached to Abraham, noted that God had declared to the latter: "In thee shall all the nations be blessed" (Gal. 3.8; see also v.16). That promise had now been fulfilled to the Jews, the children of Abraham. This is the meaning of "raised up Jesus."

Furthermore, the words "raised up" in Acts 13.22 and 33 have the same meaning, while the same words "raised up" in Acts 13.23 and 34 have the same application. Notice that in the verses which pertain to resurrection, there follow the words "from the dead," while the verses which simply denote raising up or setting up are not followed by "from the dead." Those brothers who diligently studied the Scriptures ahead of us—those such as J. N. Darby, William Kelly, F. W. Grant, and others—have explained that the quotation from Psalm 2.7 refers to the incarnation of the Lord Jesus which is the manifestation in time of the eternal Son (see also Heb. 5.5,8), whereas Acts 13.34,35 quote the words from Psalm 16 that apply to resurrection (in verse 34, note the words "from the dead").

After the Lord came down from the Mount of Transfiguration, He no longer traveled to many places; instead, He stedfastly set His face to go to Jerusalem until He arrived there to be crucified. For on the Mount He had once again received His order. There he received glory from the Father. In the glory of resurrection, the Father once again declared Him to be His beloved Son.

Although in Luke's narrative of the birth of Christ we find that He was but a babe, God nevertheless called Him Son (1.32,35), for He was already placed on resurrection ground. In baptism He entered into the work of separation which is also a type of resurrection. Hence He was again declared to be the Son of God. All the life and work of the Son of God proceeded from resurrection ground. Even His death was not that of an ordinary man, but the death of the Son of God. On the Mount of Transfiguration, Moses and Elijah appeared in order to discuss with Him the event that was to transpire in Jerusalem (His death), and meanwhile God declared Him to be the Son of God. At His resurrection, God again pronounced Him the Son of God.

This passage has dealt with the Lord's leaving His private life and entering upon His public work. It commenced at His baptism, thus indicating that whatever would be done afterwards would be done in resurrection. "The Spirit of God descending as a dove." The dove was the only bird in the Old Testament period used for atoning sin. Thus the Scripture here announced the nature of the Lord's work—that of redemption. The anointing of oil (as represented by the descent of the Spirit in the form of a dove) was for the sake of enabling Him to do the work of redemption.

This passage also tells us that when our Lord came, He must die before He lived. First the outpouring of the Holy Spirit, then becoming King. First as Savior, then as King. It is the Savior who becomes King. He is not an ordinary king. Hence whatever we do which has not passed through death is futile.

Third Section 4.1-11

This third section, dealing as it does with the Lord's temptation, follows closely upon the second one.

4.1,2 The temptation follows immediately in time after His baptism. This is clearly known from the narrative of Mark: "straightway the Spirit driveth him forth into the wilderness" (1.12). Why in such a hurry? This needs some explanation. It will be recalled that it had been at His baptism that God's approval of His personal life on earth had been declared. Except for the incident at the temple when the Lord was but twelve years of age, the Scriptures are entirely silent about His life within His first thirty years. Yet these first thirty years of His life, if we could know about them, could tell us how Jesus had lived before God as a man. But even though there was this silence, there nevertheless came one important word from God which totally summed up that period: "This is my beloved Son, in whom I am well pleased" (Matt. 3.17). After closely monitoring His every thought and action during those thirty years, God concluded that there was not a single thing He was not pleased with in His Son. Whether Jesus was qualified to be the Savior was something which had to undergo the closest scrutiny of God. And in the end, the paschal Lamb was approved by God at His baptism, which event concluded His personal private history.

Commencing from chapter 4, however, the Lord began His work. Only now could He take up His work of being Savior. No one can work for God if He is unfit as a person. Before a person's *work* can be accepted, he *himself* must first be approved by God. This is a basic principle in the Scriptures. The Bible never indicates that God will accept a person because of his work. It always maintains that the acceptance of one's work is due to the approval of the person himself.

Yet, though the Lord had fulfilled God's demand, He must now manifest His condition before His Enemy. Genesis 3, Job 1 and Matthew 4 — these three chapters reveal many things about the Devil very plainly. Job was an upright man, and God had proclaimed him so, but Satan disputed the fact. So God removed His protective hedges around His servant, and Satan tried his best to tempt Job. The outcome was that Job stood firm, and God again declared him righteous. Now, the same thing was to happen to our Lord. Satan tried to tempt Him, and as a consequence Satan's mouth was shut once more. Before the time of Matthew 4, Satan could not say, "Jesus I know"; but after that time he, by his evil spirits, was able to say that indeed (see Acts 19.13-17). This was why God took Christ to the wilderness and let Him be tempted without any reservation. By enduring the temptation, Jesus not only satisfied God's demand but also sealed the Enemy's mouth.

In studying the story of the Lord's being led to the wilderness to be tempted, it is proper for us to notice the relationship between Genesis 3 and Matthew 4. Failure to understand Genesis 3 will invariably mean a failure to comprehend Matthew 4. In Genesis 1 it is recorded that God had declared that the man the Lord created was good. Then in Genesis 3 is found the temptation narrative. First the approval, then Satan came on the scene to prove that God's approval had been premature. It would appear as though Satan had come out on top. In the instance in Matthew 3 with respect to Jesus, God had again approved. But in Matthew 4 we find that Satan once more tried to overturn that approval. It would take weeks to fully understand Genesis 3, but here we will focus only on its relationship to Matthew 4.

Let us at the outset mention two features to be learned from Genesis 3. The first is that the man whom God had created has his own place eternally fixed. He may receive life, but he can never be God. Yet this is the focus of Satan's temptation. He tempts people to cross the boundary to God's territory so that the worshipper might become the worshipped, just as he is. We can be like God in all things except in His deity. This was the nature of the first temptation to have ever occurred in the world.

The second feature is what can be deduced from what Satan said: "Ye shall not surely die: . . . your eyes shall be opened, and ye shall be as God knowing good and evil" (vv.4,5). Before man had been tempted to eat the forbidden fruit, he was unable to discern good and evil, nor did he have the sense of good and evil. Such knowledge belonged to God, not to man. Adam and Eve did not know good and evil, and therefore they must inquire of God. If God said good, they too would say good. Man and woman in the garden of Eden were not independent; they were not to make independent judgment. The fruit of the tree of the knowledge of good and evil caused them to declare independence against God, in that they would now know good and evil themselves without the necessity of communing with God. And this is what is meant when reference is made to man having fallen. The first sin of man was to do away with the need of depending on his Creator. Formerly, he was a fool without God; man could not live a day without Him. He had to maintain communication with his Maker. All issues were only to be solved through communion. Through faith and prayer, man came to know. But now man has fallen, sin having entered the world. Sin has caused man to be independent of his Creator God.

Here, then, are these two features from Genesis 3. (1) Man overstepped his boundary and moved into God's territory; (2) man declared independence of God. The first man (Adam) fell terribly after being tempted. Our Lord is the Second Man (see 1 Cor. 15.47) And should the Lord fail in His hour of temptation, the consequences will be irretrievable. But, praise God, He passed through temptation and completely overturned every work of Satan.

The entering into temptation by our Lord as recorded in Matthew 4 was something deliberate and not accidental. God removed all the hedges and permitted Satan to tempt. The first earthly temptation happened in *the garden of Eden*, which had the best environment by which man could have overcome but did not. This temptation with the Second Man occurred in *the wilderness*. The first man had all his needs satisfied, for in the garden there grew many trees, not just one. If he needed food, there was plenty. And in the midst of the garden, there was particularly the tree of life. Hence, his temptation was not one characterized by need but by pleasure. But the temptation our Lord endured was one characterized by need. He had fasted for forty days, and He was hungry, truly hungry. The fact of the matter was that He was hungry after the very first day. Therefore, the Lord Jesus must have been near to starvation after forty days. He was really thinking of food. Thus was set the scene for Satan's temptation of God's Son. God had taken away the physical resistance of the Lord Jesus. And with that, the Tempter commenced to say to Him, "If thou art . . ."

4.3,4 Please notice the word of Satan and the reply of the Lord, for quite a contrast is presented. The one word is "the

Son of God," the other is "man." And this was where the focus lay throughout the Enemy's series of temptations. Satan had just heard the word (recorded in Matthew 3), "This is my beloved Son," so he tempted the Lord to act as the Son of God. If the Lord indeed be the Son of God, He should manifest himself as such. Yet had Jesus *taken* the place of the Son of God, he would have fallen. Truly His essence *is* the Son of God, yet on earth He stands in the position of man: "who, existing in the form of God, counted not the being on an equality with God a thing to be grasped, but emptied himself, taking the form of a servant, being made in the likeness of men" (Phil. 2.6–7).

Adam was a man, but he wanted to surpass man's place and intrude into God's domain. The Lord is originally God, but He condescended to take the place of a man. And thus He could be Savior. The word "man" pointed to His own self. How glorious this was that the Lord should stand in the position of man. As to His Person, He is the Son of God; as to His authority He stands in the place of man. As a man He never invades the place of God, though He did use the authority of God. The manifestation on earth of His deity is for the work of saving men; He never uses it on himself. As to redemption and work, He stands in the position of a man. Before the Father and for himself, He is "man."

"If thou art the Son of God, command that these stones become bread" (v.3). This temptation is not that of sin, for food is the natural demand of the human body. *Others* cannot turn stones into bread, Satan intimated, but *You* can. And by so doing, it would be perfectly legitimate: it would not be sin. What was the motive behind Satan's temptation? Satan tried to cause the Lord to remove himself from standing in the place of a man, thus precluding the salvation of believers. For we believers need a *man* to be our Savior, and with such a man as He, there can *be* redemption. By tempting the Lord to turn stones into bread, however, Satan aimed at sending the Lord back to heaven and nullifying His incarnation.

The reply of the Lord was that "man shall not live by bread

alone, but by . . ." (v.4), quoting from Deuteronomy 8.3. It was as though the Lord were saying, "You are wrong, Satan, for I came here to be man. God has declared My essence, but My mission here is to be man." Not by bread alone shall man live, "but by every word that proceedeth out of the mouth of God," said the Lord. He would not die because He was tempted. He lived by the word of God. The Holy Spirit led Him to temptation, not to death. Our Lord refused to act on His own without having God's word. Truly He was hungry. Truly He had the power to save himself. And truly, even His hunger sensation had been created by God. Nonetheless, He would not do anything without the command of His Father. He refused to take even the most legitimate action.

This temptation to tempt the Lord to act according to His own judgment our Lord would not succumb to, and this is something we too need to learn: "The Son can do nothing of himself, but what he seeth the Father doing: for what things soever he doeth, these the Son also doeth in like manner" (John 5.19). In the Greek original, the word "of" here is "from" or "out from." The Son is never the source of anything. The Son only does what He sees the Father doing and only says whatever the Father says. Sin, though, means man does what God has not said: and as soon as man initiates, there is sin.

Now that is the lesson which we have been learning these several decades. I am not fit to initiate anything in the work of God. Only what God himself does remains in eternity. Whatever is done by you or me will be destroyed. Whatever is not planted by our Father will eventually be uprooted. Truly, what we ourselves have planted will all be demolished. We can only do for God's sake, not for our own.

The failure in the garden of Eden was due to (1) man's desire to stand in God's place, and (2) his wish to be independent rather than to commune with God and be dependent upon Him. But here, the Lord Jesus (1) stands in the place of man, and (2) refuses to do on His own even the legitimate act of turning stones into bread. These are the very opposite responses to the two features found in Genesis 3.

"It is written" is employed three times by Jesus. Our Lord uses the words of the Scriptures to deal with Satan. In the area of mental assault, if you lay hold of a Scripture word inwardly and hurl it at Satan, the matter is immediately resolved. "Man shall not live by bread alone." Bread causes man to live; this is a natural law set up by God himself. The word of God enables man to live; this, too, is a law—a spiritual law also established by God.

4.5,6 The second in this series of temptations of the Lord Jesus was fiercer. Satan set the Lord on a wing or pinnacle of the temple and said to Him, "If thou art the Son of God . . ." He could not forget this refrain of his. His primary expectation was to tempt the Lord to be the Son of God so as to destroy His intended redemptive work. The first temptation tested the will of the Lord, whether He would follow God's will or his own. Now, however, this second temptation tried the Lord's faith: "cast thyself down." Satan was very clever: He too would use Scripture: "for it is written . . ." This Scripture quotation comes from Psalm 91, verses 11 and 12. But he omitted to add from verse 11: "to keep thee in all thy ways" (interestingly, in English, seven words; in Hebrew, only three). He wanted man to do a spectacular thing. This was testing the Lord's faith.

4.7 The reply of the Lord was: "Again it is written." Many brothers and sisters act on only one Scripture verse, but oftentimes we need the "again it is written" of our Lord. If it is found in only one place, exercise care. It is more dependable if it is confirmed in another place. Especially in spectacular things, great care should be employed in this area of our Christian life. The ordinary conduct for a Christian is to walk in a pathway, not to jump from a tower. Here, our Lord cited another word from the Scriptures (Deut. 6.16), He declaring to the Tempter: "Thou shalt not make trial of the Lord thy God."

What is the difference between trusting God and tempting or making trial of God? In Satan's view, hurling oneself from the pinnacle of the temple was an act of trusting God. But the Lord said this was not believing, but tempting, Him. In outward appearance, believing God and tempting God look almost identical. Where the difference lies is in the fact that a person believing has the word of God given to him whereas a person in tempting God ends up using God's word by coercion. God has spoken, and you act accordingly—this is faith or trust. God has not spoken, yet you nonetheless find a Scripture verse and use it—this is tempting God. Having God's own word, that is faith. Lacking God's word yet grasping one anyway to test out if God will act, that is tempting God. If the Lord has spoken, no venture forward is a risk. But if He has not spoken, any attempt at taking one or two words out of context will be disastrous.

4.8-11 Now followed the third temptation. Verse 8 reads: "unto an exceeding high mountain, and showeth him all the kingdoms of the world, and the glory of them." This was totally different from the other two temptations. In the earlier two, there were the words, "If thou art the Son of God"—which words were used to entice the Lord to disclose himself. But now in this third temptation, these words were absent. Satan could find no way to cause the Lord to manifest himself. Though the Lord was in very truth "the Son of God," He nonetheless came forth as "man." So now Satan tried to tempt Jesus as *man*, as though Satan were saying, "If You insist upon being man, all right, I will tempt You as man." And if so, then the words, "the Son of God," would not be relevant in this third temptation.

Satan took the Lord to an exceedingly high mountain. There he exhausted all his miraculous wonder powers. In the twinkling of an eye, he displayed before the Lord the glory of the kingdoms of the world. In the Scriptures, the glory of the kingdoms of the earth include three elements: (1) the material wealth of the nations; (2) the praises and approval of men; and (3) the authority of the nations in reigning over men. All three were laid before the Lord and would be given to Him if He worshipped Satan.

Satan was actually paying the greatest price here. He had never paid such a price before. This needs some explanation. Our Lord is indeed the Second Man (see 1 Cor. 15.47), in contrast with the first man in the garden. Just as the test in the garden had been a temptation of mankind, so too is this test in the wilderness a temptation of the human race. The Lord is not being tempted here as an individual, He is being tempted as the Second Man. What was Satan trying to accomplish in paying such a price? He had already been defeated twice, but he now grew desperate. This third time his wile would no longer be in words nor in the framing of the temptation. His treachery would now be in using material things to accomplish his aim. And in so doing, his foolishness and his real character would thereby all be exposed. "If thou wilt fall down and worship me"—how foolish was this temptation: he plainly announced his ultimate aim: he was now willing to lose all the kingdoms of the world and their glory which he had obtained through his having tempted the first man: today, for the purpose of obtaining the worship of the Second Man, he would sacrifice the kingdoms of the world and all their glory. Idols are indeed dead, but Satan behind these idols is living. His purpose has always been to stand in God's place to receive worship. Let us therefore never belittle this matter of worship.

In the instance now before us, the Lord Jesus not only cited Scripture, He also spoke. In fact, He first spoke, then He quoted Scripture: "Get thee hence, Satan." He explicitly mentioned the name of the Tempter here. "Get thee hence" meant "Get away." Go away, Satan, for it is futile for you to be here. Such a reprimand perfectly answered the blatant and quite open temptation of Satan. The Lord had endured the first and second testings, but He would not tolerate this third one. He commanded Satan to be gone, for the latter openly sought for the worship which belonged to God alone. When we truly recognize that it is Satan, his power is gone. His temptation can only proceed under the cover of deception. But when there is light within you, and you see clearly that this is of Satan, you will have no problem in resisting. He will go away. As soon as you call out his name, the temptation cannot remain long.

The Lord then quoted the word of the Scriptures: "Thou shalt worship the Lord thy God, and him only shalt thou serve" (from Deut. 6.13). Whoever in this world desires worship, that one is satanic, and must be resisted. Satan failed in his two kinds of temptation: the one regarding "the Son of God" and the other regarding "man." With the result that "then the devil leaveth him."

Commencing from chapter 3, we have the Lord coming forth to be King. First, the King's forerunner; second, the King's baptism and His approval by God. He himself needed no savior, hence He could be Savior of other people. Third, the manifested King passed through Satan's temptations, thus proving He was qualified and worthy to be Savior. In consequence of this, we find by the end of chapter 4 that Satan must acknowledge Jesus as Savior. We know this to be true since hereafter, whenever the demons meet Jesus, they will cry out, "What have we to do with thee, thou Son of God? art thou come hither to torment us before the time?" (Matt. 8.29) (Let us note, in passing, that Satan himself is seldom the one who tempts people; one of the few exceptions, of course, was the case of Job; usually the task of temptation is carried out by the evil spirits.) In baptism, the Lord had His perfection revealed; in temptation, He manifested His worthiness to do God's appointed work.

Genesis 3 mentioned eating, so did Matthew 4. Eating is not a small matter. It is a natural demand which is created by God himself. The absolute necessity of the Lord Jesus to eat is a fully legitimate one. In His case with Satan, however, it was unlike Adam, who would eat for pleasure. The Lord would not stretch out His hand and convert stones into bread to eat; for He was not motivated by necessity but by the command of God. Had necessity been the motivation, the will of God would have been set aside. No, the Lord would not initiate anything on His own. Even the greatest need in us ought never to be our motivation for doing anything; for it can easily become the very area of Satan's temptation. Whatever is not commanded by God is the area of temptation for Satan. "Need" motivation is very easily attached to Satan, but not to God. Are we servants or are we masters? If God has not given an order, what do we obey?

Whenever we ourselves become the motivation, we walk fairly close to Satan's way. Man has no right to decide on anything, no right to choose the way of the Church or the method of work. Satan will of course say that if you wait for God's word, you wait for death. But the Lord says that man shall live by every word that proceeds from the mouth of God. Neither need nor self can be our inducement to act. The command of God is alone to be the determinant of our actions. There is no greater loss on earth than the loss of the presence of God!

Let us notice that the matter of eating was a problem at the commencement of the Lord's public ministry. And even at the end, on the cross, it reappears, for there He said, "I thirst" (John 19.28). In the wilderness He was hungry. When on the hill of Calvary, He said "I thirst"; yet even here, He would not say it except for the sake of fulfilling the Scriptures. Even in such a small matter as this, He was not careless but was governed by the word of God. By contrast, though, how proximate is our own action to Satan's temptation!

The common weakness of men is glory—the kingdoms of the world. How many have been captivated by earthly glory and away from walking in the way of the Lord. How many, for the sake of a little money, are unable to stand firm. If you have any reservation concerning your consecration, then please exercise doubt about your judgment in matters. For true and absolute consecration stabilizes us. But as soon as something appears wrong with our consecration, everything will go wrong. Jesus' stand against Satan was: "Him only shalt thou serve." This is absolute surrender to God. No man can serve two masters. This temptation of Satan's came to the Lord, and it comes also to us. But as in the case with Jesus, if we stand on the ground of consecration, Satan can only withdraw.

Since Matthew presents the Lord as King, he writes that Jesus was *"led up* of the Spirit into the wilderness." Luke presents Him as a man, and hence he too writes that the Lord "was *led* in the Spirit in the wilderness" (4.1). Mark, on the other hand, presents Jesus as a bondslave, and therefore his record reads that "straightway the Spirit *driveth* him forth into the wilderness" (1.12). The Scriptures never use any word carelessly. "Drive" in the original means to be driven as a vehicle is driven.

In all three of these temptations the Lord quotes an appropriate word from the Scriptures in answering Satan. And we may have noticed that in all three quotations He uses words from the one book of Deuteronomy. Of the five books in the Pentateuch of Moses we find that Genesis speaks of election; Exodus speaks of redemption; Leviticus, of worship; and Numbers, of the wilderness journey or testing; but Deuteronomy speaks of obedience. In our Lord's answers to Satan He especially cited the words from Deuteronomy. Three times He uses this Old Testament book to give reply to His Enemy. This is deliberate, not accidental. We cannot but notice from this how the Lord therefore stresses obedience to God. Accordingly, in our own dealings with Satan, let us not use our own words, but use only the word of God. God's word alone is able to deal with Satan and his evil spirits.

I frequently advise young brothers to memorize some Scripture passages. Paul tells us (in Ephesians 6) that we need to put on the whole armor of God. Only one item in the armor is offensive, and that is the sword of the Spirit (all the rest are defensive). If we do not know how to use the offensive weapon, we can at most be defensive people. Though defense is important, the Sword must also be used. Neither argument nor reasoning can cause the Enemy to retreat. The word of God alone can deal with him. As soon as there is word, there is light within, and

Satan will immediately depart: "whom withstand stedfast in your faith" (1 Peter 5.9). What is faith? Believing in God's word.

The Devil is real, but so, too, is the word of God. It takes the real word of God to deal with the real Devil.

Fourth Section 4.12–25

The Lord himself began to preach. After having been approved by God and also standing firm against Satan, he now commenced His ministry. Verses 12–17 record the Lord preaching; verses 18–22, the calling of His disciples; and verses 23–25, the Lord substantiating His gospel with miracles.

4.12 What the Lord did in Jerusalem is different from what he did in Galilee. Whereas John in his Gospel concentrated on the Jerusalem works, here Matthew focuses on the Galilean works. Do not mix up the line followed by Matthew with that of John. What Matthew records is edited by him. His account is not according to chronological order but according to the changes in time and teaching. He narrates everything related to the changes in time, and records whatever teaching and word are in accordance with those changes. On the other hand, Mark follows a chronological order, and so also does John.

When Jesus heard that John the Baptist had been rejected by men, He withdrew into Galilee. Now the Lord had come to be King, and so naturally one would think of Jerusalem, it immediately causing the person to consider Him as the King of the Jews. But Jesus is the King of the kingdom of the heavens; He is not merely the King of the Jews. And hence Matthew will mention His works in Galilee and not just those in Jerusalem, thus demonstrating that He is not only the King of the Jews but is also the King of the kingdom of the heavens. For we must understand that Galilee at that time was a special district in the entire land of Palestine: it was a place where both Jews *and* Gentiles lived; and thus the Scriptures often refer to it as "Galilee of the Gentiles" or "Galilee of the nations."

4.13–16 Casual mention is made here that the Lord left Nazareth for Capernaum. Galilee is a province, Capernaum — which means "village of comfort"— is a small city there. The Lord went and dwelt there. It borders the land of Zebulun and Naphtali, towards the sea. This, too, is to fulfill the word of the Old Testament prophet. Isaiah 9 is a Messianic chapter. Zebulun means "dwelling," and Naphtali means "my wrestling." One is dwelling in darkness, and the other is wrestling in darkness. The pedigree of the people living there was doubtful, for here the Jews had become mixed with the Gentiles and even traded with them. They are thus contaminated. So that Galilee was looked upon as being the most infamous place among the Jews. Yet, when the Lord came to be King, His work was mainly confined to this very place of Galilee. All the orthodox scribes and Pharisees and all the fundamental theologian-priests were be be found in Jerusalem. From the human viewpoint, then, this relocation by Jesus appeared to be rather strange. Nevertheless, this action set His work free from the Jewish coloring.

Darkness is not able to prevent light. The darker the night, the brighter the light. The Enemy of God is afraid of light. The King whom God has established is now shining on this land of darkness, shining on the people of darkness. The first work the Lord does, therefore, is to be light. Without Him, there is only darkness. Yet as we come into His presence, we are enlightened. If we are away from Him, we are in darkness — by which is meant that we do not see who we really are. Darkness does not require the addition of sins and faults: if we but fail to recognize our true natural state, then for just that reason alone we are nonetheless in darkness. But as we begin to question ourselves, enlightenment comes. Yet light comes not only to cast doubt about ourselves but also to bring in a new concept and new understanding about God. And this light also reveals God himself.

Originally man in darkness conceived a certain conception about God as well as about himself. But now the Lord comes to cause a change in man's conceptions of himself and of God. This is called enlightenment.

4.17 This verse succeeds the preceding thought. For in verses 12–17, where the Lord is shown beginning to preach the gospel of the kingdom, it is made clear that He preached it in Galilee. What He preached was the same as that which John the Baptist had preached. Verse 12 recorded that John had been imprisoned and thus his ministry ended. But then the Lord came forth to preach. Yet the message of the kingdom of the heavens had not changed at all. Without repentance, there can be no kingdom of the heavens. The foundation of the kingdom of the heavens is set on repentance. Repentance is the prelude to the kingdom of the heavens. May God give us a dependable and workable repentance. What the forerunner of the King preached was indeed trustworthy, because the King himself likewise so preached.

4.18–22 The Lord began to call those who would serve Him. The Sea of Galilee is actually a lake, not a sea. But the Jews prefer to call it a sea just as the Chinese, when referring to Green Lake, like to call it Green Sea. For the Jews customarily call a greater expanse of water a sea.

One thing we need to be alert to about the Lord's call is that this calling of Peter, Andrew, James and John did not constitute their first contact with the Lord Jesus. For according to John 1 these men had already encountered Jesus for salvation. Originally, of course, they had all been disciples of John the Baptist. But after John had proclaimed, "Behold, the Lamb of God, that taketh away the sin of the world!" (John 1.29), one by one these men had come to the Lord. So that by the time of Matthew 4 it was their second call—yet not a calling for them to be saved but a calling for them to follow Him to be fishers of men.

To believe unto salvation must always precede a call to follow the Lord. To the unbeliever our Lord never says, "Come and follow Me, and you will become Christians." So that this calling in Matthew 4 is not addressed to the world but only to those who are already children of God. Salvation precedes the calling to follow. The Lord never calls people directly to follow Him since there is no way they can follow. Consequently, the call here occurred after they had already known the Lord. This was a second call — not a calling them to know Jesus as Savior, but calling them to know Jesus as Lord; not calling them to believe, but calling them to follow.

In Christianity, there are three distinct ministries as represented by three men of the New Testament. The first of these men — the one who will open the door to salvation in Jesus — is Peter. At his call by the Lord, Peter was fishing. And hence, the first ministry is that of catching fish: a ministry of a fisher of men. After Peter's work is done, Paul will continue on. He was a tentmaker at the time of his call to follow the Lord. And so Paul's ministry was that of a builder. The third ministry is that identified with John. When he was called, he was mending nets. "Mending" conveys the idea of recovering back to the original as new. The Gospel according to John was the last of the Gospels written. His epistles were the last epistles written, and Revelation came to be the last written of all the New Testament books. So that John's ministry is for what happens after one has fished and built: problems arise. In that context, John comes to bring people back to grace and truth (the Gospel of John), to light and love (John's epistles), and to the very beginning and the very end (Revelation).

The rising up and following the Lord Jesus by these four men mentioned here in Matthew 4 was complete and instantaneous. There was no consideration, no question, nor even any thought of the future. It was easy to linger after the boats and one's father, but it was difficult to reject the call of the Lord of the universe. We can forsake all the people in the world, but we cannot forsake Him. All who follow the Lord follow with joy and rejoicing. It is instantaneous and without counting any cost. For the Voice of the call is such a loving one that it is impossible to resist. He alone is worthy of my all. As He calls me, all the rest have lost their attraction. He who does not know the Lord rejects Him. But he who knows the Lord is not able to refuse Him. To be a Christian demands absoluteness, that is to say, a counting nothing as costly. Naturally, no one would care for nothing. Yet, it is after hearing that Voice that nothing matters any more. Hence, listen to *this* Voice! The purpose of the call to follow is for the sake of the gospel. It is not for spiritual edification, but to be fishers of men. The Lord's call comes upon all who are saved by grace. May this call separate you from the world.

4.23-25 The Lord went about in all Galilee, teaching and preaching the gospel of the kingdom of the heavens, but in addition healing all manner of disease and all manner of sickness among the people. This was different from the ministry of John the Baptist. For the latter never performed a miracle. His work was not causing people to believe in him, therefore he did no miracle. The Lord, however, was to be believed, and thus He performed miracles. Those recorded here are healings. When the Lord was on earth, there were miracles and wonders performed by Him. With Him it was quite natural to perform miracles for other people because He is the only begotten Son of God. Yet after we have known the Lord, miracles and wonders should also become natural to us. Let us note that demon possession is spiritual sickness; epilepsy is psychological sickness; and a palsied condition is physical sickness. Throughout these twenty centuries since the time of Jesus, the Church too has continuously had miracles and wonders. The Church without these things is a dead Church. If it was something natural for our Lord to have miracle and wonder, it should also be something natural for us who are His followers to have these things too.

Decapolis—"Deca" means ten; "polis" means city. These ten small cities were Roman colonies.

| Division Three 5.1–7.29

Introduction 5.1–2

Matthew 5–7 records the so-called Sermon on the Mount. These chapters form the Gospel of Matthew's third division, of which there are six distinct sections after a brief introduction that provides some needed clarification, as follows:

5.1,2 Our Lord saw the multitudes, that is, the great multitudes who had come out from Galilee and Decapolis and Jerusalem and Judea and from beyond the Jordan (4.25). Though the multitudes were great, He did not continue to be with them, healing the sick and casting out demons as before. He at this moment had but one thing in mind, so He went up into a mountain (actually a high hill). Many were not able to go, but the disciples followed Him. The disciples were different from the multitudes. "And he opened his mouth and taught them." The word "them" pointed to the disciples, not to the multitudes. Let us first discuss a few errors in interpretation with respect to these chapters of Matthew called the Sermon on the Mount.

(1) During these two thousand years, the Sermon on the Mount has been a problem in the Church. Many consider this to be the Lord's word to the world. They view it as His teaching of non-resistance, and so they propagate this teaching in the world, expecting non-resistance and love of one's enemies. But as you study this Scripture, you at once perceive the error of such

teaching. For the Lord did not say these words on the plain; rather, He spoke them on the mountain. He did not address the multitudes, but talked to the disciples. This Sermon on the Mount is not Christ's message to the world that is soon passing away, it is His message to His own disciples. The world has no need of such a superior philosophy of life. What the people of the world need is light which can enable them to know themselves, a life that can deliver them from death. They need a salvation. No sinner can be saved by keeping the teaching on the Mount. This teaching is for *Christian* living. Christianity does not pass on the *teaching* of Christ to sinners; she can only impart the *life* of Christ to them. Whoever attempts by any means to give the teaching on the Mount to the *world* is grossly mistaken. For such an attempt will only prove that he does not know what Christianity truly is.

(2) There have also been many, especially in the last several decades,* who have presumed that the Sermon on the Mount is for the Jews. They maintain that the Gospel according to Matthew is the Gospel for the Jews, and therefore all these words are aimed at them. But I have already drawn your attention to the nature of this Gospel. Though the writer is a Jew, he nonetheless records more Gentile places in his Gospel than is to be found in the other Gospels. From chapter 4 to chapter 18, he narrates especially the Lord's work in Galilee, Galilee of the Gentiles. To whom, then, are the words of these particular Scriptures addressed? They cannot be spoken to the Jews only, otherwise, all the Gospels (including the Gospel according to John) would be exclusively for the Jews.

To whom do the disciples in this passage refer? To the Jews or the Christians? Not the Jews, though the early disciples were undoubtedly Jews. God in His word says the disciples, not the Jews. Whenever the word "disciples" is used in the four Gospels, it refers to those who are qualified to be Jesus' followers to hear

*Calculating back, of course, from the 1920s.—*Translator*

the word of the Lord, and not because they are Jews. "Ye therefore shall be perfect, as your heavenly Father is perfect" (Matt. 5.48). In other words, disciples are children of God. Later on, after His resurrection, He calls disciples those who believe in Him out of all nations (see Matt. 28.18-19). Therefore, "disciples" is just another name for Christian believers. They are not limited to the Jewish believers but include people from all nations who believe in the gospel and are baptized unto the name of the Father, the Son and the Holy Spirit. For this reason, the term "disciples" is not confined to the Jewish believers but is the common name of all Christians. Consequently, it can rightly be said that this teaching is not primarily spoken to the Jews.

Furthermore, in the Book of Acts, after the ascension of Christ and the coming of the Holy Spirit, all those who believe in the Lord are called the disciples of the Lord (Acts 6.1,2,7; 9.10,19,26; 11.26). So that all those who believe in the Lord Jesus are disciples. In Acts 11.26 we see that the disciples are Christians. At first they are called disciples, later on they are called Christians. Therefore, whoever tries to limit the meaning of this term disciples to the Jews is one who does not know the Scriptures.

The Sermon on the Mount is spoken to the disciples, that is to say, to the Christians. It is not spoken to the Jews. For further evidence on this point, see also Acts 11.20 where the Gentiles have already become disciples; Acts 14.22,28 where these disciples are all Gentiles; Acts 15.10 where the passage also points to Gentile disciples; Acts 16.1 where is mentioned a certain disciple named Timothy who is half Jewish and half Gentile; Acts 18.23,27 where all mentioned are Gentile disciples; Acts 19.9,30; 20.1; 21.4 wherein all are Gentile disciples; and so forth.

(3) A third error surrounding Matthew 5-7 is that many contend that the Sermon on the Mount is addressed to the people in the future kingdom, and hence it has no relationship to us today. This too is a grave mistake, for when the future millennial kingdom begins, the earth shall be full of righteousness and peace. It shall be the golden age of the world. There will not

be violence or injustice. And accordingly, it is called the Millennium Jubilee. Yet today as you read the teaching on the Mount, the environment of those who are to keep the teaching is quite different from that of the future kingdom age: (a) "Blessed are the poor in spirit" (or as in Luke's version of this statement: "Blessed are ye poor" — 6.20). Here is still poverty, but in the millennium there will not be poverty. (b) "Blessed are they that mourn." They who mourn today are blessed in the future. Will there be any need for mourning in the millennium? (c) Today the world is full of striving, therefore we need to be meek. Today is the time to be hungry and thirsty after righteousness, to be merciful and to be pure in heart as well as to be peacemakers. Today we may be persecuted. In the millennium, who will persecute? These are today's environments, not those in the future.

Looking further into this whole question, we can easily see that in that future day, there will be no darkness on earth, and hence there will be no need for us believers to be light or salt. Then, too, only when the Bridegroom is absent is there any need to fast. Yet the teaching on the Mount teaches us to fast, which clearly indicates that the Bridegroom is not here. Moreover, we read: "Thy kingdom come" (Matt. 6.10). Will there be any need to ask for His kingdom to come during the millennium? For all these reasons, we must conclude that the teaching on the Mount is for *today's* use, enabling us to observe and keep it *now*.

(4) Many put forward the notion that Christianity is really to be found in the New Testament Epistles, not in the Gospels. They emphasize Paul's epistles more than the words of the Lord. They argue that the gospel of grace is in these epistles, not in the Gospels. Yet let us hear what our Lord says about His words. Are not His words the very inheritance of the Church?

The first and foremost matter in this entire controversy is to answer the question of when does the dispensation of the law end? According to Matthew 11.13, "all the prophets and the law prophesied until John." As a consequence, the gospel begins with

Christ. Never fancy that the time of the Lord Jesus is still within the dispensation of the law. The Lord Jesus, as recorded in Luke 16.16, clearly states that "the law and the prophets were until John: from that time the gospel of the kingdom of God is preached, and every man entereth violently into it." From this we can conclude that immediately after John, the gospel of the kingdom of God is preached. And thus, what the Lord is recorded as saying here in Matthew 5–7 and elsewhere are the words of the gospel of the kingdom of God. They are not words which belong to the dispensation of the law. Although the death of the Lord yet lay in the future, the age of the gospel had already begun.

The incidents recorded in John 3 and 4 clearly happen before the Lord's death; nonetheless, whosoever believes shall not perish but have eternal life. The gospel age has already begun. The Lord's words are words of the dispensation of grace, not of the dispensation of law. As given in John 8.25, the Lord himself refers to His words as "that which I have also spoken unto you from the beginning." His words are not subject to any dispensational change. As revealed in John 12.48–50, the Lord Jesus shows us that His word cannot be changed or altered. Before His departure from this earth, He declares that His words are the Father's words which are eternally trustworthy (John 17.8,14). As far as Jesus is concerned, the words He spoke on earth are a part of His great work. Whoever is inclined to alter His word is unfit to serve him.

"Teaching them to observe all things whatsoever I commanded you" (Matt. 28.20). Who dares to say that the teaching on the Mount is not given to the Church and not given for today? How does Paul view the words of the Lord? To the Ephesian elders he said: "ye ought . . . to remember the words of the Lord Jesus" (Acts 20.35). Paul submits himself under the words of the Lord, saying: "Let the word of Christ dwell in you richly" (Col. 3.16). How solemn are the declarations of Paul in 1 Timothy 6.3–4: "If any man teacheth a different doctrine, and consenteth not to sound words, even the words of our Lord Jesus Christ, and to the doctrine which is according to godliness, he is puffed up, knowing nothing, but doting about questionings and disputes of words, whereof cometh envy, strife, railing, evil surmisings."

The words of the Lord, therefore, must be wholly kept. No one can cut off or eliminate His word.

(5) Some have put the words found in the Epistles and the words found in the Sermon on the Mount together and have discovered their similarity. The teaching on the Mount should be taken as the teaching of the kingdom of the heavens, as its truth. There are people who say that the kingdom passes away after the resurrection and ascension of the Lord. They therefore suggest that the teaching of the kingdom of the heavens given in the Sermon on the Mount is but a stop-gap teaching for the brief period in between the dispensation of law and the dispensation of grace.

But let us carefully read Acts. 1.3, where we see that during the forty days on earth *after* His resurrection, the Lord spoke to the disciples things concerning the kingdom of God. In Acts 8.12 Philip is recorded as having preached the "good tidings concerning the kingdom of God and the name of Jesus Christ." This happened *after* the coming of the Holy Spirit. In Acts 14.22 Paul and Barnabas are recorded as having exhorted the disciples "that through many tribulations we must enter into the kingdom of God." In Acts 19.8 we learn that for a period of three months Paul was "reasoning and persuading as to the things concerning the kingdom of God." We are told in Acts 20.25 that Paul customarily went about preaching the kingdom of God. And towards the very end of the Book of Acts, Paul was still preaching the kingdom of God (see Acts 28.23,31). From the epistles of Paul to the Book of Revelation, there are twenty-four places where the things of the kingdom of God are mentioned.

It can consequently be asserted that the kingdom of God is not contradictory to the dispensation of grace. The law ends with the coming of John the Baptist, and thereafter the gospel of the kingdom of God is continually being preached. The kingdom of God coincides with the dispensation of grace. And therefore, in the light of all which has been said with regard to these various controversies, it can confidently be said that the Sermon on the Mount in Matthew 5–7 is for Christians and not for the world; that it is neither for the Jews nor for the people in the future millennium.

The above words may have seemed to some to be unnecessary; but in view of so many heresies around, it was felt wise to clarify the truth. Let us not believe whatever sounds reasonable; let us believe only what the Scriptures themselves do say.

We now need to move on to other considerations in this introductory section. First of all, we need to examine what exactly is the kingdom of the heavens as presented in the Sermon on the Mount. What is it in the Old Testament? What is it in Matthew 5–7 and what is it in Matthew 13? The kingdom of the heavens in chapters 5–7 seems to be very different from that in chapter 13. In the former, the kingdom of the heavens is crystal clear; but in the latter, it is extremely mixed. This constitutes a problem to many students of the Scriptures.

In the Old Testament — in Daniel 2.44 and 7.13–14 — it makes clear that the heavens shall rule. The other prophets, such as Zechariah, Isaiah and David, also declare that God will set up a kingdom. The principal people of the kingdom will be the children of Israel; but there will also be those of the (sheep) nations (see Matt. 25.31ff.). All shall actually know Jehovah and worship God. Not only mankind will be blessed, even the beasts and other animals will be, too. This is the kingdom as prophesied in the Old Testament. It is clear that the kingdom of heaven spoken of in the Old Testament is not associated with the dispensation of the Church, nor is it the heaven or the New Jerusalem that Christians look forward to. So that it is neither for today's Christians nor is it the future heaven. It is another dispensation.*

---

*For further clarification, see footnote at the conclusion of point (7) of First Section, 5.3–16 below.—*Translator*

In the New Testament period our Lord succeeds John in declaring that "the kingdom of the heavens is at hand." What is the kingdom of the heavens? Matthew 3 indicates that John the Baptist proclaimed that "the kingdom of the heavens is at hand." Chapter 4 records that the Lord announces the same thing. By the time of chapter 5 the kingdom of the heavens has come. Yes, indeed, by the time of chapters 5–7, the kingdom has really come. Now the kingdom as prophesied in the Old Testament relates to the *environment* on earth in the future days. The kingdom as spoken of by the Lord and found in Matthew 5–7 refers to the *men* of the kingdom of the heavens who shall rule therein. And the kingdom spoken of in Matthew 13 applies to the *history* of the kingdom. All three point to the kingdom. A certain company of men come into being. Without them, this kingdom would never arrive. Thus the teaching in the Mount tells us what kind of persons these men are to be.

What the Lord therefore focuses on here is not environment, but people. Hence He subsequently said to Peter, "I will give unto thee the keys of the kingdom of heaven" (Matt. 16.19)— keys by which to open the door of the kingdom of the heavens, yet not to let out its environmental conditions but to let in the people. And we see later that the door was verily opened on the day of Pentecost, at which time the Jews came in. Furthermore, it was opened a second time at the house of Cornelius, with the Gentiles also being able to enter in. Moreover, in having cast out a demon, the Lord had declared: "then is the kingdom of God come upon you" (Matt. 12.28). So that where the Lord is, there is the kingdom of God. But Matthew 5–7 tells us that where a certain company of believers is, there, too, is the kingdom of the heavens. Wherever and whenever the believers become like the men described in the teaching on the Mount, there comes the kingdom of the heavens.

Let us not pay so much attention to the matter of environment that might induce us to think that the kingdom of the heavens will not have come until the right environment is present; for let us please understand that the kingdom represented by men is far more important than that signified by any kind of environment. It can consequently be stated that Matthew 5–7 informs us that when a very special and new company of believers comes into being, then and there the kingdom is present.

Matthew 13, on the other hand, speaks of another aspect of the kingdom. The seven parables therein show us what the kingdom is like. That is to say, when the kingdom of the heavens is preached on earth, these show us what are the *historical courses* it takes. It is very much the kingdom that is in view; only, it is its outward appearance. It is the Christianity that the world sees, the outward appearance of Christianity in this age.

Why does the Lord mention these lofty and deep standards to be found in Matthew 5–7? At the commencement of the teaching on the Mount, the emphasis is on what has already been alluded to above; namely, a certain company of persons whom the Lord is seeking to gain. The first seven beatitudes say, "they" (persons); the last two use the word "ye." All such persons of the kingdom of the heavens possess certain dispositions. This in itself would indicate a difference between grace and law. (I personally do not like the fashion of some who label Matthew 5–7 as "the *law* of the kingdom of the heavens.") What is law? See Romans 5.20 and 6.14: "the law came in besides, that the trespass might abound; but where sin abounded, grace did abound more exceedingly"; "sin shall not have dominion over you: for ye are not under law, but under grace." The law is like trying to kindle fire in the water or like seeking gold in sand. The more you are incapable of doing, the more you are required to do. This is the law as given in the Scriptures. The law that the world speaks of is command. Yet the law of the Scriptures is not given to us to be kept, but given to us to be broken, that the inability of our natural self might be exposed and sin might be magnified.

How different, though, is the teaching on the Mount. The Son of God has come. He died, was buried and was resurrected. The Holy Spirit came upon Him as noted in Matthew 3. All

His works subsequently done on earth are done on the ground of resurrection and the coming of the Holy Spirit. Although He was yet to die and to be resurrected and the Holy Spirit was yet to come on Pentecost, He has nonetheless already stood on such ground. (People who believe on Jesus as told of in John 3 have eternal life because He has already received the baptism of death before God, even though He has yet to die historically.) From God's viewpoint, the Lord has already stood on the ground of death, for He must indeed be baptized unto death to self in order to enter into His work for God. Now He has the Holy Spirit in Him and upon Him. And He now dares to give us—in the teaching on the Mount—such manner of strict command. For the heavier the demand, the greater the response of the divine life within. The life that our Lord has given us is inexhaustible. It is nothing surprising when we endure beyond our own endurance. God's demand never ends; it increases all the time; and yet the life within always carries us through. Therefore, whoever speaks of the Sermon on the Mount as constituting law knows nothing about either law or life. (Let us realize that a life lived according to the teaching on the Mount is a life lived under *grace*, not under *law*.)

Let us not despise the testing of the Lord. For through testing, the life within us is manifested. The greater the demands of God are upon this divine life, the greater is the manifestation of what is in this life. It is God who commands, but it is also God, by His divine life within us, who keeps the commandment. God himself fulfills what He demands. And hence, the teaching of the Sermon on the Mount is not law. (What is given on Mount Sinai is indeed law, because it is something which we are not able to do.) When we believers go ahead to follow the teaching on the Mount found in Matthew 5–7, we unconsciously fulfill it. The impossibles become possibles. And precisely this is what it is to be a Christian, the daily showing forth of what is impossible in oneself. For this reason, Romans 6.14 says that this which we have in Matthew 5–7 is what is truly under grace: it is God who enables me to do what He commands, for I am no longer under the domination of sin nor under the law.

The teaching on the Mount creates for this world many individuals whom this world is not worthy to have. It is not enough for these persons just to have life. There also needs to be a demand upon this life; otherwise, this divine life will not be manifested. This life is able to meet every one of the challenges of the teaching on the Mount! Without such demand, the exceedingly great power of the Lord in us may not be expressed. But when there is this demand, and that demand is met in the lives of men, *then* there is truly Christianity. On the one hand there is testing, on the other hand there is the supply of Christ. And when both are present, there is Christianity, there is the kingdom of the heavens.

The Lord is out to get a company of men who will obtain and enjoy now the environment of the future kingdom. (The Greek word translated as "a people" in Acts 15.14 may also be rendered as "men.") This is the time that God is choosing men. What kind of men are they to be? Men according to Matthew 5-7. With respect to such men as these, they are now the kingdom; and in the future, they will reign in the kingdom to come.

First Section 5.3-16

As indicated earlier, the Sermon on the Mount may be divided into six sections. In this section, we will talk about the men of the kingdom. What are the nature and characteristics of these men? It will be noted that the word "blessed" is used nine times in the passage now before us. Who are these blessed ones? Seven times the Greek original uses "they"; and two times, "ye." We shall look into both these usages in this initial section. But first, let us look closely at the *seven* kinds of blessed men that are presented here.

(1) "Blessed are the poor in spirit: for theirs is the kingdom
of heaven" (v.3). The men of the kingdom of the heavens possess
one basic characteristic: they are poor in spirit. It is not a blessed but a sinful thing for Christianity to travel the road of earthly
possessions. The persons whom the Lord truly blesses are the
poor: yet not only the poor outwardly, but preeminently the poor
inwardly.* Christianity is not to pay attention only to those who
are poor in terms of outward material things, since even some
of them may not be qualified to be the men of the kingdom of
the heavens; for though they may be poor in material things,
they may nonetheless be rich in their hearts if they continually
dream about wealth from dawn to dusk. Many may indeed be
poor outwardly, yet their hearts may be more ambitious towards
wealth and riches than those of anyone else. In short, their hearts,
far from being poor in spirit, are quite rich and full. Such individuals can have no share in the kingdom. So that essentially
this first beatitude enunciated by the Lord is a matter not of outward economic poverty but of inward character: we must be poor
in our spirit. Obviously, the outwardly rich have no part in the
kingdom; for as Jesus said on another occasion, it is hard for
the rich to enter the kingdom of the heavens (see Matt. 19.23).
But the outwardly poor may not necessarily enter the kingdom,
either, because their hearts may not be poor. In a word, the fact
of the matter lies not in a person being rich, but in his *minding*
to be rich.

Being poor in spirit is something voluntary, not environmental. At His birth, the Lord borrowed a manger. At His death,
He was buried in another's tomb. And while living, He had
nowhere to lay His head. His spirit while on earth was always

---

*That the Lord had in mind *both* the outward and inward states of His disciples
when enunciating this first "beatitude" is made clear when Luke's rendering
of this same beatitude is noted. In his Gospel account, Luke quotes Jesus
as saying: "Blessed are ye poor, for yours is the kingdom of God" (6.20).
—*Translator*

maintained in a state of poverty: He never nourished any desire for material gain. We ought to severely judge any minding within us to be rich. Paul never said that riches were the root of all evils. No, he plainly observed that "the *love* of money is a root of all kinds of evil" (1 Tim. 6.10). The outwardly rich and the outwardly poor may both be lovers of money. So that not only what is in your *hand* may hinder you from entering the kingdom of God, but what is in your *mind and heart* may equally keep you from entering. If you love God in your heart, you automatically hate Mammon. Yet if inwardly you hold on to Mammon in your heart but outwardly say you love God, you are deceiving yourself. Notice in the Greek original that the word is *"all* kinds of evil."

I should feel something is wrong if I am rich while many brothers and sisters are poor. If the Lord while on earth was poor, and if today brothers and sisters are poor, I too should be poor. It is a shameful thing to be rich when I ought to be poor. Such ones cannot enter the kingdom of God. Let us eradicate from our hearts the idea of the love of money and possessions. Christian character is expressed in an inward attitude of *loss*, not gain, towards the world. And the blessing pronounced upon those with such poverty of spirit is: they shall reign in the kingdom when its environment is finally brought in. According to the New Testament, Christians are to enter and *reign* in the kingdom of the heavens. The people of the kingdom in the Old Testament period are to be *people* (citizens) in the kingdom of the heavens. But a Christian either becomes a king (that is to say, one who rules) or he does not enter. Whoever is of kingly quality enters, otherwise he cannot enter: "for *theirs* is the kingdom of the heavens"— not to be people in the kingdom, but to be *kings*.*

(2) "Blessed are they that mourn: for they shall be comforted" (v.4). Such mourning is not for the sins of one's own self,

---

*For further clarification of these terms, see footnote at the conclusion of point (7) below.—*Translator.*

but for the current environment. Darkness, injustice and oppression are all around. Satan is being worshipped. There is the absence of righteousness, peace and truth. The Lord is being rejected. His teaching is being resisted. Poverty and sufferings fill this earth. Naturally, those who have the life of God will mourn. To "mourn" is the highest reaction. Anger and sorrow are also reactions. But mourning is the deepest as shown in Psalm 42. To witness the existing conditions makes one weep. This was the disposition of our Lord while on earth (see Luke 19.41–44). Whoever has such a temperament as this proves that God's life has been deeply incorporated in him.

Why mourn? Because there is love. Without love there can be no mourning, for there will be no such reaction where love is absent. Without love, there will be neither crying nor mourning. This, then, is a test. It is not simply an admonition of the Lord. It says, "Blessed are they that mourn." We already have this life. If we encounter such environment and yet are not sensitive to it, we should ask the Lord to give us burden. This is something we can learn. How can we live in this ungodly environment without having any feeling about it? If this be our condition of heart, then wherein are we any different from the world?

According to the Greek language, to "mourn" is to express the most heart-breaking kind of weeping. We ought to condemn on the one hand but love to the extent of mourning in weeping on the other hand. If so, then such who do shall one day be comforted. All the tears will be wiped away. Yet this is not to suggest that there will be no more feeling: it merely indicates that there is nothing left to be mourned for anymore. It means there is no longer any such mournful environment. And in *that* day we will share in the feeling which God had, as noted in Genesis, that all is "good."

(3) "Blessed are the meek: for they shall inherit the earth" (v.5). Meekness is also a character disposition. The meek one makes no demand on others, seeks nothing for self, and is fully

satisified with God's will and arrangement. He trusts in God's love which nevertheless lies behind affliction, and he believes in God's ordering—no matter the kind—as the best. He neither strives nor struggles for himself. He is willing to deny himself and take up the cross gladly. Whoever does not contend for himself, whoever accepts the cross, that one immediately becomes a meek person who is soft and tender before God. Do you want to be a crucified one or are you the kind of person who pushes himself forward on all occasions? Are you bearing the cross or are you, instead, maintaining your right?

The Lord himself was meek; therefore, He calls us to learn of Him; and the result will be that such people shall have rest in their souls. They will not be anxious for anything. In short, "they shall inherit the earth." Humanly speaking, it takes fighting and battling to inherit anything on the earth, and therefore the meek ones in such situations are finished! Yet in this beatitude, the Lord is saying that there shall be quite a surprise: the meek shall inherit the earth: one day the kingdom of this world shall become the kingdom of our Lord and of His Christ (see Rev. 11.15). To inherit the earth means to inherit the kingdom that is to be manifested.

(4) "Blessed are they that hunger and thirst after righteousness: for they shall be filled" (v.6). Hunger and thirst are excruciating sensations. To seek righteousness as the hungry and the thirsty ones is to have such a longing for it and to make such an endless search for it. The Lord has not said, "Blessed are the righteous." He says, instead, "Blessed are they that hunger and thirst *after* righteousness." When one day you are truly hungry, then you can begin to understand what is meant by hungering and thirsting after righteousness. Such a disposition as this is what God wants us to develop: it is a fear lest there be anything unrighteous in us, a fear lest any unrighteousness touches us.

Let us learn that which is righteous. The more we learn, the more our righteousness will expand. What we may have considered righteous before will now be reckoned as something we should not do. And hence the scope of our hungering and thirsting after righteousness will be enlarged in us, and the character of righteousness in us will be upgraded. And the consequence will be that such people will be satisfied, for the kingdom shall be filled with righteousness (Amos 5.24). The kind of satisfaction to be experienced in the kingdom is similar in nature to the satisfaction mentioned in Isaiah 53.11: "He shall see of the travail of his soul, and shall be satisfied."

Righteousness may indeed be increased. The more we have, the more we will hunger and thirst after it. And the more we hunger and thirst after righteousness, the more of it we shall have. But in the future, we shall be fully satisfied. The very least to be learned of righteousness is never to take advantage of other people. So that whoever has not learned this has not really learned any lesson in righteousness. Let us learn to return all that is not ours.

(5) "Blessed are the merciful: for they shall obtain mercy" (v.7). This too is a very essential character disposition. To be "merciful" means to be lenient, tolerant, uncritical, undemanding, taking no account of evil, willing to forgive and endure. This is a disposition that every Christian should early develop in his life in the Lord. What is meant by being a merciful man? He is one who can forgive and forget. This being "merciful" must be viewed in conjunction with the "righteousness" just discussed above. We should be afraid of being unrighteous, being wrong, or paying less than we should. In our giving to others, we are fearful of being unrighteous; but in others' giving to us, we are afraid of getting too much. We are strict towards ourselves but lenient towards other people.

So that a merciful man is a forgiving man. He is willing to let many things go. He is not always keeping count of how people treat him. As this disposition is gradually developed in a Christian, he begins to grow spiritually. He neither becomes critical nor judgmental. For judgment requires righteousness, not mercy. To be merciful is to give what is "undeserved" and to give to the undeserved. Such action is of great consequence: "they shall obtain mercy." This word is not only applicable to today, but it is also applicable at the judgment seat of Christ. When the Lord shall judge you in the future, He will see how you have judged your brethren in the Church today. If *today* you judge sharply, in *that* day you cannot expect leniency from the Lord: for with what measure you mete out to others, in the same measure will the Lord mete out to you in that day (see Luke 6.38b).

Let us therefore pay attention to this if this be our lack. Our today's attitude will decide the Lord's attitude towards us in the future: "The Lord grant unto him to find mercy of the Lord in that day " (2 Tim. 1.18) was the prayer of Paul. To be merciful today will have its lasting effect before God. Even at the Lord's judgment seat there will be mercy, and such mercy will be righteous. We may today affect the Lord to be either very merciful to us or very unmerciful to us at His judgment seat. He who is merciful is one who goes beyond righteousness. All who go beyond righteousness by being merciful today shall in that day receive from the Lord mercy which is beyond righteousness. Today I may barely pass. Therefore, I must lower my demands upon others. I must increase the demand of righteousness on myself and be filled with mercy towards others. Let us remember at all times how great is our debt to the Lord and how much we need forgiveness. Then we will not be so strict with other people. Yet this is not to be one act only; this is to be a developed and developing character. In not being exacting, I will become a merciful man. I will like to forgive. I will love to treat other people leniently. And the end result shall be that though I may not be perfect here on earth, at the judgment seat of Christ I may receive unexpected mercy. For this reason, as long as we have the possibility of receiving mercy, let us learn to be liberal as well as righteous.

(6) "Blessed are the pure in heart: for they shall see God" (v.8). What the Jews attend to is the cleanness in procedures, affairs and fleshly body. What is here spoken of concerns the purity of the heart. The Pharisees washed the outside of the cups and plates, but they neglected the truth and the law of God. The Lord makes it clear that it is the pure heart that really matters while the other things are non-consequential. There is no double heart with respect to God. Apart from Him, there is no other desire. This is what is meant by being "pure in heart." For the pure in heart, there is but one aim: to serve God and to please Him and also to live for others.

In this matter of seeing, let us note that it is not governed by thought but by the heart. It is based on our consecration and obedience, not on our cleverness and comprehension. No matter how clever you are, you may not see. But if your heart is pure and single, you will indeed see. If the heart is wrong, all that is done will be wrong. Please take note that it does not require an object as large as the earth to conceal the moonlight; oftentimes a single leaf can hide the light of the moon. So is it with the heart. A slight slant of the heart will cause spiritual blindness. Seeing is not the result of thinking through, it comes from having a pure heart. Singleness of heart is the test of absolute surrender. All whose consecration is not absolute are blind, but the pure in heart can see. Consecration is the sole condition for seeing the truth, whereas the slightest reservation can produce a different view. Man's opinion follows his intention, not his brain. Absolute surrender alone guarantees the ability to see.

"They shall see God": this refers not only to today's seeing, it also points to the seeing in the kingdom. At the Lord's return, we shall see as we are being seen. We shall see Him: we shall see His real image. Hence, seeing God in the future is based on our being pure in heart today (cf. 1 John 3.3,4).

(7) "Blessed are the peacemakers: for they shall be called sons of God" (v.9). It is God's delight to make peace. God recon-

ciles the world through the death of the Lord on the cross. He longs for men to be reconciled to Him. All who possess God's disposition ought to have the desire to be reconcilers of men to God. This is not only to be true in gospel preaching, it is even more so to be true among brethren in the Lord's body. Some brothers and sisters seem by nature to thrive on disputes and dissensions. They do not look for peace among the brethren. Yet whatever word which might divide the brethren should never be spoken. Have we diligently kept the unity of the Spirit? Oftentimes, we are not as diligent as we should be. We ought to persistently maintain peace among God's children. Any word which produces peace among the brethren is a good word, and any work which brings in peace among the brethren is a good work.

In order to be a peacemaker, one has himself to be filled with the peace of God. Some have turmoils within, so they expect disturbances without. Let us learn to make peace among our brothers and sisters. Agitation is not a Christian disposition; it should be condemned. We read in Proverbs 6.14–19 that he who sows discord among brethren is an abomination to God. The Scriptures command us to avoid fellowship with such people (Titus 3.10 mg.). We ourselves must not be contentious, nor should we maintain fellowship with any persons who are. To be able to make peace is a disposition which comes only from the peace of God within. And such men shall be called the sons of God. They shall be declared to be the sons of God in the kingdom of the heavens because they are truly like God.

Now all seven of the above features are inward dispositions of character, since all of them refer to the person himself, not to the deeds of the person. Hence, these seven beatitudes advert to seven types of men who possess such dispositions. These men are not merely the saved, nor are they only people who have done these things once or twice. They have learned their lessons to such a degree that they eventually become such men. Concerning these, the Lord himself acknowledges that they are blessed.

The men of the kingdom of the heavens are not the non-believers (including from among both the Jews and the Gentiles). These are in very truth the *possessors* of the kingdom of the heavens. They are blessed, for all seven promises refer to rewards of the kingdom. Let us therefore notice four things here by way of conclusion: *first* is the environment of the kingdom, which is seen and prophetically described in the Old Testament; *second* is the people of the kingdom, which is also seen in the Old Testament; *third* is the men of the kingdom, who are these seven types of persons just described here; and *fourth* is the power and glory of the kingdom, which are the seven blessings herein promised. What will be rewarded are power and glory which far exceed our present comprehension. When the blessed Lord pronounces "Blessed," those upon whom it is pronounced are blessed indeed! Who can know or imagine to what extent these blessings will become as both the power and the glory of the kingdom of the heavens are joined into one! To be saved and forgiven is one thing; but to be blessed unto the kingdom is quite another.*

---

*Perhaps a further clarification of the terms used here by the author will be of help to the reader. According to his understanding of the Scriptures, Watchman Nee sees the kingdom as having two spheres, the heavenly and the earthly. The phrase above, "the people of the kingdom," refers to the future millennial kingdom on earth, and hence the people of the kingdom in the Old Testament period become the people of the millennial kingdom. The Christians of the New Testament period are to be kings in the millennial kingdom, which thus refers to the heavenly part of the kingdom of the heavens. Christians either enter as kings or do not enter the kingdom at all but are to be cast into "the outer darkness" (Matt. 25.30) to be disciplined and further matured. Thus the author makes a distinction between "people" and "men" here, the latter referring to Christians who reign with Christ as kings in the millennium and the former referring to the citizens of the kingdom. Those who reign with Christ shall reign from heaven upon earth — that is to say, they shall rule over the citizens of five or ten cities in the earthly millennial kingdom (see Luke 19.11,17–19). At the same time, Israel shall stand at the center of all the nations, there being many (the sheep nations — see Matt. 25.31-4) left in the world.—*Translator*

5.10–11 Following are two other pronouncements of "blessed" which are different from the seven above. For the preceding seven are character dispositions, whereas the two suceeding ones are deeds. To be persecuted is a matter of conduct, not of character. Both verses 10 and 11 speak of persecution: the subject of verse 10 is persecution for righteousness' sake; verse 11, for the King's sake. One bespeaks the principles of righteousness, the other bespeaks the name of the Lord himself.

Being persecuted for righteousness' sake shows that a person is different from the world. His persecution, however, is not considered to be very severe. Accordingly, the reward stated ends with the kingdom of the heavens. But to be persecuted for the Lord's sake surpasses this other persecution, and hence the Lord declares: "great is your reward." When the Lord says great, it must be great indeed. As long as there is no conflict of interest, your righteousness may not be persecuted. It is when there is conflict of interest, however, that righteousness will be persecuted. Not so, though, with the Lord. The world hates the Lord. The moment you mention Christ, strangely enough, you even bear His reproach on your face. The relationship between Christ and the world remains the same even up to this moment. As the world hated Him then, so it hates Him now. Consequently, the scope of persecution for righteousness' sake is a limited one, while that for the Lord's sake is without bounds. You begin to realize how different the world is from the Lord. The world hates Him; so it hates you: "men shall reproach you, and persecute you, and say all manner of evil against you falsely" without any reason except for the sake of Christ. They do all this to you because you are Christians—that is to say, Christ's ones. Nonetheless, it indicates that our relationship with the Lord must be real, or else such things against the Lord would not fall upon us.

Let us therefore be ready for persecution. Let us have the mind to suffer (cf. 1 Peter 4.1). We do not expect the world to change, nor should we give the world any reason to expect us to change. Some forms of persecution are not too hard to endure because they do not defile. But slander is defiling and falsifying.

5.12 What should be our attitude towards these things? Perhaps some will say that since this is inevitable let us hold our breath and endure silently. Yet the Scripture verse says here for us to "rejoice, and be exceeding glad." For at that moment the Spirit of glory shall come upon us and give us such great joy as we have never before experienced. Lord, I praise You, and I thank You, for You consider me as worthy to be persecuted for You. Yet why should we be *exceeding* glad"? Because "great is your reward in heaven." This reward that our Lord promises must be something subjective and quite spectacular in nature, "for so persecuted they the prophets that were before you."

This, then, is Church history. Such men today are not alone, for not only is the Lord with them, the prophets are too. This so-called ninth beatitude bespeaks such elevated heights that the Lord simply declares that the reward is great. It is so great that it is beyond description. Now if it is great in the Lord's eye, will it not be sufficient for us?

5.13–16 It is not enough for God's children to have life. That new life in us must become our very nature. Why must believers possess the aforementioned dispositions? Because "ye are the salt of the earth." We are salt; we must have the salty taste. The nine "blesseds" which the Lord declares to us can give the Christian that salty taste. Yet salt which loses its savor is useless.

Life in a Christian is one thing; life developed by the Lord into character is quite another. From the Lord's viewpoint, the world is corrupt. Though it is impossible for the world to repent, it *is* possible to stop it from further corruption. The purpose of salt is to preserve things from corruption or prevent them from further deterioration. In a sinful society, family or school, many improper things have been stopped or kept from further decadence by salty Christians. Yes, you as Christians are the salt of the earth. You should salt the world to give it a salty savor. This is not done by your propaganda, but by your character. If, however, like salt, you have lost your savor, how can you be salted again? Some Christians have lost their testimony. It is hard for them to be salted again. In the eyes of the Lord they are "good for nothing, but to be cast out and trodden under foot of men." They will be cast out; they will not be respected by the world (especially during the Great Tribulation); and they will be trodden down.

On the other hand, the Lord shows us this: "Ye are the light of the world." He further explains: "A city set on a hill cannot be hid." He uses light to represent His children, and then uses the image of a city to illustrate the light. A believer cannot be hidden. As soon as you become a Christian, you are like the light, and this light is like a city set on a hill. And in verse 15 we read: "Neither do men light a lamp, and put it under the bushel, but on the stand; and it shineth unto all that are in the house." Some Christians are lights that are not shining. They deliberately cover the light. We must be lights that shine. When we are poor in spirit, we naturally shine. When we hunger and thirst after righteousness, we shine spontaneously. So, too, with the other character dispositions spoken of earlier.

There is no trial too great, for it does not try *you* but tries that *life of the Lord* in you. When that life is tested, it shines. Why do we consider the poor in spirit, those who mourn, and the meek ones as the shining light? Because the very fact that our dispositions differ from the world enlightens the world. The Lord leaves us here to manifest these dispositions so that we might prevent corruption on the one hand and condemn sins on the other. The light ought to be put on the stand, that is to say, it ought to be placed in an especially exposed position, so that then it might shine upon all around. Light is not heard, it can only be seen. Do people see the same thing in you as they have heard of you? You may testify, but can people see in your life that to which

you have testified? Light will shine — and even without any speech.
You are not only to persuade men but also to display the fact
before them that you as a Christian differ from them.

Verse 16 gives us a command. The Lord declares: "Even so
let your light shine before men; that they may see your good
works, and glorify your Father who is in heaven." Are "your light"
and "your good works" one and the same thing, or are they different? The Lord treats them as the same thing. Your light should
shine before men, and as it shines they see your good works. If
the light does not shine, your good works will not be seen even
though they may be there. The act of shining is actually the nature
of God being manifested in my life; it is not I myself. So that
it is really more than good works before men. If it were only
good works, people would simply give glory to us. The shining
before men is a recognition that we are Christians — that we
belong to Christ. We confess that formerly we were sinners, unjust and hardened, but one day the nature of God was manifested
in our lives. And that becomes the shining. As men behold the
light being emitted from our good works, they will glorify God.

This, then, is our daily testimony. Once we were in darkness,
but now the nature of God comes through in us. Such light shines
upon men and condemns sins. As people see our good works,
they give glory to God and acknowledge that Christians are different. Let us therefore judge ourselves and testify of the Lord.

Second Section 5.17–48

The first section ends with verse 16. Beginning from verse
17 to the end of chapter 5 forms a second section. The first has
dealt with the men of the kingdom of the heavens. This next section dwells at some length on the perfect "law."

5.17–20 This is one of the most easily misunderstood
passages in the entire New Testament.

First of all, what does the phrase, "the law and the prophets," mean? When the terms, the law and the prophets, are joined together, the resultant phrase has reference to the entire Old Testament ("the law" does not simply point to the Ten Commandments). "I came not to destroy, but to fulfil," that is, Jesus came not to destroy the Old Testament, but to fulfill it. From the Lord's standpoint, the law and the prophets are incomplete. He therefore comes to raise the standard and make it complete: "fulfil" is to fill full, to make something complete.

"For verily I say unto you, Till heaven and earth pass away, one jot or one tittle shall in no wise pass away from the law, till all things be accomplished." What the Lord means here is that the law must be fulfilled before it passes away. This passage does not say that the law will not pass away, for it will pass away eventually, but not till all things are accomplished. Then this problem of the law shall be completely resolved. Only when all of the law has been accomplished will it pass away at the time heaven and earth pass away. What are recorded in the Old Testament are things related to this our own heaven and earth (only in Isaiah is there any touching upon the matter of the new heaven and the new earth). Before this heaven and earth of ours pass away, every jot and tittle of the law will be accomplished. (Incidentally, it should be observed that this law has nothing to do with the Seventh Day Adventists; it is simply an abbreviated way of referring to the totality of the Old Testament.)

5.19 "Whosoever therefore shall break one of these least commandments, and shall teach men so, shall be called least in the kingdom of heaven; but whosoever shall do and teach them, he shall be called great in the kingdom of heaven." The Greek word for "commandments" here is plural in number. First of all, what are these commandments? Second, who are these great and least ones in the kingdom of the heavens? Are they Christians or are they Jews? In His seven letters recorded in the Book of Revelation, our Lord mentions twice of attempts to make the influence of the Jews present in the Church. Many, in reading the Bible, as soon as they see the word "commandments" readily assume this to be a reference to the Ten Commandments. But the commandments mentioned here in verse 19 are not the well known Decalogue of the Old Testament. For although in this section the Lord is indeed found citing five commandments from the Old Testament, only two belong to the Decalogue (vv.21,27) while three do not (vv.33,38,43). It can therefore be stated that these commandments given by the Lord are not the well known Decalogue or Ten Commandments of old.

Moreover, the great and the least ones in the kingdom of the heavens are not the Jews, as is evident from Matthew chapter 11: (a) "all the prophets and the law prophesied until John" (v.13) — meaning that from John the Baptist onward, the kingdom of the heavens is preached, and men of violence take it by force; also, (b) "he that is but little in the kingdom of heaven is greater than he [John the Baptist]" (v.11). So that these men in the kingdom (the great and least ones) are outside the Old Testament personages, they having to be different from John. (If they *were* of the Old Testament period, they would be smaller than John; yet the least of these men in the kingdom of the heavens is greater than John). The Old Testament period actually ends with John the Baptist, and thereafter the New Testament period begins. And he who is but little in the kingdom of the heavens is greater than John. It can hence be concluded that the least and the great ones in the kingdom of the heavens are definitely not men of the Old Testament. They are Christians.

Coupling this chapter 11 of Matthew with chapter 5, let us read verse 19 again. It is clear that one of these least commandments does not refer to the Decalogue. Are they from among the other commandments in the law? No, for the law ends with John. Consequently, these least commandments point to those that our Lord has fulfilled. This is why later on the Lord repeatedly says, "but I say unto you . . ." Though He begins with, "ye have heard that it was said to them of old time," He is nonetheless not emphasizing these commandments of old. The law has its eternal value. The words of prophecy in the Old Testament will not pass away till they are fulfilled. Yet right here the Lord fills them to the full, especially by virtue of raising, as He does, their moral standard. So that the teaching on the Mount is to uplift and not destroy the commandments of the Old Testament.

"Whosoever therefore shall break one of these least commandments, and shall teach men so, shall be called least in the kingdom of heaven." Whoever breaks one of these least commandments as fulfilled by the Lord, that is to say, whoever is unable to observe it, yet at the same time teaches men so, that is to say, he teaches that it is the Lord's word, that one shall be deemed to be the least in the kingdom of heavens. Even so, he is still greater than John. This is then followed by the words, "but whosoever shall do and teach them, he shall be called great in the kingdom of heaven." Great, not the greatest. In actual fact, even if you keep all the commandments except one of the least of them, and believe in all the teachings as well, you still shall become the least.

5.20 After saying the above words, the Lord speaks especially on the kinds of persons who cannot enter the kingdom of the heavens. (These are: (1) the unregenerated, (2) the unrepentant, and (3) those whose righteousness fails to exceed.) He begins by declaring in this verse 20: "I say unto you, that except your righteousness shall exceed the righteousness of the scribes and Pharisees, ye shall in no wise enter into the kingdom of heaven." This proves that the view we have taken here concerning the law is correct. For the righteousness of the scribes and Pharisees is that according to the law. If one's righteousness is according to the law, it is the righteousness of the scribes and Pharisees, and that one can therefore not enter the kingdom of the heavens. The righteousness of a Christian must exceed that of the scribes and Pharisees. And hence this must mean that he is following a higher law. The law of the Old Testament is the law of the scribes and the Pharisees; but when the Lord declares, "But I say unto you

84

. . ." — such declaration has reference to a higher law. The teaching of the Lord Jesus on the Mount is higher than that which was given to Moses on Mount Sinai. The righteousness that is derived from keeping the teaching on the Mount is higher than that which is derived from keeping the law which the scribes and the Pharisees try to observe. Accordingly, no one can enter the kingdom of the heavens unless he is one who keeps the teaching on the Mount. Such is the standard of the kingdom of the heavens.

The principal word in this passage from verses 17 to 20 is spoken in verse 20. Here is laid before us this matter of entering the kingdom of the heavens. It has nothing to do with being saved and having eternal life. Rather, it has to do with showing whether or not the life is there, since the commandments of the Lord are directed towards that life. Commandments draw out the life within. The growth of this inner divine life of God depends on the demand of these commandments. So that the words in Matthew 5 are not concerned with *having* life but with the *growth* of life. These words have no reference to Christ being our righteousness, but to His righteousness being manifested in us. Our righteousness must be higher than that of the scribes and Pharisees. Our law must be higher than their law. Inasmuch as the latter law is incomplete, the quality of its righteousness must be lower. But here is a higher and better law, one which the Lord comes to fulfill. He brings in the *spirit* of the law. The word "fulfil" here in verse 17 does not refer to a fulfilling of prophecy; it denotes progress. The commandments of God are always progressing. The Lord comes to bring all the wills of God to their highest potentials. He does not destroy the former, He instead fills them to the fullest: He expands them to perfection. Such is the meaning of "fulfil." The unmatured law produces unmatured righteousness; but matured righteousness comes from the matured law brought in by the Lord Jesus.

5.21–26 Here it speaks of the fulfilled law. "But I say unto you . . ." The better law has now come. "Thou shalt not kill" is the righteousness of the scribes and Pharisees. You indeed may not have killed today, but you are not therefore qualified to enter the kingdom of the heavens. The standard for entering in is higher than "Thou shalt not kill." The demand of God on Old Testament people was rather low, but He requires much more from New Testament saints: "but I say unto you . . ." How many times *more* demanding is this which God now says! For only by the observance of such teaching on the Mount can the righteousness which exceeds that of the scribes and Pharisees be produced and the kingdom of the heavens entered.

In verse 21 the Lord is found mentioning this matter of killing. He does not cite one of the other Ten Commandments having to do with regulating the relationship of man with *God,* for people may easily slip away from *it.* But one of them which has to do with regulating the relationship of man with *man* is easier to lay hold of and harder to slip away from. And hence, the Lord selects "Thou shalt not kill," which is undeniably one of the Ten Commandments (Ex. 20.13). Moreover, "whosoever shall kill shall be in danger of the judgment" is added from the word in Deuteronomy (19.11-13). The act of killing, however, is the ultimate step taken. A number of other things must happen before the act of killing can take place. And this is what the Lord Jesus draws attention to here.

How much stricter, therefore, is the Lord's word. He does not destroy the law of "Thou shalt not kill"; rather, He fulfills or makes complete that very law; for He condemns anger and everything else that occurs between anger and the act of killing (those such as scolding, hating and despising). The scribes and Pharisees do all these things except kill. But in the eye of the Lord, the whole process from anger to actual killing is called killing. The law of the scribes and Pharisees focuses on but one aspect; the Christian's law—as brought in by Christ—covers the entire process. For our Lord does not ask if anyone has taken the last step of killing. He asks if anyone has merely *started* down the road of killing. Have you taken the first step—that of anger?

If so, then once this first step has been taken, it means you have killed a person already even though you have not completed the process. With the consequence being that you are in danger of judgment.

Hence the judgment our Lord would dole out to us does not have to do with just the last step taken but with the very first step initiated. How different is this approach from the former law! The new commandment which the Lord enunciates on the Mount deals with the thought and intent of the heart. In short, it is a *fulfilled* law. Now as believers keep this perfect, fulfilled law, their righteousness shall greatly exceed the righteousness of the scribes and Pharisees.

The word "judgment" was used by the Jews of that time. The judgment of the Council was dispensed at Jerusalem. It can be likened to the judgment today of a nation's supreme court. "In danger unto the hell of fire." "Hell of fire" (Greek: Gehenna of fire) refers to the valley of Hinnom (or Gehenna) outside Jerusalem where people were burnt after being stoned to death. Different descriptions are employed to illustrate the differences in the degree of judgment. Here the emphasis is on "brother" (used twice in verse 22, and once more each in verses 23 and 24), for the Lord wants to especially maintain the unity of the brethren. "Whosoever hateth his brother is a murderer" (1 John 3.15). Do not conclude that *Raca* (an expression of contempt) and *Moreh,* translated as "Thou fool" (a Hebrew expression of condemnation) are severe words of scolding. They simply mean "good-for-nothing" or "you fool." Nevertheless, Christians should avoid using these words. In God's eye, it is a most serious thing for brethren to engage in contention, reviling and anger among themselves. Today's anger may become tomorrow's hate and the day-after-tomorrow's reviling. The Lord condemns every hostile motion of the heart, for each is but a step towards the ultimate act of murder. It is like a fire kindled from hell (cf. James 3.6). Salvation is eternal, and yet there is also the hell of fire.

"If therefore thou art offering thy gift at the altar [this is a preponderant act of a Jew], and there rememberest that thy brother hath aught against thee [which is due to your getting angry at him, hating him or offending him], leave there thy gift before the altar, and go thy way, first be reconciled to thy brother, and then come and offer thy gift." In the teaching on the Mount, there are three "firsts" — namely, "first be reconciled" (here in 5.24), "seek ye first" (6.33), and "cast out first" (7.5). Being at odds with one's brother hinders one's fellowship with God. So do not speak idly, do not reprimand and scold at will. Whatever does not come from love is reckoned as killing in the sight of the Lord. If any brother or sister has any grievance against you, be it groundless or with grounds, try your best to be reconciled. If there *are* grounds for grievance, and yet you fail to try to be reconciled, you have already committed the sin of killing, and you therefore need to get rid of that sin. Or if your brother holds a grievance against you without cause, he too has committed the sin of killing already, and you therefore need to help him out of his sin. Whether you sin or your brother sins, there is sin in the Church. We must get rid of any sin in the body of Christ. Then we will be blessed ten-fold or even a hundred-fold by God. When all grievances among the brethren have been resolved, the flow of the Holy Spirit will pervade the whole body of Christ.

The word in verse 23 is very weighty. The cry of the brother whom you have offended will one day come before the Lord. This becomes the greatest hindrance to our prayer being answered. Your brother's unhappiness at you may block many days of your prayer.

Concerning your brother's accusation, you ought to heed the Lord's admonition to "agree with thine adversary quickly, while thou art with him in the way." People are not forever in the way. For example, the brother who has anything against you may die. There is no manner of being reconciled if one is not in the way. Whether your brother or you yourself, both will not forever be in the way. Very important is the word spoken by the Lord here. "Agree with thine adversary *quickly*" — quickly, for the time is short:

"lest haply the adversary deliver thee to the judge . . ." All these constituents — the judge, the officer and the prison — are figures of speech. They point to the judgment seat of Christ and the outer darkness. "Verily I say unto thee, Thou shalt by no means come out thence, till thou have paid the last farthing." What is unresolved in the way will be settled in prison. Nothing can remain unresolved. Due to the Lord's life in us, it is not hard to love the brethren.

5.27–32 This passage deals with the issue of adultery. It reiterates the same principle of process as mentioned before with respect to killing and murder. Sex is natural, and is a natural urge. It becomes illegitimate, however, when sex is practiced outside of marriage: it becomes adultery. According to the law of Moses, a man commits adultery when there is actual physical union. Yet the Lord declares, as He has said before, that adultery, like murder, is a process and not a single step: "but I say unto you, that every one that looketh [look intentionally, not casually; look actively, not accidentally] on a woman to lust after her [look with lust] hath committed adultery with her already in his heart." Here, then, are three steps: (1) see, (2) look, and (3) lust. What our Lord condemns is (2) (3), not (1). When you see a woman and have sexual sensation, this is not sin. But if you actively look again and have the sense of guilt, this *is* sin. To look with lust in the heart, that is adultery. It is not in the first glance; it is in the second. From this second glance to the actual physical union, every step in the process is considered by God to be adultery. So that what the Lord condemns here is a matter of the heart. When you look the second time, your heart is already corrupted. How clean ought believers to be in this matter! The words in verses 29 and 30 are extremely grave. A Christian should keep his purity so diligently that he would rather be disabled than be unclean. He must not sin either with his eye or with his hand.

Sexual feeling is not sin; marriage is not sin. Both sex and marriage are holy (Matt. 19.6). God uses marriage to solve the problem of fornication (1 Cor. 7.2). Some may make themselves eunuchs for the kingdom of the heavens' sake (Matt. 19.12). Hence, on the one hand we must see the holiness of marriage and on the other, the uncleanness of adultery. Let us rather be disabled than be defiled.

Verses 31 and 32 may be appended to the above subject. Someone may commit adultery through divorcing his wife. There is only one permissible justification allowed for divorce, and that is fornication. Otherwise, anyone who puts away his wife by divorce automatically makes her an adulteress; and whoever then marries her, commits adultery.

5.33–37 This is the third subject to be dealt with. It focuses upon the issue of speech. In spite of the fact that the words of the scribes and Pharisees were untrustworthy before men, they dared not speak carelessly before God. This is the righteousness of the scribes and Pharisees. Why is it that the Old Testament people could swear? In what respect is swearing not good? What happens when no oath is made? All of this actually reduces the issue to honesty in conduct, not honesty in character. You swear because your word is not trustworthy without accompanying it with an oath. What the Lord shows us here is not that an oath is altogether wrong, but that it is not good enough. Honesty underscored by an oath is but the righteousness of the scribes and Pharisees, since such righteousness is operative only at the time of an oath and not when there is the absence of an oath. But for Christians, this is not sufficient ground for entering the kingdom of the heavens. For this reason the Lord declares: "I say unto you, Swear not at all; neither by the heaven, for it is the throne of God; nor by the earth, for it is the footstool of his feet; nor by Jerusalem, for it is the city of the great King. Neither shalt thou swear by thy head, for thou canst not make one hair white or black." Your swearing or uttering an oath is futile because even your hair will not hear you. Yet, we may still not understand why the Lord forbids us to swear till we come to verse 37: "let your speech be, Yea, yea; Nay, nay: and whatsoever is more than these is of the evil one."

If anyone wishes to enter the kingdom of the heavens, he cannot afford to neglect the various issues thus far presented: those of chastity, of hate, and of speech. And with respect to this latter issue, Jesus makes clear here that our words should be simple. The purpose of speech is to reveal fact, not to confuse it. Our Lord joins speech and swearing together in order to show us that when a Christian speaks forth, he need not swear or utter an oath as an accompaniment to what he says. The act of swearing suggests the presence of lying.

As a Christian, I should not have any special moments for truthful speaking, since all through the day I speak as before God. Therefore, my word *without* an oath ought to be as trustworthy as when it is *accompanied* by an oath. It is yea, yea, without the need of adding anything else or the need of calling heaven to be witness. Furthermore, if there be the case that my words are not being trusted in ordinary days, therefore compelling me to quickly declare that I do not lie because I am a Christian — this has the same flavor about it as though I were to utter an oath. So let us daily prove the trustworthiness of our words alone. Then we need not especially plead for trust by means of these unacceptable devices. We should not add color to our words, neither enlarging upon nor diminishing them. When our speech is closer to fact, it becomes more simple.

He who is disciplined in word learns to make his word the same as fact. If your word is more or is less than the fact, you have already commenced down the pathway of the lie. Let your word be simple, as though it has been refined by God. "Whatsoever is more than these is of the evil one." By only slightly altering your speech, your word comes from Satan. How very serious it is to use the mouth of a Christian to utter the word of the Devil. This shows how important our speech is.

A lie comes from Satan: "When he speaketh a lie, he speaketh of his own: for he is a liar, and the father thereof" (John 8.44). James, in his Epistle, declared that the tongue "is set on fire by hell" (3.6). Lies and inaccurate words all come from hell. If the righteousness of a Christian in this area of life does not exceed that of the scribes and Pharisees, he cannot enter the kingdom of the heavens.

As indicated earlier, Matthew 5.1-16 deals with character; but from verse 17 onward, it deals with conduct. and thus far we have discussed: (1) brotherly love, (2) chastity, and (3) speech. All these must be diligently learned before the Lord. Let us pay special attention to the mind of the soul and the tongue of the body. For in these two areas is where Satan is actively at work. Paul said that as brothers our conduct should be: "lie not one to another" (Col. 3.9). He also said to "speak ... truth each one with his neighbor" (Eph. 4.25). For a Christian to lie is truly a horrible state of affairs because lying puts one outside the kingdom.

5.38-42 Here, a fourth matter of conduct to be discussed is what we can call Christian reaction. Our lives from morning to night are full of reaction. As other people make a move, we too move. Not that we *initiate,* but that we *react.* After others speak or act, we speak back or react. They move first, and then we respond to their move. Let us note that what we now find before us in this passage is not something spoken to the world or to international politicians. The Lord is not teaching politics or economics here. For something of that nature, we can go to Genesis: "Who so sheddeth man's blood, by man shall his blood be shed" (9.6). This declaration of the Lord in Genesis is political in nature. But we Christians are not politicians. So that the particular reaction being spoken about there is not for us but for government, because government is based on law, and politics follows the law. However, what the Lord talks about in the Matthew passage now before us concerns the reactive conduct and walk which should characterize believers. Let us therefore look closely at what the Lord teaches.

"An eye for an eye, and a tooth for a tooth" — such is the righteousness of the scribes and the Pharisees. Under Old Testament law, if you were to knock out one of my teeth, I would legitimately be able to knock out one of yours. And so, the first knocking out would be sin, but the second knocking out would not be sin but righteousness. Yet all who embrace such an attitude of righteousness as this cannot enter the kingdom of the heavens. The one who reviles first and the one who reviles next must both remain outside the kingdom of the heavens. To exceed the righteousness of the scribes and the Pharisees is, according to the teaching on the Mount, to "resist not him that is evil."

What then follows in the Lord's teaching are three parables. If in each of these situations our reaction will be merely just and equal, we cannot enter the kingdom of the heavens. For he who reacts on the Old Testament law basis of an eye for an eye and a tooth for a tooth is one who seeks merely to be just, and that is precisely what the scribes and the Pharisees do: yet it does not lead them into the kingdom of the heavens. The righteousness of a Christian must exceed that of the scribes and Pharisees. This is because the life we as Christians have within us is a life that refuses to hurt people either (1) in initiating hurtfulness or (2) in reacting against it in kind. What the world judges as wrong is the first strike; but the second strike is deemed by the world to be self-defense. Even killing is sometimes acceptably called self-defense by the world. But the life within the Christian will not only not hit first, it will not hit at all. For there is no such element in it as smiting. The divine life within the Christian does not know how to smite first, nor does it know how to smite back: there is no characteristic of smiting about it at all. The life of the Christian is the life of Christ. This life will neither commence with hitting nor follow up with hitting. Needless to say, this is beyond the comprehension of the world; yet such conduct is not an "ism" or a movement or political or social tactic. It is simply the active and reactive behavior of the Christian.

"Right cheek . . . the other." This is not what man can do. Even if some may do so, in their hearts they may be thinking that there will be a day of reckoning in the future before God. So that their conduct is equally invalid. In turning the other cheek, there must not be any hate resident within the person. Yet this kind of reaction which comes forth from within is not expended or manifested just once. The patience and love that is expressed is long-enduring in nature. The love in me is greater than the hate in you. You ask for one mile, I can go two miles. You contrive to take my coat, I am willing to give you my cloak as well. It means that no one can provoke me beyond measure. What is in me is much stronger than what you can do. Now *that* is true Christianity.

My reaction, if it is truly Christian, is something the world cannot and does not have. It is more than mere patience. It is *grace,* of which patience is but a part. And no one can exhaust the Lord's grace in me. Let us see that what is taking place here is that God is testing me. Yet, as a matter of fact, it is not *I* whom God tests, but actually He is testing *himself,* in showing me, if He be allowed to do so, what the Lord who abides in me can do. God is well able to supply all the demands, yea, even *more* than what is demanded. Who, then, is able to "finish me off"? The inner reality is always greater than the outward trial. And *this* is what is termed true Christian reaction.

Here is neither resistance nor non-resistance. Turning the other cheek after having had the right cheek smitten is not non-resistance. Our Lord has not preached resistance; nor has He preached *non*-resistance. On the contrary, He says that there is a reaction within you which is greater than the evil of men. Here is a transcending power which the world does not know. There can be no person on the earth today more *positive* than a Christian who displays this kind of reaction. Here, too, is the most *powerful* person on earth, because this kind of Christian is able to control himself. Yet let us not mistake this as a sign of weakness: we have yet to meet a stronger person, for this kind of Christian is so strong that *he can afford not to care for himself.*

Let us look at this matter of reaction more closely. As we have seen, to react is to take some action in response to what others do or say. Of the three parables told of in this section, the one concerning the coat and the cloak demonstrates for us how we must lay down the material things of the world; that of the other cheek to be turned and smitten especially has reference to our dealing with the glory of men; and the parable of the one and two miles points to the issue of freedom. With respect to this latter parable, any forcing of me to go your way encroaches upon my freedom. But the one who truly knows God is capable of letting go his freedom entirely. For God's demand is greater than that of the evil person. He who is evil demands the right cheek, the coat and the one mile, but God demands both the right cheek *and* the left, the coat *and* the cloak, first mile *and* the second. God's demand doubles that of the evil man. It is relatively easier to deal with the demand of the evil one, but it is very hard to cope with God's demand. No matter how people treat you, they cannot require higher of you than that which God requires of you. Many problems are created due to an unsettling relationship between us and God. If you have an absolute consecration before Him, you will feel that all the demands *men* make on you are *far less* than what *God* has asked of you.

Now reaction is very quick in happening. When people act, you respond almost immediately. And such response leaves no time to think. It gives you time neither to pray nor to consider. Hence Christian reaction is far more advanced than many other forms of righteousness. This form of righteousness requires more thorough learning before God; otherwise, you may indeed offer your left *cheek* when you *remember* but stretch out your left *hand* when you do *not* remember. How we need to have our consecration absolute so that when things happen we may react rightly without even thinking or remembering or considering or praying. So great and habitual is the grace of God upon us that even without consideration or thought our reaction is right.

And finally: "Give to him that asketh thee, and from him that would borrow of thee turn not thou away" (v.42). One brother once said, "You cannot give everything to men, but you can at least give something to every man." He who has arrived at such a place is undoubtedly one who has no reservation before God. How we need to look to the Lord for protection. These situations of which the Lord has been speaking will expand our capacity. The more we do, the larger our capacity, *till there is not a single thing in the world that has a grip on us.*

Romans 13.4-6 refers to those who have authority on earth. Both Romans 13 and Matthew 5 are the teaching of Christianity as it ought to be displayed. Concerning the personal life of a Christian, let us follow Matthew 5. Concerning the government and its system, let us follow Romans 13 and not Matthew 5. We do not believe in confusion, lawlessness and anarchy. We believe in restraint and control. But what Romans teaches us pertains to our relationship with government. Today, in the Matthew passage now before us, we are concerned with how we should be disciples: what we must do as disciples when we are faced with problems. This has nothing whatever to do with government. We are not to be non-resistant or to just endure, but to offer our other cheek. When compelled to go one mile, we are able to go with someone two. When forced to give up our coat, we can also give up our cloak. The teaching on the Mount is not aimed at the outsiders—the unbelievers, the people of the world—for them to observe. It is never to be taken as the rule of government. "Ye" refers exclusively to individuals. It has nothing at all to do with system and law. It is entirely directed at the Christian himself.

5.43-48 This is the fifth part of the second section—it showing how we should treat our enemy. The first part of verse 43 is found in the Old Testament, but the second part of the same

verse is not found there. "Hate thine enemy" is not in the Old
Testament. So that when our Lord enunciates His teaching, He
quotes on the one hand the Old Testament word— "love thy
neighbor," and on the other hand the word of His contemporaries
(the rabbis)—"hate thine enemy." The rabbis of Jesus' day had
added these words to the Old Testament word. Our Lord is here
intending especially to correct the teaching of these contemporary
rabbis.

Verse 44 defines the basic life attitude of the Christian in the
world. We should love our enemies. We are not just to treat them
well but to love them from our heart. You may treat a person
quite well without there being any love in your heart at all. If
so, you fail to keep the word of the Lord here. Two different terms
are used in Greek to describe love: (1) *phileo,* which is to love with
human love; and (2) *agapao,* which is to love with God's love.
Human beings are inborn with a nature to love, but this love
is subject to environment; you love when there is something
lovable, and hence, it is relative and contingent upon the other
party. It is not under one's control, nor is it a self-initiated love.
Such is the love of all men. But God's love is altogether different.
It does not ask for a reason to love; nor is it affected by the other
party, nor does it change with time. Even though you are a sinner, God loves you. If you curse Him, He still loves you. Such
love takes initiative, and thus you cannot cause Him to love more
or to love less. God's love is full of strength; it is within Him
himself.

Today God gives us a commandment that we love as He has
loved. The reason to love is within itself; it does not lie in the
opposite party. For this life of his which is now within us is love.
It cannot *but* love. The very expression of it is love. For this reason,
we love our enemies. If your love is inherited from the *garden of
Eden,* you will not be able to love your enemy. But when the love
of *God* fills you, to love the brethren is most easy, and even to
love your enemies is easy, too.

The Lord has put this love in us, therefore He commands

us to love our enemy. This inner strength overcomes all the hatefulness of men. It exceeds the righteousness of the scribes and Pharisees, since they could only love their neighbor, for the teaching of the rabbis added on the word: "hate thine enemy." But the fulfillment of the law by the Lord is to love one's enemies. The kingdom of the heavens is far superior to all the kingdoms of the world; accordingly, the men of *that* kingdom must be bet·· ter than those of the worldly kingdoms. Our righteousness must exceed that of the scribes and Pharisees. No one in the world has the power to destroy this love of God in my heart, which can verily swallow up the enemy. No enemy is able to stand before the love of God. Give it the opportunity, and this love of God will come forth from within—and conquer.

"And pray for them that persecute you." Love without prayer is undependable. Inside is love, and outside is prayer before God. Pray for their forgiveness; pray that the Lord will not require retribution on those who persecute, whether now or in the coming age. Pray that the Lord will bless them. As you pray for those who persecute you, you shall discover the love of God filling your heart. Then you will be able to really love them. Hence, there must be prayer alongside love. Yet we are not to pray that our enemies will be like us, but to pray that God will bless them.

"That ye may be sons of your Father who is in heaven" (v.45a). Thus will it be proven that you are truly the sons of God and that His life is truly in you. To be sons of God, you need to be born of God. But to be called the sons of God you must be like Him, in that your life overcomes the hate of the enemies (see also 5.9). What can qualify you to be called the sons of God? The answer is to be found in the two parts of the rest of verse 45: (a) "for he maketh his sun to rise on the evil and the good"— the sun shines on its own; it will shine irrespective of good or bad. The power of the sun lies within itself, not in men. So, too, the love of God is not at all affected by men. And (b) the Lord then uses rain as a parable here also: "and sendeth rain on the just and the unjust" — rain falls without regard to the just or to the unjust; it falls on its own, it not being subject to the conduct of men. The strength of love lies in the love itself. And therefore, both the just and the unjust are being shown love. Since this is what God is and does, this ought to be true of the sons of God as well. Only thus can we be called the sons of God.

"For if ye love them that love you, what reward have ye? Do not even the publicans the same?" (v.46) If people love you and you love them in return, what reward will you have? Not to mention the scribes and Pharisees, even the hated and despised publicans (tax collectors) do the same. The publicans were the greediest people of that day. Though they were rich, they loved those who loved them. Accordingly, what reward can there be?

Let us realize that the teaching on the Mount deals with reward and not with gift. Gift is grace given freely by God to sinners. Reward, on the other hand, is for those who have already been saved by grace. Due to their glorifying God by their good conduct, they are rewarded with the kingdom. Eternal life is absolutely according to grace through faith. But the kingdom of the heavens as a reward is altogether obtained by works. If you love those who love you, what reward will you have? You have to answer, None.

"And if ye salute your brethren only, what do ye more than others? do not even the Gentiles the same?" (v.47) Here is being brought into view the relationship that must exist by brethren towards non-brethren. It is good to salute your brethren; but if you salute them alone, where lies your excellence? You are no different from the Gentiles. The Gentiles here refer especially to the Romans who were even then oppressing these early disciples of the Lord. Even the Romans, noted the Lord, greet their own. The word "more" in Greek here means "better." Why does the Lord use this word "better"? Because this corresponds in meaning with the word "exceed" used in the first part of this section. There must be better love, then there will be exceeding righteousness. The righteousness that exceeds becomes here the love which is better.

Augustine of old once said: In the world there are three kinds of people. Of the three, one kind returns love for love and hate for hate. This is human. The kind that is lower than this returns hate for love. This is devilish. But the kind of people which is higher than the first sort returns love for hate. This is divine.

God is calling us to love divinely as his sons: "Ye therefore shall be perfect as your heavenly Father is perfect" (v.48).· The heavenly Father is the standard. What a standard that is! Not only should we be like Him, we should be perfect as He is perfect in our conduct. As the life on the Throne never fails, so the life within us never fails either. If we are no different from the world, we are undone. At least the world should know that we are aliens, that we are different. The life lived according to the teaching on the Mount will cause the world to know that we are indeed different. If we fail here, our victory in other matters is useless.

We have now covered two sections of the teaching on the Mount. First, 5.1–20 has spoken to us concerning the character of the men of the kingdom of the heavens. Second, 5.21–48 has dealt with the righteousness that exceeds. We shall now move on to the next section.

Third Section 6.1–18

This third section now before us deals with the hidden man. Three things are mentioned: (1) alms, (2) prayer, and (3) fasting. Verse 1 of chapter 6 warns: "Take heed that ye do not your righteousness before men." This is the general theme. Verses 2–4 deal with alms; 5–15, with prayer; and 16–18, with fasting. All three are forms of righteousness. Giving alms is visible and is related to other men. Prayer is related to God, and fasting is related to one's self. Regardless of whether towards men, God or self, none of them must be done with the purpose of having such righteousness seen by men. Alms, prayer and fasting will all be rewarded, but if they are seen by men, the future reward is canceled. Christians should cultivate the habit of doing these

righteousnesses secretly. As they practice righteousness, they need
to avoid the temptation of two extremes. One is to do all of these
things before men and to be influenced by men. The other is
to do all according to one's own idea without any consideration
of men. Both these extremes are unacceptable.

6.2-4 When you do alms, do not make many noises
before men to attract their attention. For this is as the hypocrites
would do, whose purpose in giving alms is to have glory of men.
"They have received their reward." The word "received" is a term
in Greek used in accounting. It means the account is settled right
then and there. But the Lord's way is that as you do alms, you
should expect to have your account settled in the future before
God. But now this account is closed. For this reason, you should
avoid the glory of men or the praise of your brothers and sisters.
Let your alms be done with simplicity and in secret. Let it be
accomplished so fast that your left hand does not know what your
right hand has done. Let it be done in secret, and your Father
shall see it in secret. "Thy Father who seeth in secret shall
recompense thee" — this statement is used three times in this
passage. It underscores the fact that whatever we do is noticed
by the Father. Even a cup of cold water will not be overlooked.
The Father will recompense you. Giving alms is the first practical form of righteousness. The two thousand years of Church
history are full of alms-giving. Alms must be given as much as
possible, but it should not be done before men.

6.5-15 The second righteousness that needs to be practiced in secret is prayer. Prayer is for the manifestation of the
glory of God as well as to acknowledge our own inadequacy. This
is why we seek after God. Yet how sad that men will take advantage of glorifying God to glorify themselves. They pray to be
heard of men. The hypocrites pray in the synagogues and on
the streets with the intention of being seen by men. But in so
doing, they have received their reward: they have received it from

men. The Lord does not speak here of the answer of prayer, but of the reward of prayer, for it is in the same category as the reward of fasting mentioned below. Hence, the reward of prayer does not refer to the answer of prayer. It is a recompense according to works. Prayer, therefore, has not only answer today but also reward in the future at the judgment seat of Christ. It will be remembered at the judgment seat as a righteousness that is to be rewarded. So that whoever prays to be heard of men now will have no possibility of being rewarded then at the judgment seat.

Prayer is a kind of righteousness. I hope that brothers and sisters will not be lacking in such righteousness. He who does not pray will receive no answer today and no reward in the future. In reality, prayer is our intimate communion with God. If anyone uses it as a means to be seen by men, he is a very shallow person. It should instead be our greatest secret. The Lord shows us that when we pray we should enter an inner chamber (synagogues, corners of the streets, and inner chamber are all symbolisms in this passage). An inner chamber has reference to a secret place where no one can purposely show off his prayer. To "shut thy door" is to shut out all that is of the world and to shut oneself in so as not even to be able to answer the doorbell. It leaves the person alone with God in prayer. It is a righteousness as well as a reason for God to reward us. This must be something which greatly pleases Him. So that the purpose of prayer is more than receiving answer, it also involves future reward. "Pray to thy Father who is in secret, and thy Father who seeth in secret shall recompense thee." Our Father watches our every action.

Alms are to be done in secret; but prayer is not only something to be done in secret but is also something in which we must be careful as to our words. Thus prayer is a greater form of righteousness than alms-giving. The Lord has to continue further in teaching us how to pray. Prayer must not only be in secret, it must also be devoid of vain repetitions such as the Gentiles are guilty of voicing. Prayer should be simple. "Vain repetitions" in the Greek language conveys a sense of the sound of water running through stones: it makes the same sound all the time. Its sound is monotonous and repetitious. Also, "much speaking" is a phrase which in the Greek points to the sound of a wheel rolling over stones. Thus the Lord uses these two expressions to describe the sound of prayer. It is like water slapping against stones and a wheel rolling over stones. They are totally meaningless. Hence in our praying, let it not be seen by men nor be done in the form of much meaningless speaking.

In public prayer, we are more or less affected by men. We not only pray to God but also pray to be heard by men. Our heart is not able to concentrate wholly on God. Some may not be able to stop praying because of the amens said by the brethren. Thus their prayer is not measured by the depth of their heart desire but by the number of amens elicited from the brethren. This nullifies the effectiveness of prayer. Prayer must be measured by heart desire; it should never exceed heart desire. Let us not quit praying in the meeting; but by the same token, let us not pray *only* in the meeting. Pray not only in public, pray also in private. If the words in your secret prayer are simple, then do not let them be far different in your open prayer. There is no need for much speaking, "for your Father knoweth what things ye have need of, before ye ask him." The answer to your prayer is according to your heart desire and attitude of prayer, not according to your words. Do not try to force God, for He already knows what you need. Then, why pray? It is that I may express my attitude of willing to believe and depend on Him.

"After this manner therefore pray ye." The prayer which then follows in this passage has been given to us by the Lord to serve as an example; it has not been given for us to repeat afterwards these same words.

"Our Father who art in heaven." This is the newest appellation by which men are now to address God. (Formerly, He was called "the God Most High," "the God of the heavens," or "Jehovah.") People of the world are not the children of God, and therefore all who do not have the life of God are not His children.

Only those who have His life within them can call God Father.

The prayer which follows touches upon *three areas* which *concern the things of God*—(a) "Hallowed be thy name"; (b) "Thy kingdom come"; and (c) "Thy will be done, as in heaven, so on earth." This phrase— "as in heaven, so on earth" —applies to all three of these things. It serves as a qualifier for all of them and is therefore not used exclusively to be only a part of the third statement that deals with the matter of God's "will." God's name is sanctified in the heavens; only on earth is it not being sanctified. In the heavens is the kingdom of God; only on earth is it missing. And the will of God is done in the heavens; yet only on this earth is His will not being obeyed. Accordingly, we need to pray.

The words in this so-called Lord's Prayer far exceed our thoughts. It would appear that ever since the creation of the world man has never come to God and prayed what He wants. The significance of this prayer lies in the fact that God himself has come from behind the veil and told us what He desires. This is the first time God became man and told us the prayer that strikes the mark. Here we realize immediately what the kingdom of the heavens is, that it has been extended to include this earth. God calls us to pray what He desires, that which He considers to be essential.

In the Scriptures the kingdom of the heavens is concurrently historical and geographical. The mistake of past Bible commentators has been to treat the kingdom of the heavens as purely historical. But today the course of history is less determinative in this matter of what the kingdom is than is geography. "If I by the Spirit of God cast out demons," declares the Lord Jesus, "then is the kingdom of God come upon you" (Matt. 12.28). This statement is geographical, not historical, in content. Wherever the Lord casts out demons, *there* is the kingdom of God. So that today it is more a matter of geography than of history.

Today God expects you to pray that His name might be sanctified. How His name has truly been taken in vain on earth! Even idols are called gods. "Hallowed" means unique and different. Only God can use that name. But the world has not honored His name as holy. Hence God wants us to pray that as His name is hallowed in heaven so shall it be hallowed on earth. This is the first among the things of God for which He desires prayer.

The second thing is, "Thy kingdom come." The millennium is to be the time when the kingdom is fully manifested. In the Old Testament period there were only prophecies about it. But when John the Baptist and the Lord came, they proclaimed that "the kingdom of the heavens is at hand." There is reason to so proclaim it because now there are men for the kingdom, now there is the Exemplar of the kingdom of the heavens, and now there are the principles of the kingdom being enunciated. Matthew 13 tells us that the history of the outward appearance of the kingdom of the heavens has also come. What we are shown today is far from what the future millennium will be, since the kingdoms of the world have yet to become the kingdom of our Lord and of His Christ (see Rev. 11.15). Nonetheless, there are fragments of the kingdom of the heavens which have appeared here and there as miniatures of it wherever the people of God are located. Casting out demons through the authority of the Holy Spirit, for example, indicated that the kingdom of God has come. Let us continue to pray: May Your kingdom be more strongly demonstrated on earth, for the whole earth is Your kingdom.

The third matter among God's concerns requiring prayer is: "Thy will be done, as in heaven, so on earth." What is prayer? It expresses man's desire. Yet the highest expression of prayer is for man to utter *God's* desire. Why should the Lord want His disciples to pray, saying, "Hallowed be thy name . . ." etc.? Who can hinder God's name from being hallowed? Who can block God's kingdom and God's will? If this is what you ask, it shows you do not even know the basics of prayer. According to our foolish thinking, there should be no need to pray. Why does God not have His will done on earth? Does He not know our needs before we ask? Is it not by His own power that His will is done? Why, then, should we be asked to pray at all? Let me observe that if we truly know the reason for prayer, we will begin to be good Christians.

Let me answer in the following fashion. First of all, I do not know the reason for men having to pray, I only know the fact. God has made a decision that whenever He is going to do a thing, He will wait till some on earth pray for it, and then He will do it. This is basic Christianity which God has revealed to us in the entire Bible. This will help us to settle the reason for prayer. Take, for example, the following Old Testament passage: "Thus saith Jehovah, the Holy One of Israel, and his Maker: Ask me of the things that are to come: concerning my sons, and concerning the work of my hands, command ye me" (Is. 45.11). He will wait till He is asked. He knew how many He would deliver from Sodom, but He waited for Abraham to say it. The Lord Jesus was to come to this earth, but He needed people such as Simeon to be vigilant and persistent in prayer. The Holy Spirit was to come on the day of Pentecost, but He waited for the one hundred and twenty people to pray. The very need of prayer is to show us that God will not do His will alone. Without question He has His will, but He wants us to pray before He will do it. So, the meaning of prayer is (1) God has a will, (2) I touch the will of God and I pray, and (3) God answers prayer. I use my mouth to utter the will of God, and God hears my prayer.

This prayer is offered by the Church, and after much prayer the kingdom shall come. Take special notice of the prayer for this age. The fundamental spiritual principle of it is that though the will of God is already formed, God will not move until some on earth agree with His will and pray accordingly. Then God's hand will move. So that we may justifiably say that the millennium could come either early or late. This early or late factor hinges on the matter of men's prayer. In spite of the fact that today we may not be allowed to preach the gospel openly, we can at least pray.

The will of God is not what we ordinarily think of as the many pieces and bits of God's will. Today we need to learn to be men and women of stature. God has a *supreme* will which includes within it all the many fragments of His will. When that *great* will of His is eventually fulfilled, all the small wills shall automatically be fulfilled as well. For this reason, we must set apart a time each day to do this work of prayer. If we do not pray, God will not have His will done. This is the mystery of prayer in the Scriptures: God has His will in heaven; His Spirit comunicates that will to us and causes us to desire that will; we then pray; and finally, God does His will. "Verily I say unto you, What things soever ye shall bind on earth shall be bound in heaven; and what things soever ye shall loose on earth shall be loosed in heaven" (Matt. 18.18). God wants *us* to do first, and then *He* will do. Our prayer is first, God's act is next. Binding and loosing sum up all actions. "Again I say unto you, that if two of you shall agree on earth as touching anything that they shall ask, it shall be done for them of my Father who is in heaven" (v.19). We can see from this, then, that prayer is not only a matter of God's will, it is also a matter of the will of the Church. It would appear as though God's action in heaven is governed by us who are His Church on earth. The Lord forgive me for saying this.

We ought to give our all to pray till God begins to move. Thus prayer will not only be answered but be rewarded, too. Prayer becomes the greatest work. The will of God is like a river, and prayer is like a pipe. No matter how large and manifold is the will of God, it is circumscribed by the "prayer-pipe" of His people. Many years after the Welsh revival, someone asked Evan Roberts this question: "I have not seen you for eight years; what have you been doing in those years?" His reply: "I have been praying the prayer of the kingdom." Oh, that people would offer themselves to God for prayer like that!

The prayer in Matthew 6.10 is not our prayer, that is to say, it is not a praying for things concerning ourselves but a praying for the things which God wants to accomplish. God has an opportunity to tell us what we should do. The basic meaning of prayer is that God has a will, but He will not do it all by himself; so He puts this will on men's hearts till men also will it and pray for it, and then He will begin to answer this prayer. And precisely for this reason, the Lord himself desires to teach men how to pray. Hence real prayer never originates from the earth, it always begins in heaven. What God lays stress upon here is that He wishes His kingdom might come upon this earth. The main difficulty lies not in heaven but on the earth.

In chapter 3 of Matthew, the Baptist is found declaring that "the kingdom of heaven is at hand" (v.2). In chapter 4 we read that the Lord too said that "the kingdom of heaven is at hand" (v.17). And here in chapter 6 we learn that He now wants the disciples to pray: "thy kingdom come." In this present age God must first get individuals to be the men of the kingdom, and then, through these men to bring in the kingdom of the heavens. So that the first consideration is that we need to obtain our place in the kingdom of the heavens. But, then, what is our work to be? It is to pray till the kingdom of the heavens comes. First of all, are you a man of the kingdom of the heavens? Is the kingdom of the heavens yours? If it is not yours, all is vanity of vanities. But secondly, you must not simply work, but take time to pray that the kingdom will indeed come in all its fullness. And when such voice is urgent enough, so that the will of the Church and the will of God are merged into one, the kingdom will soon thereafter come.

"Give us this day our daily bread" (v.11). The aforementioned segments of this prayer of the Lord's is concerned with the Name, the kingdom and the will. All these are related to God. But the Lord does not want us to forget ourselves completely. For as soon as the person who prays comes under attack, his prayer will cease immediately. The content of prayer is important, but so also is the one who prays. So that what follows are *three matters* which the person who prays asks *concerning himself.* The first is: "Give us this day our daily bread." All men of the kingdom of the heavens are poor. There is none rich, for his very riches will put him out of the kingdom. It is indeed an imposing problem when daily bread is lacking. Prayer is on the one hand so lofty, yet on the other hand it falls so low as to be able to reach down to "the rice bowl." This, however, is nothing to be surprised at. Only with the protection of the Lord can the above-mentioned prayers concerning the things of God persevere. If we truly trust the Lord for our living, we cannot afford to ask weekly for our bread; we shall have to ask daily. During the two thousand years of Church history many children of God have traveled this path.

Following the prayer regarding daily bread is another prayer: "And forgive us our debts, as we also have forgiven our debtors" (v.12). As we are indebted to God daily, we need to ask for a conscience void of offense. Not necessarily sin, but certainly debt. What needs to be done is too often left undone. This is debt, a liability. It is not easy to maintain a conscience void of offense. What should we do? By asking God to forgive our debts we shall thereby have a good conscience. Such prayer will be answered. A good conscience is a must, without which we would make shipwreck concerning the faith (see 1 Tim. 1.19). This is because faith leaks away through a bad conscience. As soon as there is accusation, faith leaks away. Hence, we must always ask God to forgive our debts. This must not be dragged on to the next day.

Nevertheless, there is a condition for asking God's forgiveness—which is, that we must forgive our debtors. Forgiving debt is not a matter related to salvation but to fellowship. It lies within the realm of God's government and discipline. Without having forgiven our debtors, we cannot ask God to forgive our own debts. The Bible tells us first of all of our relationship to God, and then, secondly, of the relationship among the brethren. We deceive ourselves if we remember our relationship with God but forget our relationship with the brethren! Anything between the brethren, however slight it may be, will take away God's blessing. As we have said before, debt may not be sin, but it is certainly something left undone which needs to be done. If we forgive our brother's debts completely, we will also have our own debts completely forgiven by God. If we find fault with our brother and continue to talk about it, we shall find our debts wholly remembered before God. Let us therefore forgive from the heart, and then God from the heart will also forgive our debts.

There are two statements in verse 13, yet they in fact constitute but one thing, each of the two simply reflecting either a negative or a positive aspect. When we begin to live for God and do the work of prayer on earth, we need to ask Him, *first*, to supply our material needs, *second*, to keep our conscience free from accusation, and *third*, to deliver us from Satan's hand. "Temptation" is a weighty word. We have already read in 5.39: "whosoever smiteth thee on thy right cheek, turn to him the other also." Should this verse unfortunately fall into the hands of the unbelieving Gentiles, they might today tempt us by in fact smiting our right cheek. What should we do? We should ask the Lord not to bring us into such temptation—the negative side of this one thing in verse 13. This prayer gives us a great protection. We will accept whatever the Lord has permitted to fall upon us, but we will not wait daily for people to tempt us unnecessarily. We pray that whatever is not allowed by the Lord will not come to us. How ever could we stand if this were not so? But when God-permitted temptation does come, we must nonetheless endure.

We read on the positive side of verse 13 this: "deliver us from the evil one." We ask the Lord to deliver us from Satan's hand in terms of bread, conscience and temptation. Satan's hand upon man's body results in the palsy, his hand upon the sea results in waves, and upon man's heart it results in hatred. Let us pray to God that He will deliver us from the Enemy's hand. So the three things asked for God are foundational; and the three things asked for ourselves are protective, in order that we may do the work of prayer on earth.

But after all the above, there comes still another word. It also speaks of *three things,* which is *concerning our praise:* "thine is the kingdom, and the power, and the glory, for ever. Amen" (mg.). This word is closely related to the preceding word that speaks of asking God to deliver us from the Evil One. Since the *kingdom* is Yours and not the Enemy's, since the *power* and the *glory* are also Yours and not his, we ought not fall into the hand of the Evil One. This is a most powerful reason why we will not fall into the Evil One's hand. "Behold, I have given you authority . . . over all the power of the enemy" (Luke 10.19). The authority given includes the actual power of the kingdom, for the kingdom is God's. But then, too, the authority and the power are also God's. And so does the glory belong to Him as well. Hence we cannot fall into the hand of the Evil One. Otherwise, God will not be glorified.

The kingdom is one thing, the actual power is another. If the kingdom is weak, people will not obey. Therefore, there must be the kingdom on the one hand and power on the other. In the New Testament the name of the Lord represents authority and the Holy Spirit represents power. When God moves, the Holy Spirit is His power. As the demons encounter the Holy Spirit, they are cast out. For the kingdom and the power and the glory are all the Lord's. Hence we are completely delivered from the power of the Devil.

"After this manner therefore pray ye." All our prayers are based on this one. This so-called Lord's Prayer stands as the pattern. In the New Testament are to be found many prayers that lack the ending of, "We ask in the name of the Lord." Some think this so-called Lord's Prayer is not given to us because it has no such ending. Such thought is a total mistake; for this prayer, please carefully note, is not a form of liturgy, but a pattern.

6.14–15 is a footnote to verse 12, that is to say, it can especially explain the word to be found in verse 12. Why is this? Because just here is the most common failure among Christians. So the Lord repeats two very simple words. And these words are what God's children need. Without these two words, the Church will suffer much. An unforgiving heart can easily give ground to

Satan. So that unless this is dealt with, it will destroy us as candidates to be men of the kingdom as well as destroy the very work of the kingdom.

Now the teaching on prayer ends with verse 15. We can readily perceive the importance our Lord attaches to prayer. For in the case of alms, mentioned before, there are only four verses; and for fasting, which follows this portion on prayer, there are merely three verses. But for prayer itself, there are many words and many verses. We should at least take out five, ten, or fifteen minutes each day to pray for the coming of the kingdom of the heavens — which is the main emphasis of this so-called Model Prayer of our Lord. In the long duration of this age, may we be ranked among those many who have prayed what is called for by this prayer.

6.16–18 deals with the question of fasting. To fast is to refrain from satisfying the legitimate demand of my physical body. The stomach has been created by God, and eating is not sin. Yet in Christianity there is a self-imposed fasting which must never be misconstrued as indicating that Christianity is against eating. For this fasting now under discussion is something voluntarily and gladly done. Due to some *spiritual* need, the *physical* demand of the body is temporarily set aside. Paul was "in hunger and thirst," but he also was "in fastings often" (2 Cor. 11.27). Sometimes he was so pressed circumstantially that he could not eat or drink. To fast is to not eat. When is there fasting? When the bridegroom is taken away. This means that when there is sorrow or problems, the legitimate demand is put aside; that when there is spiritual burden, we do not ever hold on to the natural burden of hunger but lay it aside for the sake of the spiritual burden.

Fasting is a voluntary act. Here we must once again speak of reward. Christian fasting is not Christian advertising. If alms and fasting become advertisements of oneself, there can be no reward from the Lord. If fasting is done to be seen by men, then just as in alms-giving, you are finished, for you have already received your reward. When fasting for the Lord, you should anoint your head and wash your face. At the most difficult time, show forth your best. When you suffer the most, you anoint your head and wash your face even more. All who are motivated to do primarily before men are shallow people. Living to be seen of men is the greatest loss that can ever befall a Christian. Any brother or sister who continually lives to be noticed by others is shallow in his or her entire walk before God. A person who would truly live only to be seen of God must have something in his life unknown to men. To be shallow means to be exposed. To be deep, on the other hand, means to be unseen. A shallow person is most useless to God. He is as a hypocrite. Therefore, let us learn to do righteousness secretly before God. He who enters the temple only to commune with God has no concern for people. But he who communicates with men simply to be seen of them is a hypocrite so far as God is concerned.

What the Lord condemns here is fasting that is done to be seen of men. It is done on purpose. On purpose means with intention. Fasting with such intention as this is not accepted by God, for such intention is to obtain glory from men. Whoever designs to seek men's glory is not approved of God. We must firmly deny all glory that comes from men in order that we may be blessed of God.

In conclusion, therefore, the Lord has taught us (1) to not let the left hand know what the right hand is doing in alms-giving, (2) to enter our inner chamber and shut the door when praying, and (3) to anoint the head and wash the face while fasting. Here is a different purpose and intention: instead of wishing to be seen by men, we seek to be hidden and do things in secret. And thus our secrecy is also with purpose. Let us learn to be in secret, let us design not to be seen by men. A person who truly knows God deliberately hides his spiritual strength. Yet let us beware, too, lest some of us would even use hiddenness to manifest ourselves. For this is even more a thing to be condemned.

Fourth Section 6.19-34

This section runs from verse 19 to the end of the chapter. It can be entitled "The Life of Faith" or "First Seek Righteousness."

We have been discussing at some length, now, concerning what the man of the kingdom of the heavens should be like. And we have spoken, first of all, about his character; then, his better righteousness that, like Jesus, fills up the law; and thirdly, his hidden righteousness. But now we wish to look at his attitude towards material things.

In launching out from the sanctuary to the wilderness, we shall be confronted by the issues of clothing and eating. The Lord is not unmindful of the problem created by material things. He shows us here that in order not to seek after clothing and eating in the manner of the Gentiles, we must seek first the kingdom of God and His righteousness. Not that clothing and eating are unconcerns, but that the heavenly Father himself will take care of these. He who forsakes the kingdom of the heavens for the sake of clothing and eating is a fool. If he would simply refrain from seeking after such things, the person would soon see that the Father would take care of him in this regard. He would not only have clothing and food, he would also have the kingdom. But should he seek only these things, he will get only clothing and food but lose the kingdom in the process.

6.19-24 These verses comprise the first part of this section. It is addressed to those who would be wealthy. "Lay not up for yourselves treasures upon the earth, where moth and rust consume, and where thieves break through and steal." The Lord does not want us to lay up treasures upon the earth but to lay them up in heaven. Lay up we must, but not for ourselves; and lay up in heaven and not on earth. How do we lay up in heaven? "He that hath pity upon the poor lendeth unto Jehovah" (Prov. 19.17). We may lend to the Lord. There is not another borrower who is so trustworthy as He. How very undependable it is to lay up treasures upon earth. To lay up treasures in heaven is to sell all and lay it at the feet of the apostles to be distributed, or to give to those whom the Lord has raised up to care for us, or to give to the preaching of the gospel. All such actions are like depositing money in the bank. The Lord's purpose is to deliver us completely from the power of wealth. Let us seek opportunities to send our money to heaven for deposit. Let us spend time and concentrate on finding ways to achieve such an attempt. Let our money go out, and then we will commence to accumulate wealth in heaven. Many believers have their money in all sorts of earthly banking facilities, but they have none of their wealth in heaven's treasury. This is indeed a most foolish plan.

Why are we not allowed to lay up treasures upon the earth? Because "where thy treasure is, there will thy heart be also." This the Lord knows for sure. Where is our heart? Let us ask ourselves where our treasure truly is.

Following these words, the Lord then tells us of the tremendous connection between this treasure and our spiritual insight. The eye is the lamp of the body where the light is focused and also diffused. If therefore your eye is single the whole body is full of light. What is meant by the eye being single? It is to lay up treasures only in heaven. The people with the most problems are not those who lay up treasures only upon the earth, because their eyes are also singly focused. The people who experience the most difficulty are those who try to lay up treasures in heaven as well as upon the earth. They are the most distressed. Their eyes are not focused, and they cannot see clearly. But lay up *all* treasures in heaven, and the eye will be single, and the whole body will be full of light.

Spiritual light and treasure are closely related. Many are not spiritual not because their spirit is wrong but because of their money. He whose whole body is full of light is a person full of revelation. He is a single-eyed person. There must be a day when you come before the Lord and say, "Lord, I put all into Your hand." You turn your back to the world and always send your treasure to heaven. Then your eye will be single, and your whole body will be full of light. Many who are unclear in Scripture truths, whose path is not straight, and who fail to see clearly church truth are affected by the influence of wealth and possessions. Many problems come from double-mindedness, from inadequate consecration. But what keeps you from seeing is money. For there within the heart is a secret desire.

Verse 23 presents the negative side. "Evil" is the opposite of "single." It means that one is willing neither to forsake the world nor the kingdom. This makes him a double-minded person. A man in darkness is a man of double-mindedness. The reason why he is unable to understand the word of God is because there is a problem with his consecration. If consecration is a problem the eye will become undependable, and the whole body shall be full of darkness. Finally, the Lord gives His judgment: "If therefore the light that is in thee be darkness, how great is the darkness!" Light will turn into darkness. Many try to make light out of darkness and teach it as doctrine. How great must be its darkness! Hence, we should be fearful of any doctrine arrived at through imperfect consecration. If I have not offered myself, or if my consecration is faulty, the thought of my heart, however dependable, is extremely unreliable. Faulty consecration produces wrong judgment. The sharpness of the teaching on the Mount is evident in its demand on our absoluteness in serving God.

In verse 24 the Lord raises a new thought: "No man can serve two masters." A single eye means one serves either God or Mammon (Riches). One of the greatest temptations of today's disciples is the desire to serve two masters. But God himself and Mammon cancel each other out. You cannot force the mingling of what God will not tolerate. When the influence of Mammon conflicts with God's interest, it is always the latter that suffers. (This is like mixing sweet water with salty water; the sweet always suffers.) If the problem of money and riches is not solved, your problem as a Christian is unresolved. During these few recent years, we have talked about offering our all. It is not without reason.

For the nature of God is diametrically opposite to the nature of Mammon: "either he will hate the one, and love the other; or else he will hold to one, and despise the other." Today God is calling you to make the choice. You are to forsake everything so that you may preach the gospel. Whenever riches goes out, the fire of the gospel is kindled.

What has thus far been considered of the Lord's message in this Fourth Section is addressed to those with wealth. What now follows is addressed to others who are not.

6.25-27 Here, the Lord begins to speak to the poor. The love of money is not an exclusive longing of the rich, it is found among the poor as well. "Be not anxious for your life." Why? Because our life is more than food, and our body is more than raiment. Are you not, says the Lord, of much more value than the birds? Verses 26 and 27 speak of food, and verses 28-30 of clothing. The problem of food as presented in verses 26 and 27 is rather simply stated. God feeds many living creatures in the universe, and all without any problem; why, then, should men have a problem? You list everything else in your account, why do you not also put God on your list? That item — God himself — has not been counted into your life and thought. Think of it: you have God!

If you truly seek after the kingdom of God and His righteousness, you will begin to learn to trust in God. The life of faith is not for the preachers alone. It is for all who seek the kingdom of the heavens. The life of faith means that I count God in my life and thought. When there is no "raven," there will be a "widow." If there is no "widow," there will be a "raven" (see 1 Kings 17.1-16). When both are absent, the Lord is still present. What, then, is the use of being anxious? "And which of you by being anxious can add one cubit unto the measure of his life?" How utterly useless is your anxiety. Anxiety cannot cause the hungry to be full. It is God who feeds the hungry. All anxieties are vain. You do not need to worry about things which are manageable; and your worry will not help in things which are unmanageable. Of all the useless things in the entire world, anxiety tops the list. Let us learn to trust the heavenly Father in feeding us in at least the manner that He does in feeding the birds. Fear does not glorify God, and anxiety disgraces Him the most.

6.28–30 These verses deal with the problem of clothing. The lilies of the field form no weaving factory, yet "even Solomon in all his glory was not arrayed like one of these." "O ye of little faith"—here the subject of the Lord's lesson in this part of His teaching is pointed out. "The grass of the field"—this is not speaking of the beautifully arrayed lily, but common grass: "if God doth so clothe the grass of the field, which to-day is, and to-morrow is cast into the oven, shall he not much more clothe you?" Brethren of little faith and much doubt must learn to trust. Let us not live on earth as those who do not have God.

6.31 This verse joins food and clothing together: "Be not therefore anxious, saying, What shall we eat? or, What shall we drink? or, Wherewithal shall we be clothed?" As you become anxious about food and clothing, your usefulness is lost. Your heart ought to be emptied of all things such as these so as to be wholly at the Lord's disposal. But when your heart is filled with anxiety, your hands are not able to take up the work of the Lord.

6.32 This is the Lord's word to Christians: "after all these things do the Gentiles seek; for your heavenly Father knoweth that ye have need of all these things." You must *believe* this; for only then will you seek first the kingdom of God and His righteousness.

6.33 This verse consists of the Lord's command to us: "seek ye first his kingdom, and his righteousness; and all these things shall be added unto you." The first half of this command is to be done by us; that is to say, we must seek first His kingdom and His righteousness. Not seek first food and clothing, but seek first the character of the kingdom, the reactions that excel the world's, and the hidden righteousness. The second half is done by God. The phrase, "all these things," means food, drink and clothing. ". . . shall be added unto you." What is meant by "added"? It means you will obtain the kingdom and righteousness *plus* all these things. The kingdom you get; and the righteousness you get; but food and clothing are much easier to get, so these are *added* to you. If you are right with the kingdom and its righteousness, you will have no problem with food and clothing. If the kingdom is given to you, and the righteousness is given to you, will not food, drink and clothing also be given to you? As a matter of fact, all these will be *added* to you.

6.34 This verse concludes the above thought: "Be not therefore anxious for the morrow." The Lord knows how much of our anxiety is for tomorrow, for the future. The world has little of today's anxiety. Let tomorrow's anxiety be taken care of tomorrow. God's grace is always sufficient for actual needs but not for imaginary problems. Tomorrow's anxiety belongs to the realm of imagination. Learn, therefore, to live a life without anxiety. He who is always worrying is unfit for the kingdom of God. We may be the poorest people in the whole of Shanghai, but we are the least anxious too.

Not to be anxious and worried does not mean not to work, not to labor. We must work with our hands to earn our clothing and food in a proper manner. But after we have done that, let us not be anxious anymore.

Fifth Section 7.1–12

This fifth section in the teaching on the Mount we may entitle as "The Government of God"—which is to say, how God governs His children. How can we consider this passage of Scripture to be one section? This becomes evident when one looks at verses 2 and 12 together. In the second half of verse 2 the Lord is recorded as saying: "with what measure ye mete, it shall be measured unto you." The measure is the balance. In verse 12 He is recorded as saying: "All things therefore whatsoever ye would that men should do unto you, even so do ye also unto them." The meaning of both verses is the same. Verse 2 begins and verse 12 concludes. If these two verses deal with the same subject, it is logical to assume that all the verses in between must likewise treat the same subject. This is a principle in Bible study. Any other explanation is bound to be incorrect. Hence I believe these twelve verses comprise one integral section dealing with one single subject. They should not be treated as fragmentary words.

7.1 "Judge not, that ye be not judged." Here the Lord cannot be referring to the realm of politics or government at whatever level. For Paul in Romans 13 distinctly states that God does indeed ordain on earth many judges and rulers, who obviously must judge. Hence the word here in Matthew 7 cannot have anything to do with earthly government. 1 Corinthians 5.12 states: "what have I to do with judging them that are without? Do not ye judge them that are within?" This treats of the judgment in the local church such as excommunication. But the word "judge" here in Matthew 7 means to not gossip, to not carelessly conclude as to people's motives and intentions because one does not know. It would also convey the idea of not picking out flaws in others or criticizing them. Its meaning would include as well the idea of not considering one's own opinion as fact, of not letting personal affection, interest, inclination or a spirit of revenge intrude into any discussion concerning others' affairs.

To judge means that I and *my* word stand on the same side: it means that I speak according to my subjective sentiment, not according to an objective view. The person who judges is undoubtedly one who has not been delivered from self. Interestingly, later on in this passage we find the Lord saying, "Thou hypocrite . . ." (v.5). But is this not an example of the Lord himself judging? Is He not contradicting himself? Not so, for the Lord speaks here according to *objective fact*. The one who inveighs most strongly against judging is James, yet he himself condemns many people. But he, like our Lord, speaks *objectively*; he does not speak according to his own whims, likes or dislikes. And hence, what he does is not what is being forbidden here by the Lord in Matthew 7. The judging which the Lord *does* forbid, however, is that kind in which one's own personal feeling is involved. It may not be false or incorrect, and yet it is judging in the manner spoken against by the Lord Jesus. Let us clearly understand that even speaking truthfully may be a case of judging when one's personal feeling is involved; for if your inward sense is joyful when it should be mournful, or if it is a judgment expressed for reproving when it should be for restoring—then *that* is judging.

"Judge not, that ye be not judged." This is God's government. This is the way He disciplines and educates His children. This way is administered along a fundamental rule, which is, that as you judge others, God will allow others to judge you too. When you are being criticized, do not be agitated, for you have also so criticized others. This is God's government. "Whatsoever a man soweth, that shall he also reap" (Gal. 6.7). Such is the government of God.

The more advanced one grows, the stricter will be his judgment of himself and the less and more lenient he judges others.

7.2 Verse 1 speaks of the fact of judging; verse 2 emphasizes the "how": "with what judgment ye judge, ye shall be judged: and with what measure ye mete, it shall be measured unto you." Oftentimes what a brother does becomes the talk of your mouth, and what you do becomes the talk of other people. In reprimanding others, you are fearful of not being strong enough. But in being reprimanded just a little yourself, you cannot tolerate it. Many believers are like that. The heart of God's children should be full of love. Even your reproof should be filled with love. Without love, nothing is right.

7.3 From verse 3 onward, several things are mentioned. "And why beholdest thou the mote that is in thy brother's eye, but considerest not the beam that is in thine own eye?" We see fault in other people because we ourselves have fault. If you can see the mote, which is a tiny thing, in your brother's eye, why can you not see the large beam in your own eye? The more unclean one is, the more he is able to see uncleanness in others. The holier one is, the less he will find fault in others. A good-natured person finds no fault whatsoever. But the more one knows his own faults, the easier it is for him to find faults in other people. Due to sin, human nature is especially interested in sin. Why is it we so easily have a deep impression about Abraham's lie and David's adultery, but it takes a great deal of time and effort for us to discover their good points? This is because our nature as sinners is close to sin. A person who approximates sin in his own life can recall immediately the shortcoming of another as soon as the latter's name is mentioned. But a person who approaches holiness in his own life remembers the niceness of another when his name is heard. You can test this out yourself. The beam in your own eye, strangely enough, causes you to notice even the tiniest mote in your brother's eye. What you have much of inside you, this you tend to comprehend and see more of the same in other people.

7.4,5 Verse 4 deals with seeing, verse 5, with casting out. The former verse tells us how the beam in your eye induces you to see the mote in your brother's eye. The latter shows you that because of the beam in your eye you cannot cast out the mote in your brother's eye — that is to say, you are not able to help him. To criticize is one thing, to help is another. Criticizing is costless, but helping is costly: "ye who are spiritual, restore such a one" (Gal. 6.1). You need to be spiritual before you can restore others, and to become spiritual yourself is a costly affair to one's self. It is easy to see a fault in others, but this is of no help. Judging in the sense which Jesus inveighs against here does not restore anything. You yourself must first be restored. If you have not cast the large beam out of your own eye, you are unable to cast the tiny mote out of your brother's eye.

"Thou hypocrite, cast out first the beam out of thine own eye . . ." We ourselves must be judged strictly before God; and only then will we be able to help other people. The injunction to "judge not" which the Lord talks about here is concerned with judging without oneself having been legitimately judged and yet voicing one's own opinion. But with the beam cast out, we are enlightened; and thus we may then be able to help our brothers to see light. Now this is no longer judging.

7.6 "Give not that which is holy unto the dogs, neither cast your pearls before the swine, lest haply they trample them under their feet, and turn and rend you." Here is an example of a cross-over construction in the Greek grammar, which can be diagrammed as follows:

Give not that which is holy   Neither cast your pearls
unto the dogs   before the swine
Lest haply they trample them   And turn and rend you
under their feet

Dogs and swine stand as definite types in the Scriptures. According to Leviticus 11, both are unclean animals. A dog is totally unclean, both within and without. A swine is unclean inside but clean outside, for it "parteth the hoof, and is clovenfooted, but cheweth not the cud" (Lev. 11.7). Dogs therefore typify the perishing; while swine typify the hypocrites or nominal Christians. (Some have taken the dogs to represent sinners and swine to represent church members.) Today if you cast the holy things to the dogs, they are unable to discern that these are holy. Hence, not being satisfied, and even being displeased, they will turn and rend you. And if you cast your pearls before the swine, they do not realize the preciousness of these objects; they will therefore trample them under their feet.

When you are judging people, remember that those living

in the world around you not only include the brethren but also include dogs (sinners) and swine (nominal church members). In your eyes your judgments are most precious, and are like things which are most holy. But the dogs will bite and tear you apart, and the swine will trample them underfoot. You will speak in vain, for they have no understanding. The holy things here refer especially to the things of Jesus' teaching on the Mount. If you base your judgment of the world on the higher teaching of the Mount, the world will turn and rend you. And if you take the teaching on the Mount as the moral standard to be observed by the false brethren (the nominal church members), they will trample it under their feet, because they have no affection for it. The world will use this as their ground of attack, and the nominal church members will not treasure it. There should therefore be a difference in the measure you use. Whatever measure you mete out to your true brethren, they will mete out the same to you. But with those of the world, they will either turn, bite and rend you, or else trample the measure under their feet.

7.7-11 "Ask, and it shall be given unto you; seek, and ye shall find; knock, and it shall be opened unto you" (v.7). The Lord uses the words of verse 8 to prove the promise of verse 7. These two verses have three levels of meaning. "Ask" is without action and is therefore an expression of desire. "Seek" has action involved in it, yet it has not found the place. But "knock" has arrived at the place. All prayers are heard by God. His answer is most generous. In verses 9 and 10 the Lord is found citing a case which *assures* us of this tremendous promise — and without any reservation. Why is it so that if you ask, it shall be given you; if you seek, you shall find; and if you knock, it shall be opened to you? Because of God's word in verse 11: "how much more shall your Father who is in heaven give good things to them that ask him." The children of the world seem to be more clever than the children of light. None of *them* ever asks for a stone or a serpent. But we, as the children of light, are not so clever. We sometimes mistake a stone for a loaf and a serpent for a fish. The Father always answers us, but not necessarily according to what we ask for. When we pray amiss, God responds with a correct answer. In answering prayer, God does so according to *His* knowledge, not according to ours. The Father gives us good things, He does not necessarily give us things we ask for.

7.12 When you look at this section as a whole, you notice that everything mentioned is couched in pairs; such, for example, as: your measure versus others' measure, your beam versus your brother's mote, giving holy things to the dogs and being bitten versus casting pearls before swine and they being trampled, earthly fathers giving good gifts to children versus the heavenly Father giving good things to us. In verse 12 we have the concluding word: "All things therefore whatsoever ye would that men should do unto you, even so do ye also unto them." The way to treat men is governed by how you want men to treat you rather than how men actually treat you. The Christian attitude and action towards men follow the highest principle. They are not affected by fact. All the Christian's strength comes from within, not from his circumstances. This is because within the Christian is the life of Christ. I as a Christian must therefore act by this inner strength.

God will treat us in the way we treat others. So that (1) to the brethren, let us be liberal; and (2) to the unbelieving Gentiles and false brethren, let us not carelessly give spiritual things to them. Here God's word also speaks of the discipline of God. We can see especially in verse 11 how the heavenly Father gives good things to His children as human fathers give good gifts to their children. Since men so give, the Father in heaven gives also. Thus the deeds of the heavenly Father are influenced by men's deeds.

Verse 12 is a conclusion: "All things *therefore* ..." — that is to say, based on the teaching immediately given above — "... whatsoever ye would that men should do unto you, even so do ye also unto them." This is the concluding word. "If ye then, being evil, know how to give good gifts unto your children, how much more shall your Father who is in heaven give good things to them that ask him?" This is brought in as an answer to prayer. In verse 11 it says, "If *ye* then," not "if we then." This is most beautiful. Though it is a minor point, it nevertheless shows how our Lord is the God who is separated from sinners. The summing up of the law and the prophets is that we love our neighbors — expecting good and not evil for them. The Lord declares that He does not come to destroy the law and the prophets, but to fulfill them. If the law and the prophets seek the profit of the people, how much more the teaching of our Lord? He comes to fulfill, not to destroy.

Sixth Section 7.13-29

This is the last section in the teaching on the Mount. It may be entitled, "The Calling of Disciples." The Lord uses three different words to tell us how He calls us to be His disciples. From the first section to the fifth, we have been told how those who seek the kingdom of the heavens should behave. From verse 13 of chapter 7 onward, which is the sixth and last section, it is the Lord calling us to be such ones.

7.13,14 The *first* word here is: "Enter ye in by the narrow gate." The Lord acknowledges that this is narrow. You must enter this gate in order to walk in this way. How is this gate entered? Previously, as people of the world, you were naturally proud and arrogant. Now you need to consecrate yourself to the Lord and capitulate to Him. You have to enter through this opening of His appointment. Unless you do, you will never be able to walk in this way. You ought to form a determination in your heart to offer yourself, to surrender yourself. The Lord is telling us now that we must enter through this gate. Having heard the teaching on the Mount, we need to have a singular consecration, that is, we need to have a special dealing with the Lord. Then we will start on this way. It is impossible to be a man of the kingdom of the heavens casually.

"For wide is the gate and broad is the way, that leadeth to destruction, and many are they that enter in thereby. For narrow is the gate, and straitened the way, that leadeth unto life, and few are they that find it." The teaching on the Mount touches upon the reward and discipline of Christians. The "life" here refers to that in the millennial kingdom. In some places in the Scriptures "life" points to eternity. However, even "eternal life" or "life" or "live" in the Scriptures sometimes alludes to the millennial kingdom, such as for example in Mark 9.43–47, Luke 13.28–29, Romans 5.17 and Galatians 6.8. All these passages point to life in the millennial kingdom.

Here we must make a clear distinction between reward and initial salvation. For instance, the phrase "in the world to come eternal life" (Mark 10.30) refers to the kingdom. In certain Scripture passages we find that some may be disciplined in the kingdom, such as: "shall be in danger of [Greek: unto] the hell of fire" (Matt. 5.22), or "to enter into life maimed or halt, rather than having two hands or two feet to be cast into the eternal fire" (Matt. 18.8). These passages speak of the discipline to be exercised or experienced in the kingdom. Nevertheless, our salvation is sure and certain. He who has eternal life may "be *hurt* of the second death" (Rev. 2.11) but not experience the second death itself. A Christian may suffer loss, and this seems to be unavoidable in the case of some people; nevertheless, they will not be lost eternally. Hence, the loss must be experienced during the kingdom period.

The gate that leads to destruction is wide, and the way is broad. But the command of the Lord is for us to enter by the narrow gate, for this alone leads us to millennial life and reward. Today the Lord is calling us to accept the teaching on the Mount, which is this gate and this way. Let us respond to the Lord's call.

7.15–23 This is the *second* word of this final section. The teaching on the Mount has been delivered. Now we must beware of false prophets. All who enlarge this gate or alter this way are false prophets. False prophets come to cater to your taste. They change the word of the Lord. They put on sheepskins so as to appear outwardly as the Lord's. Inside of such garments, however, are grievous wolves. They do not have the life of Christ. False prophets are those who are clothed with sheepskins but speak wolves' words. The teaching on the Mount is spoken by the Lord. But the words of the false prophets are spoken out of themselves. By their fruits they can be recognized. For fruits are produced according to their nature. It is not a question of fruit or no fruit; it is a question of what *kind* of fruit is produced according to its nature. *Men's* teaching can be ferocious, cruel, fierce and crushing; it cannot produce beautiful character. The character formed as a result of teaching out of one's own self is totally different from the character produced by the teaching of the Lord. Man's fierce teaching can only produce evil character. You cannot pick grapes from thorns. Correct teaching alone produces proper character. All trees which do not bear good fruits shall be hewn down and cast into fire. This ferocious teaching is not only found in the world, it is also present in Christianity. By looking at the character produced, we can see the incorrectness of such teaching. Any teaching that differs from the teaching on the Mount is a bad teaching.

"Not every one that saith unto me, Lord, Lord, shall enter into the kingdom of heaven" (v.21). It does not read "No one . . . shall enter" but reads "Not every one . . . shall enter"; for some can only say, Lord, Lord, with their mouth, but they do not let the Lord be Lord in actual living. "Not every one"— this word is concerned with the kingdom and not salvation. The will of the heavenly Father has been revealed in the teaching on the Mount. All who keep this will may enter the kingdom of the heavens.

In the words of the Lord found in verses 22 and 23, we see

that He uses the personal pronoun "me" without watching himself. He unconciously reveals His Person here. "Many will say to me in that day [the day of judgment], Lord, Lord." How precious is this word. He casually divulges His Person as the future Judge. In studying the Scriptures, these are the kinds of places to notice with a careful eye.

The word in verse 22 is especially relevant to the brethren who overemphasize spiritual gifts. These have nothing to do with salvation. Spiritual gifts are produced through the Holy Spirit coming upon us, whereas spiritual fruit is produced through the Holy Spirit indwelling us. These two are different. For the work of the Holy Spirit in us is two-fold: one is for spiritual life, the other is for power in service. The gifts outpoured do not make life more holy. For example, the Corinthian believers were highly gifted, but they remained as carnal Christians (see especially 1 Cor. 1.5–7 with 3.1–3). It is therefore possible to be endowed with much gift and still be carnal. For gifts have no relation to inner life. They may help others' life, but not one's own life. It is also likely that the more the gift, the prouder one may become. Such a person may not know the teaching on the Mount and may be shut out of the kingdom. We must have an accurate estimate of the value of spiritual gifts. We do not despise them; we shall even encourage people to seek for such gifts. But we confess that life is also much needed, even *more* needed.

"I never knew you" (v.23). This means, "I do not approve of you." In other words, the Lord is not pleased with people who only have outward gifts but not the life of the kingdom within. "Ye that work iniquity"—according to the Greek, this word means "lawlessness." You do everything according to your own will and not according to the will of God. You who have not been dealt with by the cross inwardly and yet are full of activities outwardly are not any closer to the kingdom of the heavens than those who are the farthest from it. The Lord considers your works and the fruits of your works as falling short of the life according to the teaching on the Mount.

By comparing these three chapters of Matthew with 1 Corinthians 13 we will readily see that what the Lord teaches here is nothing but that of "love." Work is not as essential as your character. Even prophesying, casting out demons and doing mighty works have the possibility of being lawless activities. This is where our problem lies. Inner grace is far more important than outward gift. Men ought to know that life is of greater consequence than works. The fruit of the Holy Spirit is far more necessary than gifts. Love is more significant than power. Those who know this today are humbled by it. Woe to those who come to this knowledge too late. May God be gracious to us in causing us to take the teaching on the Mount as our standard hereafter. This is the standard of true Christianity. We would enter through this gate. And from now on we would also make this teaching on the Mount our way.

Let us recapitulate. We have seen two gates and two ways. The narrow gate and the straightened way do not refer to Christ himself, who spoke truly when He said elsewhere, "I am the door of the sheep" (John 10.7) and "I am the way" (John 14.6). No, the gate and the way allude here instead to His teaching on the Mount. When a Christian walks on *this* way he has to leave many things outside the gate. Either he may shut both himself and his wealth outside, or he may leave the wealth outside and go in himself. Between these two, each of us must make a choice. This way is never stumbled upon; it has to be found. Few are those who walk in the way of the kingdom of the heavens. Loneliness is the price for pleasing God. All who look for excitement are prone to go the way that displeases the Lord. How very few are there among Christians who practice the teaching on the Mount! This is nothing to be surprised at, however, since few are the people who really want to please God. If you are a sparrow, you will have a flock of sparrows on the ground. But if you are an eagle, you will be counted singly, for loneliness is the price for soaring high. "Enter ye in" (v.13). The first step is to enter, without which nothing counts.

Having heard the teaching on the Mount, we should beware
of false prophets who try to introduce new teaching to the Church.
As recorded in Acts 20, Paul too predicted the same, he declaring: "after my departing grievous wolves shall enter in among
you, not sparing the flock" (v.29). These wolves are false teachers.
They are "ravening wolves" in sheepskin clothing. Some think
evil fruit must be sordid, immoral things. It may not necessarily be so, because Satan sometimes uses people with very good
morality but who become his instruments of false teaching.
Sheep's clothing may denote moral conduct and pleasant temperament; inside, however, are wolves. When Satan tempts people,
he transforms himself into an angel of light (2 Cor. 11.14). His
most successful tactic is to mix false teaching with good morals.
Such false prophets will emerge for the purpose of changing the
men of the kingdom of the heavens by changing the Lord's demand on them. Whatever lowers His demands and makes them
easy are the works of the false prophets. Throughout the centuries there have been false prophets in the Church who have
attempted to change the teaching on the Mount.

The Lord now uses the parable of the two trees. Here, on
the one hand, are good trees such as a vine or a fig tree; and
on the other hand, here are evil trees such as a thorn or thistle
tree. A thorn tree bears a kind of black berry fruit which looks
like grapes but is not. A thistle tree also bears fruit, which appears as unripened figs but is not. What may look alike are not
necessarily the same. The Lord says that "every good tree bringeth
forth good fruit." In verses 17 and 18 we find Him reiterating
this point again and again. This is a fact that cannot be changed
or confused. The tree here does not refer to life; rather, it points
to teaching. The good tree means the teaching on the Mount,
and the evil tree is the teaching of the false prophets. The teaching
of our Lord alone produces men of the kingdom of the heavens.
The teaching of the false prophets may produce people who look
like such men, but the Lord declares that they are not.

The apostle Paul tells us that spiritual fruit comes from the

Holy Spirit (see Gal. 5.22). The Lord shows us here that spiritual fruit comes from teaching. True teaching is that which the Lord teaches and which the Holy Spirit applies in us to produce good fruit in our lives. The Lord's teaching plus the Holy Spirit's working result in such fruit. Without the inner operation of the Holy Spirit, teaching is of no avail. With the indwelling Holy Spirit and yet without the coming of the Lord's word we will not avail ourselves of the Holy Spirit. For there to be fruit produced in us we need both the teaching and the Holy Spirit. The teaching on the Mount is particularly effective in stimulating us to bear fruit. This is because, the greater the demand the more manifested will be the power of the Holy Spirit in us. The progress of a young brother or sister depends on the demands of the teaching on the Mount as well as the knowledge of life. If anyone teaches evil doctrines, he will be hewn down and cast into the fire, says the Lord.

Verses 15-20 contain the parable, and verses 21-23 are the explanation of the parable. "Lord, Lord"— the crying of the lips spoken of here may be grapes, but it may be thorns too; for some who cry may be submissive to the Lord, while some others may rely on themselves. No one can obey the Lord without having his heart fully yielded. Thus the vine and the thorns are separated. Only those who are obedient are fit to enter the kingdom of the heavens. Verse 22 explains the evil fruit, and verse 23 tells why those who bear such fruit cannot enter the kingdom of the heavens. Verse 22 suggests that there are fruits that look like grapes and figs, yet the Lord discounts them because these are mere outward appearances. Verse 23 demonstrates that the Lord knows whether the act of prophesying is doing God's will. If it is not, it is "lawlessness." Whoever does a thing on his own without doing the will of God is a lawless person.

"Depart from me." This is an explanation. It explains the earlier phrase in this passage, "cast into the fire," which denotes that there cannot be an entering of the kingdom. The kingdom is gained only through obedience. Works cannot substitute for obedience here. No one can make toil and labour an alternative to obedience to the will of the Father. We read in verse 13 that "many" are they who travel the broad way; we also read, in verse 22, that "many" are those who will be disapproved by the Lord and can therefore not enter the kingdom of the heavens. It is rather meaningful to join these two "manys" together.

7.24–27 Now let us look at the two foundations. This is the *third* part of the sixth section. "Therefore" (v.24) is the term used to conclude the words spoken before. This foundation is the word of the Lord. "Rock" is the word spoken by the Lord himself. The foundation of all works is the rock. Every believer is seen as building a house. Some build upon the rock, while some others build upon the sand. Everyone is building; only the foundations are different. "Rock" is the word of the teaching on the Mount given by the Lord. If you build upon this, it is most secure. What is meant by building a house? It is that work which results from hearing the teaching of the Lord. The kind of teaching we hear will produce the kind of works we perform. The foundation and the house are intimately related. In the various works of a Christian will be found the principle of the teaching he has heard.

This house is not built merely to be seen by men, nor is it built only for the sake of standing against the rain, the wind and the flood. Before the day of judgment comes, it may appear that that which is built upon the rock and that which is built upon the sand are the same. But when judgment comes, the house that is built upon the sand totally collapses. This is parallel to what Paul in 1 Corinthians 3 says about wood, hay and stubble which will be burnt. Here in Matthew the work is tested by rain, water and flood; there in 1 Corinthians, it is tested by fire. Hence, we must not live according to our own ideas, but live according to the Lord. From this we see that the "rock" is the word of the Lord, and the building of the house is our works.

"And every one that heareth these words of mine, and doeth

them not." To us it might appear that the phrase "doeth them not" means that there is no doing of any work of building; yet the Lord states that "[he] built his house upon the sand." Consequently, his not doing is likewise to be construed as the building of a house, but in his case he builds a house upon the sand. Hence everyone builds, hence all who live work. Some, after they have heard the Lord's word, build upon the rock, while some do not follow the Lord's word and instead follow their own thought. Any work which is done without following the Lord's word but is done by following one's own idea is like building upon the sand. For when the rain descends and the flood comes and the winds blow, that house shall fall completely.

The difference between these two builders is that one is wise and the other is foolish. This corresponds to the two kinds of virgins mentioned in Matthew 25. Once having become disciples of the Lord, there yet remains the possibility of having one's house collapse. May we from this day onward have all our works done according to the principle of the teaching on the Mount. We cannot follow any other principle. Only by following the teaching on the Mount shall we be reckoned as true Christians. Now that we have heard the teaching on the Mount, we today should accept this principle of the Lord and live on earth accordingly. Then no trial will overwhelm us. Even the final testing of judgment will not vanquish us.

7.28,29 Finally, in verse 28 we have "the multitudes." The more the preaching, the more the hearers. Our Lord originally began speaking to the disciples, but the multitudes also came to the Mount to hear Him. "The multitudes were astonished at his teaching: for he taught them as one having authority, and not as their scribes" (vv.28b–29)

4 | Division Four 8.1–9.35

Introduction

Chapters 1 and 2 make up the first division; chapters 3 and 4, the second division; and chapters 5–7, the third. This fourth division tells us how the Lord exercises His own authority. Chapters 8 and 9 are full of miracles just as chapters 5, 6 and 7 are full of teachings. The words in chapters 5–7 were not preached at one time but most likely uttered on different occasions. Matthew, however, compiles them together. The same is true with chapters 8 and 9. What things have happened do not occur at one time, but evidently at different times. But Matthew gathers these events into one as well. For example, according to Luke and Mark the healing of Peter's mother-in-law precedes the cleansing of the leper, but in Matthew it follows afterward. This is because Matthew is a compiler, not a chronicler. Both John and Mark are chroniclers, while Luke and Matthew have their specific plans. What the Spirit of God moves them to write is not according to chronological order, but in accordance with the grouping of related teachings or actions. If anyone wishes to find out the chronological order of events he must look at John's account, if these occur in Judea, and at Mark's, if they occur in Galilee. So that of the four Gospels, the authors of two of them are chroniclers and the authors of the other two are compilers.

Had the purpose of the Lord's coming to the world been for teaching alone, the Book of Matthew should have ended at the conclusion of chapter 7. For enough had been given with those first seven chapters without any need of further compilation into chapter 8 and beyond. But the Lord did not come for the presentation of new doctrine and teaching only, He had other purposes to fulfill as well: He wished also to perform miracles. For Him to have done miracles should come as no surprise. The surprise would have been had He done *no* miracles. If one knows the Lord Jesus at all, he would be astonished not to find any miracles in the New Testament Scriptures.

Concerning miracles themselves, it is interesting to find that there are three different words for them in the Greek New Testament: (1) *dunamis,* active power; (2) *teras,* something strange that causes the beholder to wonder; and (3) *semeion,* a sign, mark, or token.* Unfortunately in our own day we focus our attention especially on power. And as to the matter of wonder, miracles are really nothing to be amazed at by those who are in the Lord. But why are miracles sometimes called signs? There is no denying that what the Lord did on earth were all powerful acts, with some of these miraculous acts known as wonders and still others known as signs. Now with respect to this latter category of miracles, we ought to note here that signs have specific purposes behind them; for when God performs a miracle, He has a certain intention behind it, by which is meant that He intends to arrive at a certain aim. For example, in the case of Jonah, the Scripture passage uses the word "sign" to show that God has a particular signification in the story of this prophet and the great fish.

All the miracles to be found in Matthew 8 are therefore God's signs. They are not only powers and wonders, they are signs too. Otherwise, Matthew would have no need to *compile* them. To

---

*"A sign is intended to appeal to the understanding, a wonder appeals to the imagination, a power (*dunamis*) indicates its source as supernatural." W.E. Vine, *An Expository Dictionary of New Testament Words* (Old Tappan, N.J.: Fleming H. Revell Co., 1966), IV, p. 228.—*Translator*

simply record events is primarily a matter of history, but to compile them is chiefly a matter of purpose. And thus we come to understand that the miracles performed below the Mount as told about in chapters 8 and 9 are God's signs. We must not treat them as mere wonders and powers. Hence, the miracles cited by Matthew in these two chapters have deeper implication than mere appearance. Though our Lord does miracles, He does not expect people to believe in Him because of *them*. On the contrary, He considers those who believe in Him due to miracles to be untrustworthy: He cannot trust himself to them (see John 2.23-25). In John 4.48 He is recorded as saying in a disapproving, negative way that "except ye see signs and wonders, ye will in no wise believe"— this thus indicating that He had no desire to perform miracles for them. There does not seem to be much difference in nature between believing the Lord through wonders and worshipping demons.

Nevertheless, the Lord, being the Son of God, can and does perform miracles quite easily. Yet the purpose in Matthew 8 is not to induce people to believe in the powers and wonders of God but to cause us instead to pay attention to God's objective behind them.

First Section 8.1-17

This is a section which puts together five incidents: (1) the cleansing of the leper; (2) the healing of the centurion's servant; (3) the healing of Peter's mother-in-law; (4) the casting out of demons; and (5) the healing of many sick. The Lord will perform miracles below the Mount because His coming to the earth is not only to pronounce the teaching on the Mount but also to heal the sick and cast out demons. Unless the sick are healed and demons cast out, the teaching on the Mount, however good it is, will be of little use to us. The teaching on the Mount is backed up by the power of the Lord. As this power proceeds, redemption results. For redemption is based on two things: (1)

price, and (2) power. To deliver the children of Israel out of Egypt the lamb was the price paid and the ten miracles were the power demonstrated. Our Lord, too, must pay the price, and He must also manifest His power. For this reason, Matthew cannot cease to write at the end of chapter 7. He must continue to write and to compile. By doing so, his readers will come to know and to recognize that by God having accomplished the work of redemption, it can therefore now be easy for them to follow the teaching on the Mount.

Peter is noted in Acts 2.22 and 10.38 as mentioning how the Lord did mighty works and wonders and signs while on earth. When Christ performed these miracles on earth He demonstrated the power of the kingdom. It is as much as reiterated in those few words of Hebrews 6.5 that read: "the powers of the age to come." What is the age to come? It is the future age, the kingdom age. Thus the powers of the age to come reflect the power of the kingdom. Due to rejection of the Lord by the Jews, the kingdom is not able to manifest its full power in this present age. It can only demonstrate "patience" (see Rev. 1.9). So that people who receive grace today are not at all the same as people who received grace in the day of the Gospels. At that time their spirit and soul *and* their body *all* received grace, for the kingdom and power and glory were all the Lord's in full manifestation while He was here on earth. But today, in the time of the Lord's rejection, we are *spiritually* blessed but we *may* not be *bodily* blessed. It is possible for some people today to receive physical healing as well as spiritual life. But it is equally possible for some others to receive spiritual life without having sickness healed. The miracles noted in the Gospels were universal, while the miracles of today are individual and exceptional. For what is recounted in the Gospels are things which were done at a time when the power of the kingdom was especially being manifested due to the physical presence of the Lord on the earth. This is not to suggest, of course, that now there is not the power of the kingdom, because the Book of Hebrews says we may taste the powers of the age to come today. But a *taste* is not a full meal; yet neither is it going hungry. There *is* power, and we have a *taste* of it; but it is a *fore*taste only, and thus it cannot be universally experienced. Nonetheless, as the age to come is approaching, we *are* able to taste *more* of its power.

8.2-4   Matthew 5 speaks of "the poor in spirit . . ."; Matthew 8 tells of "a leper . . ." The former shows us what men ought to be, while the latter exposes what men actually are.

Leprosy in the Scriptures is a type of sin (see Lev. 13, 14). Leviticus 13 tells of the uncleanness of leprosy, and Leviticus 14 relates the law of the leper in the day of his cleansing. In all of recorded Old Testament Jewish history right up to this very moment in Matthew's narrative, there is no record of any Jewish leper having ever been cleansed. Miriam, the sister of Moses, had indeed had leprosy for a brief moment of time under God's judgment of her, but she was not a leper in the constitutional sense; and, of course, Naaman the Syrian general was not a Jew. Apart from these two, who were *miraculously* cleansed, there is no case in the Old Testament record of a leper having been cleansed by himself in the natural process. Leprosy is a very different phenomenon from a cold or tuberculosis. So the Scriptures utilize leprosy to typify sin. It may be dormant for five or possibly eight years before it breaks out. One may be totally unaware of its presence, yet leprosy is being cultivated continuously in his body. He is altogether unconscious of it, yet the germ of this disease does not neglect him. Whoever has leprosy is unclean, and whoever touches it likewise becomes unclean.

Yet leprosy is not to be judged by the person who has it. It is to be examined and judged by the priest of God. From the record of Leviticus 13 and 14 we must conclude that the leper here in Matthew 8 must have been examined, judged and declared to be such by a priest at least once. So that from this we may say that in type, to sin is one thing, to be pronounced as having sinned by the priest of God is another thing. The peo-

ple of the world have not only sinned, they have been pronounced
as sinners by the Lord himself.

The question in Matthew 8.2 does not at all center around
the power of the Lord but the will of the Lord. For the power
of God is governed by God's will. Hence the leper rightly said,
"if thou wilt." This is a lesson for us to learn before God. In stretch-
ing out His hand and touching the leper, our Lord seems to take
a great risk. If He is not able to cleanse the leper, He himself
will become leprous and unclean. There is no middle ground
here. Either sin will contaminate Him, or sin will depart from
us. But thank God, sin cannot defile the Lord Jesus. He stretched
out His hand and touched the leper, saying, "I will; be thou made
clean."

The work of the Lord is mainly accomplished by the command of His word. As a matter of fact, in the Scriptures God's
work is primarily done through His word and command. That
is one of the reasons why the Lord is called the Word of God
in the Scriptures (see John 1). Apart from His word, God hardly
does any work. In Genesis 1 and 2 we see that all His works were
done by His word, except that He formed man out of the dust
of the ground. Where the word of God is, there are His creation, miracles and work. The Lord did not by His touch alone
remove the leprosy from that man. His touch of the leper was
accompanied by His word: "be thou made clean." And hence it
is the *word* which does this work of miracle. That word is everything. How powerful is a word that proceeds from the mouth
of God. He commands, and the work is done. On the other hand,
His silence is death to us. What we should be afraid of is His
silence. But once He opens His mouth, work immediately follows.
There will be power and miracle. This is a fundamental, heavenly
principle.

"And Jesus saith unto him, See thou tell no man; but go, show
thyself to the priest." It is useless to tell any other man. This man
who is now cleansed must go and see the priest for the second
time and let the latter judge if he is cleansed. Other people may

not believe that the man had leprosy before, but the priest knows because he had examined him before.

Here, the phenomenon of leprosy heads the list of physical deficiences to be dealt with by the Lord. This is because God wants us to know (in type) that human uncleanness must be the first to be perceived. We feel the power of sin and sense our weakness, but we are not aware of the uncleanness of sin. Weakness is what men sense within; uncleanness is what is terrible before God. So that our sin has two aspects: (1) the weakness within us, and (2) the uncleanness before God. Today our knowledge of sin seems to be limited to the difficulty noted in Romans 7. Rarely do we recognize the problem severely cited in Romans 3. This explains why in Matthew 8 leprosy is mentioned first, and palsy or paralysis (weakness) is next on the list.

In dealing with sin, every saved person must have dealings with regard to these two aspects of sin. *First,* he needs to deal with its uncleanness and to receive pardon. This is sin according to Romans 3. *Then,* he is able to overcome the power of sin discussed in Romans 7. The first and foremost consequence of the work of the Holy Spirit upon us is to cause us to be convicted that we are unclean before God. After this leprosy is cleansed, there will remain no consciousness of uncleanness. And thus we dare to see the priest and dare to fellowship with God's children.

8.5-13 This portion narrates the story of the *second* sick person. His physical illness is not like the disease of leprosy which is contagious and unclean. His is palsy—that is to say, he is a paralytic, the characteristic of which is to be left absolutely strengthless. Thus the Scriptures show us here the other aspect of sin. Sin not only renders us unclean before God and makes us feel guilty in our conscience, it also reduces us to weakness, especially in the realm of our will. Conscience convicts us of the uncleanness of sin in the sight of God, and the will reveals to us the weakness caused by sin. This latter demonstrates to us the power of sin upon us. It is our will that is impressed by this power. So the palsy here signifies the non-existence of strength as well as the heavy weight of sin.

The centurion asked the Lord Jesus on behalf of his palsied servant. In the Gospels, apart from the six or seven times in which healings come as the result of the patient's own personal petition of the Lord, all the rest of the healings come as a consequence of the request made by other people. In other words, the sick are brought in by others. This fact should encourage all the children of God to do their best in bringing people to God.

After the Lord heard the centurion, who addressed Him as Lord, He answered, "I will come and heal him." When people called Him "Lord," which is the same as calling Him "Jehovah," He accepted it with no hesitation. There are many similar instances found throughout the Gospels. Readers ought to take note of these places for such instances can help us to know the Person of the Lord Jesus. Among the Jewish people none but God is addressed as "Lord." But Jesus of Nazareth *is* Lord, as is confirmed by the fact that He neither corrected it nor rejected it when individuals called Him such. "I will come and heal him." The promise is based on need. There is no other reason. The centurion did not mention how faithful his servant was. He merely said that his servant was sick. And the Lord immediately promised to heal him. The only reason why people get healed is because they are sick. The grace of God comes upon the needy. Many reasons offered by people hinder them from receiving grace rather than helping them to obtain grace. God works when there is need. Let us therefore learn to believe.

"Lord, I am not worthy that thou shouldest come under my roof" (v.8). The will of the Lord may be altered. In many situations, God's will cannot be changed; but in other situations it can be, as the instance now before us exemplifies. "I will come and heal him"— that was initially the Lord's intention. The Lord was willing to condescend himself to do more, for He is aware of the weakness of man's faith. This is just as His touching the leper was an expression of His condescension in order to make it easier for the leper to believe and receive healing. In other words, I do not need to climb high for He lowers himself. The willingness here to "come" is also the Lord's way of making faith easier. The Lord purposely lowers the condition and makes the environment easier. This, then, is the will of the Lord. Yet all this is based upon the weakness of man. This centurion, though, was able to climb to a higher ground, thus obviating the need of the Lord's condescension. And willingly, the Lord changes His mind. The will that our Lord forms on the basis of man's weakness may be changed through man's strength. This is why the experiences of God's children may vary.

"Only say the word, and my servant shall be healed." The centurion desired only a word from the Lord, he firmly believing that the Lord's work would indeed be done as a result. The word needs no other support. Such faith is great. A faith that requires support is not great. "Only say the word" is the secret that Christians must learn in their lifetime.

How is it that this centurion was able to believe that his servant would be healed with just a word from the Lord? This we do not read from the Biblical account itself, but it is evident that he has been taught by the Holy Spirit. Verse 9 reveals the reason, which our Lord reckons as most precious: "I say to this one, Go, and he goeth; and to another, Come, and he cometh." There is no other reason or explanation but one, the centurion appears to be saying, which is, that my word carries power. When I say go, they go, for they are under my authority. So here we find a secret: that one's word has power. Not all words have power; only the word of authority has. There is authority in word. The Lord's word is as valuable as His coming. We may probably say that the Lord's word is even more powerful than His touch. Certainly His word is more precious than His touch. Even so, men usually deem "touch" to be more precious than "word." Yet this is meeting the Lord at a lower level. Thank God, though, that some people require only a word from the Lord. They have no need for Him to come to the house. This higher level of understanding our Lord declares as faith — great faith. In His eyes, in fact, He has never seen so great a faith on earth as that manifested by this centurion.

Authority, word and faith — these three are here joined together. Faith is not only connected with the word of God, it is also joined with the authority of God. At the time one knows the authority of God, it is very easy for that one to believe in God's word. There is practically no need to lower the condition. He has no need to rely on some help to faith. For he recognizes basically the authority of the word. God's command is as powerful today as it was in the day of creation. In creation God had neither used skill nor method. He only used word. He commanded, and the miracle was done. He had absolutely no need for any other help. To those who truly believe, environment neither helps nor hinders. For them, God's word is the sole foundation of faith. These are such who recognize the authority of God. All who are struggling for faith lack adequate knowledge of God's authority. Once I asked Miss Margaret E. Barber* this question: "How can man believe God?" Her answer was: "Man ought to know God." If I do not know God, how can I believe in Him? But if I know Him, I just naturally believe Him.

"So great faith." This faith *is* great, for it needs neither help nor crutches of support. It is based solely on God's word! on God's authority! Authority is the basic principle by which God governs the universe. If you believe in this authority, you will readily see that there is nothing God's word cannot accomplish. In the natural world we speak of laws; in the human world, of power; and in God's world, of authority.

"Many shall come from the east and the west . . ." (v.11). Because of their faith, many "shall sit down . . . in the kingdom of heaven." That is, the Gentiles will be received into the kingdom.

---

*Miss Barber was a missionary from England who was a great help to Watchman Nee's spiritual life.—*Translator*

"But the sons of the kingdom shall be cast forth into the outer darkness" (v.12). They shall not have the light of the Lord's countenance. Accordingly, there is darkness. They weep because of repentance. They gnash their teeth because of pains. The children of Israel ought to possess the greatest faith, since the Scriptures are theirs, and the servants of God have always been in their midst. But for the Gentiles to believe is indeed great faith, that which the children of Israel do not have. This is not to suggest, however, that religious education adversely causes people to depart from God whereas the unfavorable environment of the Gentiles enables them to gain God.

But whence comes this great faith among the Gentiles and such a lack thereof among the children of Israel? To answer such a question we must first know what is meant by being called the children of Israel. The Pharisees and the Sadducees are all children of Israel. Their relationship with God is quite neutral. They do not oppose Him but rather approve Him. But approval is no substitute for consecration. The Gentiles who oppose God cannot be neutral when they eventually turn to Him. Since the children of Israel are neutral, it is hard to find great faith among them. Yet this great faith, surprisingly, is found among the Gentiles. But among the children of Israel, many doctrines have become so popular that they can be held without any cost. Many spiritual things have turned into rituals that require no obedience. Such things require only lip-confession without demanding inward affection. And that is why so great faith is not found in Israel.

This incident about the centurion is the one time that our Lord was so greatly moved in a positive way. While He was slandered and rejected everywhere on earth, He met one with so great a faith. It was like a cup of water in the desert that could satisfy His great thirst. So He declared that such people are those in the kingdom of the heavens. And thus there in Matthew 8, it is revealed already how the Gentiles are to be brought in as the Jews are being rejected.

With faith comes wholeness; there is no need to wait. Before the Lord had said to the centurion, "as thou hast believed, so be it done unto thee" (v.13), the latter's faith was already such in principle. But now, *with* this word from the Lord, the centurion gladly acquiesced. To the one with faith, when the word is spoken it is sufficient for him. He asks for no further words. The Lord has spoken, and so all is settled: "the servant was healed in that hour." With authority comes miracle. God comes forth through the word, and by faith, healing is done.

8.14–15 covers the *third* instance of sickness. It is a fever which is contagious. In the Greek, the word used here for fever suggests a very high fever. The Lord Jesus came to Peter's house and saw His disciple's mother-in-law lying in bed with a fever. Fever is also a type of sin. It signifies the restlessness of sin. Fever is the opposite of rest. The nature of sin is uncleanness and disabling, and the result of sin is to be without peace. Fever speaks of the current consequence that sin brings in. (So that it becomes quite evident to the reader by this time that Matthew is indeed not merely a recorder, he is also a compiler with purpose and design in his selection of incidents to be placed together in his Gospel narrative.) Sin produces unsatisfaction and unrest in our soul. It causes impatience and anxiety. This is illustrated to us by fever. Why is it that the world needs so much amusement? Because its people need these many stimulations to help them forget their distresses. But the Christians are satisfied within, and therefore they do not need these stimuli. The more the unrest and unhappiness inside, the greater the desire for outside stimuli. Drinking, for example, is to wash away sorrow. We have no sorrow, so we have not the need of washing it away with alcohol. (Yet let it be clearly understood that the Lord does not advocate asceticism, either.)

The Lord touched the hand of Peter's mother-in-law, and the fever immediately left her. She now had rest, and thus she could arise and serve Jesus. This indicates that healing is for service.

8.16-17 The *fourth* kind of sickness cited here is the kind which comes through demon possession. The entire person falls under the power of Satan. To be demon-possessed means both the body and the mind come under the power of a demon. Ordinary sickness is but being *physically* ill. But to be demon-possessed is a sickness more than physical in nature, for the will, mind and body are all being possessed.

The Lord healed all sicknesses that came through Satan. He saved the *total* man. With just a word He cast out the evil spirits. For the word of God represents the authority of God. To cast out demons is always done with authority, never with power. For it is in the *name* of the Lord, and not by any power, that demons are cast out. For in and of itself, the Name, too, stands for authority. The Name is the authority inherent in the Lord; it is objective. Word is the authority that comes from the Lord to man; it is subjective.

Fifth and finally, the Gospel writer mentioned that the Lord "healed all that were sick" (v.16c). There is no need to analyze each case. All sicknesses which were brought in through sin and through Satan were healed. This summed up all the healings mentioned above.

The word in verse 17 comes from Isaiah 53.4. But Isaiah 53 has reference to the cross, whereas Matthew 8 does not refer to the cross but is simply a narration of the healing of the sick by the Lord. Nevertheless, this that the Lord Jesus has done has already fulfilled the word of Isaiah 53.4. For all the works of the Lord are based on the cross. This may be confirmed by what is found earlier in Matthew 3. We learned there that our Lord did not begin to work until He had been baptized in the river Jordan. This is to say that all the Lord's works in God's eyes are done only on the ground of death and resurrection. And hence His work of healing the sick and casting out the evil spirits is reckoned as taking our infirmities to the cross and bearing our diseases there. Though historically He at this point is as yet to die, according to spiritual reality these acts of healing are already the aftermath of the cross.

This section ends at verse 17. All these miracles are signs not only recorded but also *compiled* by Matthew. Please note, for example, that in his compilation of chapter 8 he deliberately placed the servant of the centurion *here* and not elsewhere, for he had further interest in the centurion. Again, Matthew purposely placed here in chapter 8 the many possessed by demons but, interestingly enough, left unmentioned the particular demon-possessed one he did mention in the very next chapter! This is because besides the individual significance of the sicknesses selected, Matthew also had in mind some special meanings to be derived from these sick ones themselves. The order in which they are presented in chapter 8 has even additional significance beyond what has already been mentioned, as will be seen next.

Let us note that the first sick one who was healed was a Jew. This is evident from the fact that the priest was mentioned. In all of Jewish history this was the first case of a leper having been cleansed. It was therefore a great event. And in the light of that fact, the priest, upon knowing the case, ought to have come and worshipped the Lord. But he did not come, if the silence of the Scripture can be our evidence. Here we are shown in type the meaning not only of this particular *sickness* but also of the *sick person* himself. This particular sick person represents in type the Jews who have received grace on earth. This has reference to the work which our Lord did at that time, for He *touched* the sick one. The priest who failed to come to the Lord represents in type, of course, the Jews who have rejected the Lord and His work of grace.

The second sick one in Matthew's compilation was a Gentile whose healing came through faith. This healing of a Gentile represents the grace which our Lord extends to us all in this present age. Today if a Jew is to receive grace he, too, must stand on this new position of faith to receive it. But let us notice as well that in the story of this Gentile servant being healed, the grace of our Lord is dispensed without His even entering the house. The Lord was not present; He only used a word. Today all who receive grace receive it on the ground of faith and not sight. And such is the very characteristic as to how the Gentiles in the world are to receive grace.

The third sick person cited in chapter 8 who was healed was a Jewess. Peter was a brother in the Lord, and so was his wife. Both Peter and his wife are in the Church. Peter's mother-in-law, though, is *related* to the Church but not *in* the Church. From this we can conclude that after the days of grace upon the Gentiles are over, the Jews will again have opportunity to receive grace — that is to say, the Jews who are related to the Church. By this is meant that for the sake of the Church, the grace of God will once more come upon the Jews during the millennial kingdom. Please note that when this third sick person was healed, it was an instance again of the Lord touching — He *touched* her with His hand.

With the first sick one, the Lord was present; in the case of the second, the Lord was absent; and in the instance of the third, He was again present. With the fourth and fifth sick people selected by Matthew for chapter 8, we find that the Lord had cast out all the demons and healed all the sick. This would suggest that in the kingdom age the *whole* world will receive grace. For in the instance of chapter 8 He healed *all* the sick; and at the time of the kingdom, we know that there will be no infirmities. Hence, we see here that the very *identities* of the sick as well as their particular *sicknesses* all have signficance. How harmonious and therefore beautiful! While Matthew was engaged in compiling, the Holy Spirit was engaged in attaching the proper significance to each element in the Gospel writer's compilation!

Second Section 8.18–9.8

The section now before us tells of three incidents: (1) the cross-

ing of the sea; (2) the casting out of demons; and (3) the
forgiveness of sins.

8.18–28a—the crossing of the sea. Our Lord works to gain
men, so He must avoid the crowds who seek for thrills. In order
to maintain the purity of His work, He decides to sail to the other
side of the Sea or Lake of Galilee. In verses 19 and 20 we are
told of two men who came to talk with Jesus. This is inserted
as a parenthesis to the story of the lake crossing. In verse 19 we
are told of a scribe who ventured to declare to the Lord: "Teacher,
I will follow thee whithersoever thou goest." The Lord was deeply
touched by his zeal and did not in the least doubt his sincerity.
Yet He did not accept him. In His reply He did not give the
least encouragement to the man. And why? For two reasons: (1)
There is never a person who can follow the Lord without his first
having been called, since he will easily drop out along the way
if he has not been called. He who comes on his own will depart
on his own. It is the divine calling upon us that keeps us going,
holds us from falling, and helps us from looseness. Our Lord
never attempts to stir up the excitement of anyone who is not
clear on the issue of calling. "Ye did not choose me," says the Lord,
"but I chose you" (John 15.16). If on a given day in your so-called
following of the Lord, you do not choose Christ but yourself,
what then will happen? Our "choice" is totally undependable,
for how easily our heart may change. But with the Lord, "the
gifts and the *calling* of God are not repented of" (Rom. 11.29).
So we must be a people who, in our walk, are being held not
by our supposed original choosing of the Lord but by His calling of us.

(2) There is a second reason for the Lord's lack of encouragement of this would-be disciple. This man thinks more highly of
himself than he ought to think. He over-estimates himself. He
has not learned to know his own weakness. He is overly self-
confident. He is even bolder than Peter, for he utters these words
on the very first day of his supposed discipleship! He seems to

see everything except his own weakness. How very many people are like him. They fail to keep their early vows. They may start well, but they end badly. All because they do not know their weakness. My promise can never be substituted for God's promise. The Lord never encourages those who are not called, nor does He ever endorse those who do not know their own weakness. So His answer was: "The foxes have holes, and the birds of the heaven have nests; but the Son of man hath not where to lay his head" (v.20). This does not mean He has no pillow but that He has no place of His own. The foxes have their secure holes, the birds have their established nests, but the Son of man is rejected on earth. Do you want to follow Him? Many are zealous without having counted the cost. If they really knew the cost, they would not make such an easy and bold promise. The phrase "the Son of man" found in Matthew 8.20 is the first time this appellation is used in the New Testament. It signifies His rejection on earth. But in the future kingdom when He is highly exalted He will still use this Name.

One of the disciples now stepped forward and said, "Lord, suffer me first to go and bury my father." Unlike the scribe, this person was *already* a believer and disciple. We know this for a fact because he had confessed Jesus by calling Him "Lord" whereas the scribe had addressed Jesus as "Teacher." In this disciple's home there were most likely many people, possibly his brothers or relatives. "Suffer me first"—this is a wrong approach, because the primary governing principle of every disciple should be, "In the beginning God." To bury his father or not was a small matter. The real issue here was: "suffer me first." His father might have already died, although according to Greek grammar it can also be possible that he might not be dead yet. If so, then this disciple had wanted to wait till after his father had died to follow the Lord. How did Jesus answer him? "Leave the dead to bury the dead." You do not need to bury the dead. In the Lord's answer, the first "dead" refers to the *spiritually* dead — the unregenerated. The second "dead" means the *physically* dead — the disciple's father.

Those who believe in the Lord should not spend much time on funerals. Preceding that statement the Lord had said, "Follow me." This is the second time the Lord had called him to follow. He had been called once, but now he is being called *again* by the Lord because he now wanted to go back to bury his father. *We* may forget our calling, but the *Lord* never does. Calling keeps us from the world. The Lord will never take the second place. It is a reasonable thing to want to bury one's father, but the Lord's demand is higher than any earthly father's. His is the highest demand. Who is worthy to be His disciple? He who puts Christ in the first place. All Christians who have problems in their lives will find a common cause for their problems in their inadequate consecration.

The highest glory lies in the Lord's acceptance, not in my giving. That He is willing to accept me, this is amazing grace.

In our following the Lord, if there is any unfinished business, that may hinder us from following. Hence the Lord says to "leave the dead to bury the dead."

Both the incident of the scribe and that of the disciple are parenthetic. For the Lord had commanded to depart to the other side of the lake. In verse 23 we read about the Lord commencing to cross the water. The word "tempest" (v.24) in Greek is not the term used for any ordinary tempest. It refers to a storm caused by an *earthquake* or some similar tremendous upheaval. This particular tempest is therefore quite special — in fact, Matthew termed it "a *great* tempest." It may therefore be viewed as the Enemy's attempt to create such a natural phenomenon to destroy the Lord. The Enemy had raised up such a terrible storm by which to swallow up the Lord in the lake. Yet the Bible describes the Lord's reaction in this way: "but he was asleep." This is truly a beautiful word — a word of peaceful rest. Peace so filled His heart as though nothing was happening. With such peace, there is naturally rest.

The disciples came and woke Him up. They cried out together, "Save, Lord; we perish." According to their past experience (for they were all veteran seafarers), they knew there was no hope of survival. And the Lord said, "Why are ye fearful, O ye of little faith?" Our Lord never blames us for praying, but He does reproach us for being afraid. As a matter of fact, He *loves* to have us bother Him with prayers. What He reprimanded them for was that they had troubled themselves with fear before they had troubled Jesus with prayer. What had the Lord wanted them to believe? The object of faith is the word, the promise. The disciples had forgotten His earlier clear command. They were of little faith because they did not remember the Lord's word found in verse 18. The Lord had given commandment to depart to the other side of the lake. This should have been sufficient for them to believe. If the disciples had truly believed in His word, they, too, could have gone to sleep just as the Lord had done. Our prayer should be the expression of faith, but the prayer here was a sign of unbelief. Many prayers are the result of our believing in God. But many a time when God has already spoken we need not pray anymore. We should stop praying. If we continue to pray because the word has yet to be "cashed in," then by this we show our unbelief. God takes no pleasure in our prayer of unbelief. If we truly believe in the Lord's word, we will sit in the bow of the boat and laugh at the wind and wave. They can even grow ten times more fierce than before, but where can they possibly send us?

Let us notice here that the Lord *may* be compelled to act — that is to say, when we are weak He can be constrained to do what it is unnecessary for Him to do. The way many prayers are answered is for no other reason than to comfort us. These prayers give us no help other than psychological aid. In the case at hand, in spite of the great tempest these disciples could have still reached the other side, but like most men's hearts, these disciples looked for calmness of wind and waves. Jesus comforted His disciples and answered their prayer of unbelief: "there was a great calm." Here, the Lord showed forth His authority over the natural world.

In verses 1–17 we witnessed the great faith of the centurion. In verses 18–28a we saw how the Lord used a word to overcome a natural phenomenon, just as in the earlier cases He had exercised His authority over sin and demons. Later on He will again use a word to overcome demons. All these manifest the authority of the Lord. With respect to this great tempest, clearly Satan was at the back; hence the Lord *rebuked* the winds and the sea, after which there was a great calm. We certainly ought not to be like superstitious people, but we also ought not to be like common people who consider *all* tempests to be mere natural phenomena. Rather, we should learn to distinguish between the natural and the supernatural. In the event we discover that there is a supernatural force behind what we see or experience, we must pray if we do not have a word from the Lord. If there is word, we then must believe. Verse 27 reveals that our Lord is no ordinary man, since "even the winds and the sea obey him." He has authority, and His authority is manifested in His word.

Verses 28b–34 tell us how the Lord overcomes the demons. Matthew records two men possessed, while Luke mentions only one of them in his narrative. Matthew reports the total number of men in order to show forth the authority of the Lord. These two who were possessed with demons did not dwell in the place of the living. They were exceedingly fierce in their behavior. According to verse 29 the demons recognized what men had refused to confess. Many times the demons know more than men. When the Lord had come up out of the waters of the river Jordan God had declared: "This is my beloved Son, in whom I am well pleased." In the wilderness Satan had said twice, "If thou art the Son of God . . ." So Satan and his hosts all confess this fact. Dust is the food of the serpent. But here is a man who is the Son of God and in whom there is not a grain of dust. Hence Satan could not swallow Him up as He crossed the lake in the little boat.

This passage also reveals to us that the demons' work on earth has a time limit. After this event they will not be able to live. So the word in verse 29 was said according to the time the demons had. From verses 30 and 31 we are given a hint that the demons mentioned in the Scriptures are the disembodied spirits of the former world (Gen. 1.1–2). These disembodied spirits seek for bodies to possess. A disembodied spirit's existence is apparently a painful one, for if the Lord would not allow them to possess human bodies any longer, then they expected to at least be allowed to dwell in the swine as an alternative. They would rather possess the swine if they cannot possess men. Yet all who are experienced in casting out demons know how these creatures are most reluctant to depart from the human body. It takes the powerful name of the Lord to cast them out. Even so, they will only reluctantly leave. Yet these demons in the incident now before us, upon being permitted to go into the swine, found possessing animals was not as good as possessing men, so they caused the swine to rush madly down the slope into the sea to perish in the waters (v.32).

According to Luke's account, as soon as the demons had been cast out by the Lord, the men came to their right mind (8.35). This cannot be explained medically. The Lord alone has the authority to cast out demons. He does not need to move a finger. He merely utters a word, and the demons are cast out. All the works of the Lord are accomplished by His word. Many a time we sense the need of power, though what we really need is authority. *The more we know God the more we shall use authority and the less we shall use power.*

"And they that fed them fled . . ." (v.33). The Jews may tend sheep but they are not permitted to feed swine. Keeping swine was against the Mosaic law. Hence these swineherds had violated the word of God for the sake of profit.

"And behold, all the city came out to meet Jesus: and when they saw him, they besought him that he would depart from their borders" (v.34). How strange—here, through the Lord's help, they had retrieved two of their citizens, though they had lost numerous swine in the process. Their beseeching the Lord to leave indicates that they calculated the swine to be far more valuable than the two men. Though they themselves did not own these swine but were only herders, the multitude from the city nonetheless asked the Lord to depart from their territory. So here we have two requests: the demons had asked to enter the swine, and the people asked the Lord to depart from their area. The people made the request because they reckoned that the Lord's continued presence would be harmful to their illegal profiteering; so they wanted Him to leave.

In the Bible swine are always used to typify nominal believers; being unclean animals inside (not chewing the cud) but clean outside (they parting the hoof), they easily represent nominal believers who may have the outward appearance but lack the inward reality. Also in the Bible, the demon-possessed are used as a type for sinners. We see, then, in this present story of the two demon-possessed ones, that two sinners received salvation. In verse 18 we saw the Lord give commandment to His disciples to depart with Him to the other side of the lake. And immediately after their departure, a great tempest arose. But the Lord braved this danger in order to save two sinners. Sinners such as these two received much grace before God. On the other hand, we also see the many nominal believers, as represented by the two thousand swine (see Mark 5.13), perish in the depths of the lake.

At the name of Jesus, all demons must submit.

Being demon-possessed and being insane are two different conditions. Let us note the following points. (1) The insane one is confused in mind but not in will. The demon-possessed may at times be confused in mind but at other times clear in mind, though his will is definitely unable to control his body. A demon may or may not possess the mind, but it certainly possesses the will. The affected element in an insane person is the mind, while that in a demon-possessed person is the will. So insanity is in the realm of the mind, whereas demon possession is centered in the realm of the will—although sometimes even in a demon-possessed person his mind may also be confused.

(2) Insanity is basically a sickness of the physiological brain. The derangement can be quite fierce, and even at its dormancy it may not be completely healed. But the demon-possessed becomes a totally other person when the possession is active. When the demon departs or goes into hiding, the man seems to be completely well.

(3) Medical doctors diagnose both insanity and demon possession as illness. But when we Christians encounter an insane person, our spirit does not sense being defiled, just as we do not feel defiled while contacting an ordinary sick person. When, however, we meet a demon-possessed person, our spirit will be conscious of the power of darkness and its defilement. Our spirit will rise up against it. Insanity is therefore purely a physical illness, whereas demon possession is a supernatural illness. The latter has nothing to do with heredity. It may not have any relation to stimulation. It is totally supernatural.

(4) Now it is true that many insane people commence with mental illness but later become demon-possessed. Some may at first have become mentally deranged through fear and have then turned to be demon-possessed. Such cases are not easy to deal with, for although we can cast out demons we cannot cast out insanity. Such people need to have the demons cast out on the one hand and maintain a state of rest on the other. Here, doctors can be of help towards their recovery.

(5) The demon-possessed are one hundred percent healed, and the sickness will not pass on to the next generation. Mental illness, however, may become hereditary. The insane do not have supernatural knowledge, but the demon-possessed have such knowledge.

9.1-8 What we have here is the third part of this present section. It shows how the Lord has authority to forgive sins. "His own city" is Capernaum. "Be of good cheer" (v.2) is used by the Lord a number of times. It can be helpful to us if we would locate all the "be of good cheers" to be found in the New Testament.

Why, though, in this instance, "be of good cheer"? Because "thy sins are forgiven." Sin is man's fundamental problem. The word "sin" is cast in the plural in Greek here. It refers to man's sinful deeds. (Sin in the singular number signifies the sinful nature which cannot be forgiven but must be dealt with by the cross; sinful deeds, however, need to be forgiven.)

"And behold, certain of the scribes said within themselves, This man blasphemeth" (v.3). In Mark's account of this event we have the following record of what the scribes said: "Why doth this man thus speak? he blasphemeth: who can forgive sins but one, even God?" (2.7) No one, of course, *can* forgive sins but God himself. Men can only punish but not forgive. What are to be forgiven are all sins of unrighteousness. And the only righteous result is judgment. The one who is sinned against is the only one who can forgive. If my book is stolen, I have the authority to forgive; and such forgiving is not unrighteous. Likewise, all the sins we commit today are sinned against God. So God alone can forgive. When the Lord said, "Thy sins are forgiven," there could only be one of two possible explanations: either (1) Jesus is indeed the God who can and does forgive, or (2) He is an imposter and a blasphemer. Because these scribes did not know Jesus, they automatically accused Him of blaspheming.

But the Lord is God, so He knew the thoughts of these scribes (v.4). From His viewpoint, "to say, Thy sins are forgiven; or to say, Arise, and walk" (v.5) were both equally easy. Here, again, forgiveness of sins is done by a word. In that word the sins of the palsied one were all forgiven. The issue does not lie in saying the word, it lies in having the authority to forgive. But in order to demonstrate to the watching world that He did in truth have the authority to forgive, the Lord turned to the paralytic and said again, "Arise, and take up thy bed, and go unto thy house" (v.6). Why did He do this? To let people "know that the Son of man hath authority on earth to forgive sins." He employs the visible to prove the invisible.

In the New Testament there are these two different bases by

which forgiveness could be administered: (1) the authority to forgive as expressed by the word here; and (2) the work of the Lord on the cross. Yet even before the Lord had accomplished the work of redemption on the cross He already could forgive by His authority. This is because forgiveness is not just His work; for even without using His work the Lord can proceed to forgive sins because He has authority. In short, it is because He is God. As a result, the man who was brought in on a bed now walked home carrying the bed.

When the multitudes saw the palsied one healed, they could not fail to believe that his sins were now in actual fact forgiven. So they "glorified God, who had given such authority unto men" (v.8).

Third Section 9.9–35

This section can be quite simply entitled, "Grace."

9.9 The first incident is about the call of Matthew himself. From the books written by Jewish rabbis, it is known that at that time the position of the publicans or tax collectors was listed as the lowest of all occupations. This is because (1) during that time all publicans embezzled and extorted; and (2) these publicans collected revenues for imperial Rome and in the process oppressed their own Jewish countrymen, so that they were considered traitors. Society at that time despised these publicans, and Matthew was one of them. Nonetheless, "at the place of toll"—which was the very location where Matthew had so often committed his crimes—the Lord called him, saying, "Follow me." And Matthew rose up and followed the Lord. This man had absolutely no way nor strength to rise up and follow the Lord except he had indeed heard the call of the Most High God. Let us all see that the call of the Lord stands between the world and me. It stands between my money and me. It also stands between my profession and me. Matthew offered no excuse not to respond.

He did not even say that he must settle all his accounts first before
he could arise and follow. For when the divine call comes, man
has to obey. His own future is forever destroyed. His lifelong am-
bition is cast into the dust. The call destroys my entire being
and reconstructs me. It burns the bridges behind me so that I
will not be able to go back to the world. Thus Matthew arose
and followed the Lord. In the eyes of unbelievers this is incom-
prehensible. Matthew was not a child, nor was he mad or foolish:
he was one who knew how to calculate. Yet, in the face of this
call, he could neither resist nor deny. It is not that we are able
to meet the challenge but that the call has drawn us.

9.10-13 Matthew not only followed the Lord, he also in-
vited many publicans and sinners into his house (v.10). He did
not look at his own experience as anything special. He believed
that all could be attracted by this call. Matthew tried to spread
the gospel through invitation. Not many days before, he had been
a powerful though despised publican, but now he had been
changed and had become a disciple.

"And when the Pharisees saw it, they said unto his disciples"
(v.11). This was the habit of the Pharisees. They rarely spoke to
the Lord; they generally spoke behind His back.

"They that are whole have no need of a physician, but they
that are sick" (v.12). In the world, there is actually not a single
person who is really healthy. People may think of themselves as
healthy, and therefore they do not consider it needful to have
a physician. Some others are actually told they are healthy, and
so they ignore the plain fact that they are sick and need a physician. Many are the spiritually sick, but few confess they are such.
The Lord comes to save only those who know they are sinners.
All who are sinners and yet refuse to confess to be such are unable
to receive grace from the Lord. Sinners who are in darkness and
are not being enlightened think they have no need of the Lord
Jesus. But as soon as they realize their sins, it is easy for them
to accept Him. Hence, the basic problem with the world lies not

in knowing the Lord, but in knowing themselves. Those who do not know themselves cannot take the Lord seriously. But those who truly know themselves treasure Jesus of Nazareth very much.

The Pharisees were familiar with the Scriptures. So here the Lord quoted a passage from them: "I desire mercy, and not sacrifice" (v.13), quoting from Hosea 6.6. Mercy is what God does for men, while sacrifice is what men do for God. God loves to give, not to receive. This is what the Lord came to the world to tell us about God. It is absolutely impossible for man to sacrifice without first knowing the grace of God. We must first accept the Lord as the Sin Offering, then we may present ourselves as a living sacrifice to God. First is Romans 3, then follows Romans 12. For man, the first thing in order is to receive God's mercy, not to sacrifice right away. Let us do according to God's delight.

"Go ye and learn." To study the Scriptures is one thing; to learn the Scriptures is quite another. The publicans and sinners are those to whom God shows mercy. But you Pharisees, says Jesus in so many words, are the people who sacrifice; yet God my Father delights in these sinners more than in you; for I do not come "to call the righteous, but sinners." No one can serve the Lord Jesus first. Each must first accept the Lord as his Physician. To be a Christian, one must first enter in as a sick patient. Then he can help others as a nurse.

9.14–17 Here is another incident. The disciples of John came to ask of Jesus. These are different from the Pharisees. The latter speak behind the back, whereas the disciples of John come to speak directly with the Lord. The Pharisees discuss the Lord with His disciples, while the disciples of John ask the Lord directly about His disciples. Their attitudes are quite different. Many who know God have few questions. The more distant one is from the Lord, the more questions he has.

In verse 15 we see that the Lord showed them that His coming to the world to work was the beginning of a new age. He himself was like a bridegroom, and His disciples were the sons of the bridechamber. As long as He was with them they had no reason to mourn. But He knew this situation could not last long, for He would soon be rejected and crucified. So He explained that "the days will come, when the bridegroom shall be taken away from them, and then will they fast." At that latter time fasting would then indeed be meaningful.

The reply of the Lord goes deeper than their question. The disciples of John merely asked about fasting, but the Lord spoke not only of the *fact* of fasting but also of another aspect of fasting. Fasting that is not real is like the ritualistic fasting of the Pharisees. The fasting spoken of here in Matthew 9.15 is real fasting, while verses 16 and 17 refer to the ritualistic kind of the Pharisees. For these latter verses touch upon law and grace. A garment is outside, wine is inside. A garment signifies outward conduct. No one puts the grace of God within the context of the old conduct. Nor can anyone mend the hole in the garment of his old conduct with the grace of God. For the undressed cloth has shrinking power, and a worse rent can be made. Hence, you cannot mix law and grace. If you do, grace will lose its sweetness, and law will lose its fear. With the result that you end up with neither grace nor law. The work which Christ came to do is to take away the old garment completely and put on the new garment.

Yet He did more than this: He also accomplished the inward work. Wine represents the Holy Spirit as life. The Lord spoke of the new wine, which has the power of expanding. If it is put in the old wineskins it will rend the skins. The Lord gives us the Holy Spirit, and the Holy Spirit is the new life in us. This power of the Holy Spirit moves and expands. It will not cease working till it breaks all the old habits, old life and old decisions. This new life demands a new wineskin. What is within is called wine, what is without is called the wineskins. There must be new habits, new life and new decisions in order for anyone to be a Christian. Whether it is the story of Matthew the tax collector or the discussion of fasting, it is all a matter of grace.

9.18-26 What we have seen above are the sick and the mournful. In this lengthy portion now before us we will see the dead, the blind and the dumb. All these incidents have as their emphasis the nature of the Lord's work on earth. The works of our Lord are all based on grace, not on law. His purpose is not in putting new wine into the old wineskins but in putting the new wine into the new wineskins. He has no intention to rend the old skins. He is not intent on destroying the law; rather, He is for new life and new living.

On earth our Lord met not only the sick and the mournful, He also encountered the dead who needed a new life. He answers the sick as a Physician and answers the mournful with the new wine. Without Him, life is indeed quite sorrowful. Now He answers the dead with life.

This daughter typifies especially the Jewish people, for her father was a ruler of the synagogue (cf. Mark 5.22). But the daughter was now dead. The request recorded in verse 18 is the greatest kind. The ruler made the request because he believed. When men come before the great God, they may ask for great things. Yet no one is ever able to ask beyond what the Lord can do.

On the way to the ruler's house, another incident interposed itself (vv. 20-22). At that moment a woman with an issue of blood began to exercise faith in the Lord. This faith caused her to have the assurance that her illness would be healed by her simply touching the border of Jesus' garment. She touched it, and in response the Lord said to her: "thy faith hath made thee whole." And the woman was made whole from that very hour. This incident, however, delayed the Lord's journey to the ruler's house so that by the time the Lord had arrived, the daughter was thoroughly dead.

Yet the damsel was raised from the dead (vv. 23-26). Here we can learn a few basic lessons. The damsel was twelve years old, but so had the woman an issue of blood twelve years. What is the meaning of an issue of blood according to the Scriptures? Leviticus tells us that "the life of the flesh is in the blood" (17.11).

An issue of blood thus signifies the wasting away of life, hence further signifying a journeying towards death. How strange that shortly after the damsel had died, the woman received healing, and after the woman was made whole the damsel was called back to life.

Here the Bible shows us what the nature of the Lord's work on earth is. The elements to be found in this passage of Scripture can serve as kinds of types or signs for two groups of people without grace. During the period of human history when the Lord God was being gracious to the Jews, the Gentiles were as it were experiencing a time of an issue of blood. But now the Lord had come to the world during the days when the Jews as a nation were rejected and dead. They had lost their kingdom. The Lord therefore came to heal the Jews so that they might again receive grace from God. This is typified by His going to heal the damsel. But while on the way, the woman with an issue of blood met the Lord. Or we may say, the Lord meets the Gentiles. All the Gentiles who have faith are healed. Only afterwards will the Lord heal the Jews. In other words, we may say that the purpose of the Lord's coming is to heal the Jews; but in the midst of His purpose and work with the children of Israel He encounters the Gentiles. So He heals the Gentiles first, and then He will return to heal the Jews and revive the nation of Israel. His ultimate purpose is for the damsel, but His work is done first for the woman. He comes to give life. He comes to save the Gentiles as well as the Jews. He gives life to all.

This is a point worth special notice. Before God men are not just sinners, they are also the dead ones, they having thoroughly died. To look upon oneself as simply a sinner is still an overestimation of oneself. One ought also to reckon himself as one of the dead. So that towards sin I am a sinner, for I sin; and towards God I am numbered among the dead because I can do nothing. One needs to stand on such a twin-ground to really receive grace. How useless we are, for we cannot even move, just as the dead are unable to move. If we truly arrive at this point in an estimation of ourselves we will struggle no more; because if we have truly given up all hope of ourselves, as seen in Romans 7, then we shall begin to look up to God, and life will commence to be manifested in us.

This passage of Scripture also shows us the two sides of the Lord's work on earth. On His side He gives life. On our side we believe. All the works of our Lord are done within the context of the interaction between these two sides. One side is what the Lord does by His sovereignty, and the other is what we receive by faith. He has sovereign authority, but we need to believe. He is sovereign, and life is in Him. He took the hand of the damsel, and the damsel arose. So that due to the sovereign touch of the Lord, men receive life. But on the other side, there was a woman with an issue of blood who had never prayed before, nor had she been taught to believe. In the Gospels, this woman alone signifies the characteristic of faith. The faith of the centurion is great, but it is expressed in prayer. This woman has not prayed, nor has she ever heard God's word. Her faith is therefore a naked kind of faith. It is simply faith itself, for "she said within herself, If I do but touch his garment, I shall be made whole." So the emphasis is not on the word nor on prayer but on faith itself. The result is, she was made whole.

Hence we see that the work is done partly through the sovereignty of the Lord in giving life and partly through acceptance by faith. As soon as you desire it, God will honor your wish, your decision. And as a consequence, you receive it. This woman merely touched the Lord's garment, she did not even touch the Lord himself. The garment signifies outward conduct, which may refer to the way our Lord lived on earth and how He manifested His character. This woman seemed to understand this. She understood that the Lord came full of grace — that He called sinners, that He came not to judge but to give grace. With such understanding she received grace. Truly the work of the Lord on earth is to respond to man's faith. All else is unnecessary. Just to see the Lord's manner of life is sufficient to believe, and in believing receive His work of grace. Although the Lord had not spoken a word, and the woman had not gotten any word from the Lord, she believed. Only after she had believed did the Lord speak to her. Now she had the word of the Lord. So that in the future she could face any new symptom with the Lord's word. Her faith in any second instance would now have the Lord's word on which to rely. Otherwise, in any future trial, her faith might be destroyed. It may be helpful to contrast verse 2 with verse 22.

9.27–31 In these verses we have the fourth incident, that of the healing of the two blind men. Matthew records two men, while Luke and Mark mention only one person. This is because Matthew focuses on the men whereas Luke and Mark pay more attention to the event itself. After the time of Matthew 1 these two blind men are the first who confess the Lord as the Son of David. This is a very significant matter in the Book of Matthew. The Lord came to earth to be King. Verse 28 notes that they said to Jesus, "Yea, Lord." This "Yea" to the Lord is also the first time it has thus far been spoken in the Gospels. No one should ever say "Nay" to the Lord. Only Peter said it as recorded in chapter 16. We instead ought always to say, "Yea, Lord"; for this is an expression of faith. Faith in the Scriptures is presented in its many aspects. Here is one of them. "Believe ye that I am able to do this?" (v.28) This is concerned with the power of the Lord. They believed. Then He touched their eyes, saying, "According to your faith be it done unto you" (v.29).

"And Jesus strictly charged them, saying, See that no man know it" (v.30). Why did the Lord charge them not to let any man know? He was afraid this would attract many who were only curious. Regarding His saving of our souls, He always wants us to testify to that. But with regard to sickness healed in answer to prayer, He has not required us to frequently bear witness to that. This is because of the fear of stirring up man's curiosity. Nevertheless, these two men "went forth, and spread abroad his fame in all that land" (v.31). As a consequence, their broadcasting hindered the work of the Lord Jesus.

Jesus came to this world to be Lord. As those who are dead, men have need of receiving life; but also, as those who are blind, men need the restoration of sight. And thus, I have my sins forgiven, I am filled with joy (that is to say, filled with the new wine of the life of the Spirit), and I have my eyes opened.

9.32, 33a The last incident recorded in this series is that of the dumb man who, once healed by the Lord, was able to speak. In verse 32 we are told that there was a dumb man possessed with a demon. The next verse tells of the demon being cast out and the dumb man speaking. The dumbness spoken of here is a different kind from the ordinary. Ordinarily, it is a physical ailment; but the kind here has been caused by demon possession. Some sins are the fruits of the flesh; others, though, are the results of demon activities. Likewise, some illnesses are caused by demons. Dumbness due to demon possession cannot be treated in the same manner as an ordinary case of dumbness. The demon must be cast out. Certain sins committed by some brothers and sisters are caused by the activities of demons. These demons need to be cast out of them before their sins can be dealt with.

9.33b–35 All five of these incidents show us the characteristics of the Lord's work on earth. Man needs to see; he also needs to speak. In verse 33b we are told that the multitudes marveled, in verse 34 we see that the Pharisees rejected the Lord, and in verse 35 we learn that the Lord thereafter went about all the cities and the villages. The Scriptures use "city" as the unit; hence we read here: "all the cities and the villages." This is the gospel of the kingdom of the heavens. The Lord is King. He forgives sins. He gives men joy. He heals the sick and casts out demons. Earlier, at the time of chapter 4, the gospel of the kingdom of the heavens had already been announced. Here in 9.9–35 we are given to know the nature of the gospel of the kingdom of the heavens. For that gospel includes not only the saving of souls but also the deliverance of the body. Three times — in chapters 4, 8, and 9 — the phrase, "healing all manner of disease and all manner of sickness," or some such variant wording, is mentioned. On each occasion, this phrase serves as a summary to the Lord's work on earth.

5 | Division Five 9.36–11.1

From 9.36ff., we see how the Lord sent forth His apostles — that is to say, how He sent out to be apostles the disciples whom He had earlier called. Hereafter, the disciples became apostles. This Division Five of Matthew's Gospel commences with need. When the Lord saw the need of the multitudes, He "was moved with compassion for them" (v.36). If today we are able to see men's need, the life in us will surely manifest compassion such as was the Lord's. Those who close their eyes are mostly people who close their hearts.

Verse 37 records the Lord's use of a parable. Sinners to be saved are like a harvest ready to be gathered. Actually, harvest in the Scriptures may serve as a type for two different things: (a) it can typify believers being matured to be raptured (as in Lev. 23, Matt. 13.36–39 and Rev. 14.14–16); or (b) it can typify sinners ready in coming to the Lord for salvation. Now it is true that in some places in the Scriptures preaching the gospel is likened to sowing seed (as in Matt. 13.18–23). But in other places people coming to the Lord are also described as being harvested (as is the case here in verse 37). In this present case, the Lord has already brought sinners to the point of being ready to be harvested: you therefore have no need to sow seed again: you simply use the sickle to cut. Today is the day that sinners are ready to be harvested. The work of today is therefore to reap.

If we do not know how to reap, we bear a great responsibility before God. For our responsibility today is to reap, because now is the time of harvesting, as is evident from Jesus' words recorded in John 4.35: "Lift up your eyes, and look on the fields, that they are white already unto harvest."

Verse 38 notes the Lord giving a commandment. In preaching the gospel, there is the need of supplication. Do not go out at once, but let your hearts be filled with the love for souls, and pray for them. In Matthew there are two related commandments pertaining to the spread of the gospel. One is at the end of chapter 9: "Pray ye"; the other is at the end of chapter 28: "Go ye." To pray but not go, or to go but not pray—these procedures are both useless. Here the Lord for the first time formally laid the work before the disciples. After the "pray ye" commandment, the Lord then appointed apostles (see chapter 10). And in 10.5 we see that they were "sent forth." Most likely, the ones actually selected and sent are those who had prayed.

10.1–4 The Lord prepared these disciples by giving them authority so as to make them apostles. From the time of verse 2 onward, these twelve disciples became twelve apostles. Apostles are those who are sent forth. In other words, they are messengers. In verses 2–4 we have a list of the names of the apostles. In the New Testament this list is given in four different places: in Matthew 10, Mark 3, Luke 6 and Acts 1. But the order of the names is not the same in every case.

By comparing these four lists we may discover a most amazing fact. The names listed first, fifth, ninth and twelfth are the same in every list. The first is always Peter; the fifth is always Philip; the ninth, James the son of Alphaeus; and the twelfth, Judas Iscariot, the betrayer. The Twelve are divided into three sets of four. Peter always stands at the front of the first four; Philip, at the front of the second; and James, at the front of the third. Judas is always at the last. Looking at the Twelve altogether, Peter always heads the list and Judas always ends the list. Such an arrangement has in it a distinctly spiritual relationship about it. Judas is the worst, so he is placed last. Peter is put first because he is the best.

Now the Lord was to say on one occasion to the Twelve: "Verily I say unto you, that ye who have followed me, in the regeneration when the Son of man shall sit on the throne of his glory, ye also shall sit upon twelve thrones, judging the twelve tribes of Israel" (Matt. 19.28). And as revealed in the Book of Revelation, the twelve foundations of the New Jerusalem will have the names of the twelve apostles (21.14). After Judas died Matthias took his place. He was chosen through prayer and the casting of lots, thus indicating the mind of the Holy Spirit (see Acts 1.15-26). In 1 Corinthians 15 Paul did not rank himself among the Twelve (vv.5,8), showing that he too recognized the position of Matthias.

The position of the twelve apostles is different from the position of the other apostles who came after them. These Twelve are the ones appointed by the Lord personally while He was on earth. According to Ephesians 4.11, God "gave some to be apostles; and some, prophets, and some, evangelists; and some, pastors and teachers." The apostles spoken of here are those ones to be given by the Lord after He has ascended on high. And hence, the twelve apostles represent a fixed number of men. They are not included in the apostles of the Church as appointed later by the risen Lord. These Twelve are Jews, and they will therefore judge Israel in the kingdom. They are exclusively for the Jews. Yet the Church is composed of the Jews as well as of the Gentiles. Hence, after His ascension the Lord also gave to the Church the Twelve that they, too, might become the apostles of the Church after the ascension of the Lord and the coming of the Holy Spirit. While the Lord was on earth He sent the Twelve to the children of Israel. But when He gave grace to the Church He also made the Twelve to be apostles of the Church.

If we read 1 Corinthians 15.5-7 carefully we see from verse

5 that the Lord appeared to Cephas (Peter) and then to the Twelve. From verse 7 we learn that He appeared to James, then to "all the apostles." "All the apostles" are obviously not the same as the Twelve. Then from verse 8 we also learn that He appeared to Paul too. And Paul said, "I am the least of the apostles" (v.9). So that besides the Twelve, there are many other apostles.

The Book of Acts, we know, deals especially with the works of these apostles. In the first part it tells of the works of the Twelve; but in the next part it records the works of Paul and Barnabas. And the Bible calls both Paul and Barnabas apostles (see Acts 14.14). In Romans 16.7 Andronicus and Junias are "of note among the apostles." In other words, they, too, are noteworthy apostles. And in Revelation 2.2 we learn that the church in Ephesus "didst try them that call themselves apostles, and they are not, and didst find them false." The word "apostles" here is cast in the plural number. The Book of Revelation was written around 95–96 A.D. By the time John had written this final New Testament book, all the other eleven apostles, together with Paul, had passed away. John had lived to a very advanced age. If there were to be only twelve apostles in the Church, then the local church at Ephesus would have had no need to try those who claimed to be apostles. They would have only needed to see if any one of them was John. But the Ephesian church at that time did try, and the Lord praised them for doing so. And hence this conclusively proves that there are to be in the Church more than just twelve apostles. So that besides the Twelve, the Lord gives to His Church many other apostles. And this line of apostles has never been broken. It is the Roman Catholic Church that has arbitrarily claimed that its popes are the successors to the twelve apostles. For this reason, they are the ones who have especially elevated the position of the Twelve. They have done so to support the position of their popes.

Let us pay special attention to Peter's position here. The Twelve are all formally appointed by the Lord to be apostles. Peter's position as first among the Twelve is not especially set up by the Lord. He occupies that place only because of his gift and spiritual condition. The distinction between the two is extremely important, for it has an intimate relationship to the government of the Church on earth.

Peter as a person is quite unique. He often spoke for the Twelve. Let us note from Matthew 16.16 that he answered for the Twelve, that from 19.27 we learn that he asked on behalf of the Twelve, and that it is recorded in 26.33–35 that the Lord especially talked to Peter. From all this we can see that Peter is always at the front. Note that in Acts 1.15 it was Peter who spoke, in 2.14—after the Holy Spirit had come—it was again Peter who spoke, and that in Acts 4.8 and 5.29 it was Peter once more who spoke. On the day of Pentecost, Peter represented the Eleven (the Twelve minus Judas Iscariot) in preaching the gospel to the Jews for the first time (Acts 2.14–40). While he was with John it was Peter again who preached (Acts 3.12–26; 4.8–12)—in the latter instance, before the Jewish Council at Jerusalem. Once more before the Council, Peter again was the spokesman for all the other apostles (Acts 5.29), who by this time had had Mathias added to their number. Peter does indeed appear to be the leader among the Twelve. Here in the four lists his name is always placed first. Nevertheless, whenever the Scriptures mention the twelve apostles, they never point out Peter's special position. The twelve foundations and the twelve thrones are given in such a manner that no one is outstanding. All twelve of these apostles have the same standing. According to the word given in Matthew 20.25–27, it can be stated with great certainty that the Lord has not given Peter any special position among the Twelve.

So we see on the one hand that Peter took the lead among the twelve apostles, but that on the other hand he was not in any way different from the other eleven. Though he functioned as the leading apostle, he nonetheless was not formally established as such by the Lord. This was exclusively due to his spiritual progress. Hence it was a spiritual position, not an appointed one. Furthermore, it should be noted that during a subsequent period in the early history of the local church at Jerusalem, James moved up because of his spiritual stature. Spiritual leadership therefore fell upon the shoulders of this apostle. And by the time of the second part of the Book of Acts, Paul seems to have learned of the Lord higher than Peter had. So that the line of the testimony of God now fell upon Paul. Hence this kind of position is spiritual, not formal or appointive, in nature.

The position of the Twelve is special, but leadership among them is according to spiritual condition. The Lord appoints the apostles, but He has not set up a chief apostle. The name of Peter heads the list because of his manifested spiritual condition. Moreover, though the names of Andrew, James and John do not follow a regular order, they are always listed with Peter. Philip stands at the front of the second four names. He is not as forward as those of the first group, though he is still the chief one in his group. James the son of Alphaeus heads the last group, but the last four are not as advanced as the other two groups. Their various spiritual statures are spontaneously shown in their orders. Judas always stands at the last, and Simon the Zealot is the next to the last. We need to look further into this matter of the list of the Twelve.

In Matthew 10.2-4 these Twelve are divided into six pairs. The first pair is Peter and Andrew. Actually, Andrew had met the Lord first, but Peter was stronger spiritually. In pairing these men, the Lord has not denied their natural relationship; for Peter and Andrew are not only brothers spiritually, they are also natural brothers. The Lord pairs them for service. The second pair is James and John, who are also natural brothers. The third pair is Philip and Bartholomew (the latter is not a name but a title; it means the son of Tolmai, his actual name being Nathanael). The fourth pair is Thomas and Matthew the publican. (This is the last time the author of this Gospel mentions himself, his name appearing only twice — in 9.9 and here in 10.3. It is a good thing that he mentions so little of himself, and when he does he never fails to remind the reader that he is but a publican.) The fifth pair is James the son of Alphaeus and Thaddaeus. The sixth pair is Simon the Zealot and Judas Iscariot who betrayed Jesus. The Zealots belonged to a party that strictly kept the law. Iscariot was the name of a place in Judea, the rest were from Galilee.

The Book of Acts records a great deal about Peter, not so much about John, and about James even less. Elsewhere in the Scriptures it is difficult to find the personal histories of these Twelve. Though the Twelve are apostles, the Lord does not take note of the works of the apostles but rather their works through the Holy Spirit. Such is the nature of the work in this dispensation. It is not to be done through any official succession of apostleship, but done by the Holy Spirit through men who are called to be apostles. For this age is that of the Holy Spirit.

Matthew 10.5–15 tells us what is the mission of the apostles of that time. 10.16–23 discloses the difficulties that confront the preaching of the gospel, whether at that time or in the future. 10.24–33 records the Lord's forewarnings of what we are foreordained to endure. And 10.34–42 gives an account of what He demands of us.

10.5–15 According to 10.5 the preaching of the gospel is at that time only to the Jews. Yet the purpose of our Lord's coming to this earth does not exclusively comprise the preaching of the gospel to only the Jews. He is for whosoever wills. Nonetheless, there is a procedure in His work. Hence, here He is distinguishing the procedure, not defining the purpose. According to procedure, the gospel is to be preached to the Jews first. By the time of the Book of Acts, in Acts 1.8 in fact, there is the dissolution by the Lord Jesus himself of the prohibition He gave here in Matthew 10.5. It is therefore evident that Jesus' instruction here in v.5 is a matter of procedure and not of purpose. At the beginning of His ministry, the Lord must concentrate His work among the Jews because God had already been at work among them for two thousand years — ever since the days of Abraham — to prepare them to accept God's word. Before the Son of man came, God had already given them the Scriptures. If the Lord should at that time have immediately begun preaching the gospel to the Gentiles, the fruit of His work would have been much less. Hence He began with the Jews. Samaria was the place to which the king of Assyria had migrated Gentiles, and these Gentiles had accepted the Jewish culture.

Verse 7 indicates that these apostles were still ordered to preach that the "kingdom of heaven is at hand."

Verse 8 records the Lord commissioning them to do four things: (1) heal the sick, (2) raise the dead, (3) cleanse the lepers, and (4) cast out demons. Here the power and authority of the Lord were especially emphasized: "freely ye received, freely give." In using this authority they ought not accept money. Otherwise, they will become a Balaam, the greedy prophet, and not a servant of God.

In traveling forth, these twelve apostles of the Lord were to take note of four issues: (1) the matter of money, (2) the matter of clothing, (3) that of eating, and (4) that of lodging. (1) "Get you no gold, nor silver, nor brass in your purses" (v.9). (2) "No wallet for your journey, neither two coats, nor shoes, nor staff" (v.10a). Going out to preach the gospel should not be marked by comfort as though moving into one's home. (3) "The laborer is worthy of his food" (v.10b). And this food is related to lodging. (4) "Into whatsoever city or village ye shall enter, search out who in it is worthy; and there abide till ye go forth" (v.11). A city or village is the unit of locality in the Scriptures. Stay there till you go forth.

These four matters regulated the manner by which the apostles preached the gospel to the Jews of that time. They are not for today. They were the orders concerning the preaching of the gospel then because for two thousand, or one thousand five hundred, years the Jews had had the word of God with them. But when the Lord was about to leave this world, He plainly told His followers that these requirements had passed away (see

Luke 22.35-36). These orders in Matthew 10 were not everlasting, for after three years the Lord himself annulled them. They were not for all time; they were for that specific period when the Lord was on earth. Today when we go forth to preach the gospel we are to take nothing of the Gentiles (3 John 7). Here in Matthew 10 we see that they went to the Jews and therefore they could take something. But 3 John 7 tells of those who went to the Gentiles and took nothing of them. God's servants in this current time of reaching the Gentiles with the gospel ought to have this same attitude. Even though Matthew 10 is not today's order, the spirit is nonetheless the same — that is to say, when we go out we should not bring a great deal of money, luggage and other impedimenta; and we should not worry where to stay. Instead, we should learn to look up to God.

"And as ye enter into the house, salute it. And if the house be worthy, let your peace come upon it: but if it be not worthy, let your peace return to you" (vv.12-13). Whether or not this house is worthy of peace is not decided by the apostles but by God. For the apostles to abide in the house, they must salute it with peace, since the Israelites were the people of God at least in name. Had the gospel preachers of that day dwelt in the house of the unworthy, their gospel would have been evilly affected or evilly spoken of.

"And whosoever shall not receive you, nor hear your words, as ye go forth out of that house or that city, shake off the dust of your feet. Verily I say unto you, It shall be more tolerable for the land of Sodom and Gomorrah in the day of judgment than for that city" (vv.14-15). If these apostles would not be received, they were to shake off the dust from their feet. This meant they were to have nothing further to do with the people there. Why go forth to preach the gospel? Because there will be the day of judgment. Yet if in so doing the gospel is not received by the people, heavier judgment will await them in that day. Up to this point in Matthew's record, all is concerned with the works of the apostles of that day. The works are to be done in the land of Judea and for only a short period of three years. At the coming of the Holy Spirit, however, even the field of labor shall be changed.

10.16–23 Commencing from verse 16 we shall see that the Lord is concerned not only with the current situation but also things in the future (see especially verses 22 and 23 where the Lord brings the very "end" into view). So that the scope from verse 16 onward is much wider than that which obtained before verse 15. "As sheep in the midst of wolves" (v.16). The history of the Church in these two thousand years since Jesus' days on earth has been marked by the situation described here. Even up till now nothing has changed: as the messengers of the gospel go forth, they are not armed: they cannot resist nor defend themselves: they are truly meek as sheep: and the environment into which they enter is hostile, it being full of opposers. What, then, according to Jesus, can the Christians do in the midst of wolves? "Be ye therefore wise as serpents." Let those of us in our day not be crafty as serpents, but let us be wise and watchful as serpents. Let us be those who forestall problems, let us be careful not to be boastful nor display ourselves haughtily, lest we attract attention; yet let us likewise not be deceiving and slippery as serpents, but be "harmless as doves."

The term "councils" in verse 17 refers to the ruling Jewish Council of that time (also called the Sanhedrin), which was composed of seventy distinguished members. The word "synagogues" also indicates a Jewish background. But the phrase in verse 18, "before governors and kings," shows that the scope has been extended. For by that time the Jewish nation had been destroyed and the Jews were without a sovereign king of their own. Moreover, "kings" here is in plural number. "For a testimony to them *and to the Gentiles*" clearly indicates that the scope has enlarged from merely the land of Judea to include the Gentiles as well. In the time of the Book of Acts Paul actually testified before governors, kings and Gentiles.

"But when they deliver you up, be not anxious how or what ye shall speak: for it shall be given you in that hour what ye shall speak" (v.19). *How* to speak refers to the way of speaking. *What* to speak refers to the contents of one's speaking. The Lord has promised us that when we are being judged we have no need to think in advance of the words or the technique of speaking, for God will give them to us. Oftentimes we are able to say words which we could not have ever said or even thought of saying previously. For it is not we who speak, but the Spirit of our Father who speaks in us (v.20).

"And brother shall deliver up brother to death, and the father his child: and children shall rise up against parents, and cause them to be put to death" (v.21). In Church history there have been frequent instances when, for the sake of the Lord, there has arisen a strange kind of jealousy and hatred in families against the believers in those families. Formerly, there was no such thing as religious freedom. Believing in the Lord Jesus Christ was reckoned as a crime punishable by death. During the time of the Roman Empire, for example, many of the children of God had their blood shed for the sake of the Lord. Even after the Roman Church had come into power and both before and after the Protestant Reformation, many true believers were cruelly killed. As a matter of fact, the Roman Church ended up killing more Christians than had the Roman Empire itself. All this would indicate that brother must have delivered brother to death and parents must have moved against children and vice versa. Their hatred subverted natural affection.

"And ye shall be hated of all men for my name's sake" (v.22a). Bearing the name of the Lord is sufficient to be hated of all men. For men do not hate you, but hate your Lord. However, "he that endureth to the end, the same shall be saved" (v.22b).

"But when they persecute you in this city, flee into the next: for verily I say unto you, Ye shall not have gone through the cities of Israel, till the son of man be come" (v.23). Many do not understand this word. Let us understand that for Christians to take

refuge is nothing of which to be ashamed. It is the order of the
Lord. "Till the Son of man be come" refers to the Lord's second
coming. This must be the proper interpretation since in the
preceding verse we read: "he that endureth to the end, the same
shall be saved." Here it is essential to notice the relationship between Matthew 10 and Matthew 24. Please read 24.9, 13–14, and
36–39. We find that both of these portions of Scripture talk about
"persecution" or "tribulation," "the Son of man be come," and "the
end." One particular word, in fact, is exactly the same in these
two chapters: "he that endureth to the end, the same shall be
saved." So both portions speak of the same issue. As the Lord
continues to say these things, His hearers find that His words
cover larger and larger areas beyond just the time-frame in which
He was speaking.

Now the twelve apostles went, as they had been instructed,
through all the cities of Israel. Moreover, they eventually all died.
Nevertheless, the Lord has not yet come again. How is this verse
23 to be explained, then? It must be recalled that though while
on earth the Lord had indeed sent forth the apostles to preach
to the Jews, He did not mention the two thousand years of ensuing Church history. After these twenty or so centuries of Church
history, though, God will resume His work in the land of Judea.
So that what the Lord has said as recorded in 10.23 here will
yet be fulfilled: before some people go through the cities of Israel,
He will come. Consequently, "he that endureth to the end, the
same shall be saved." Indeed, by inserting the two thousand years
of Church history into this verse, all difficulties vanish. Today,
percentage-wise, there are more Israelites believing in the Lord
than any other people. Praise God! He will return to the children
of Israel.

10.24–33 Beginning with verse 24, what is said has no
reference to time. All are principles. Verse 24 speaks of our relationship with the Lord. It is spoken in accordance with common knowledge: "A disciple is not above his teacher, nor a ser-

vant above his lord." What treatment do we expect to receive here on earth? In verse 25 "Beelzebub"—which in Greek is commonly acknowledged to be correctly translated as "the lord of flies"—is actually another name for Satan. The Jews called the Lord Jesus this name. If the Master of the house was so called, what ever differently can the servants expect? What will people say of us? Note Paul's self-deprecating though very accurate words to describe himself and those with him: "We are made a spectacle unto the world, both to angels and men," and "ye have come to reign without us" (1 Cor. 4.9,8). What our Lord received here in this world was a cross; can we possibly expect to receive a crown now? The obvious answer is, Impossible! How can we ever possibly anticipate any response, destiny or future that is any different from that of the Lord? Whoever seeks for man's glory is not worthy to be the Lord's servant. Woe to us when the world speaks well of us. When our path is smooth we should ask ourselves if the Lord has ever traveled this path. We should seriously test ourselves whether we are true disciples of the Lord.

"Fear them not therefore . . ." (v.26). Apart from sin, worry is the greatest problem. But after worry, the next greatest is fear. We are always afraid that we will not be of much use to God. Yet we are not to fear: "for there is nothing covered, that shall not be revealed; and hid, that shall not be known." This points especially to the judgment seat. Whatever is endured for God will be rewarded in that day.

"What I tell you in the darkness, speak ye in the light; and what ye hear in the ear, proclaim upon the house-tops" (v.27). This word is spoken to us by the Lord. What should we do with the revelation which the Lord has given us? All must be viewed in the light of the judgment seat. We ought to be glad, for there is the judgment seat. Let those who have the ministry of the word of God pay special attention. The ministry of God's word is based on hearing Him first. In proclaiming the word of God, it must be words which God has spoken and that you have heard.

"Be not afraid . . ." (v.28). Why? Because there is the judgment seat, and because, further, what I as a minister of the gospel say is that which the Lord has said. It is not something out of myself. Again, why not be afraid? Because those who can "kill the body . . . are not able to kill the soul." Instead, "fear him who is able to destroy both soul and body in hell." Now this One is God! Therefore, we must fear Him!

But is fear the only sentiment we have towards God? No. "Are not two sparrows sold for a penny? . . . the very hairs of your head are all numbered" (vv.29,30). Here our Lord uses two succinct parables. One concerns the sparrow, which is the smallest of birds; yet, "not one of them shall fall on the ground without your Father." The other parable is about the many hairs on our heads, which "are all numbered." Notice here that it does not say, "counted" but "numbered." The first term conveys the meaning of a total amount, but the second means that each hair is given a number. So let us learn to trust in God's care. He has even numbered our hairs. He takes care of the smallest detail.

"Ye are of more value than many sparrows" (v.31). How precious is the word "many." You may substitute for this word any number you would want. "Fear not therefore." This discloses to us where the fear of men comes from. It is due to our lack of trust in God's hand. There is nothing without God's arrangement. If we believe in His ordering, we not only will not fear but we will also praise God. If anything happens to us, it is not man's attack; it is God's ordering. It is as Madame Guyon once said—that she would kiss the scourge that thrashed her. Subjection will produce joy; faith will bring in rest. When the heart is full of rest and joy, there will not be any fear.

However, we still need to fear—that is to say, there is still a need for us to fear God: "Every one therefore who shall confess me before men, him will I also confess before my Father who is in heaven. But whosoever shall deny me before men, him will I also deny before my Father who is in heaven" (vv.32-33). In the Book of Revelation there is mentioned an overcomer, Antipas by name, who held fast to the name of the Lord (see 2.13).

The term "confess" used here is not related to initial salvation. It is related to the issue of overcoming. It is of great importance that we confess Him before men. The foundation of a Christian is set on the matter of confession. We must be willing to pay any cost, but we cannot deny the Lord. This is what our Lord demands of us here. The way of the Christian is in confessing Christ. It would therefore appear that we ought to be afraid of at least one thing—a fear of being denied by the Lord in the future (v.33).

10.34–42,11.1 Beginning from verse 34 we have the fourth issue in this fifth division of Matthew's Gospel. What does the Lord require of us? "Think not that I came to send peace on the earth: I came not to send peace, but a sword" (v.34). The Lord says, "Think not." We should refrain from thinking whether or not there is peace on the earth. Let us not dream about things. Listen instead to My word, says the Lord. The explanation for the presence of friction, hostility, belligerence and sword here is given in verse 35: "I came to set a man at variance against his father, and the daughter against her mother, and the daughter-in-law against her mother-in-law." Due to the intrusion of the Lord into the situation, there is strangeness that arises between parents and children. The Lord comes to demand the highest place in men. Men usually give that highest place to parents and/or mothers-in-law. But with the coming of the Lord, that place is now given to Him. Indeed, the Lord demands of us that we push back everything in order to serve Him. Hence, family relationships cannot be the same as before. The Lord's coming touches the very depths of relationship. It therefore causes problems in the family: "a man's foes shall be they of his own household" (v.36). The result is that household members become enemies.

In verses 37 and 38, there are mentioned three more special demands of the Lord Jesus. The Latter is always demanding that He have the first place. These words are out of the ordinary. Who is this Man who makes such a demand? I would have to declare that if not a madman, He must be the Son of God. But yes, He is truly the Son of God. And because of this, He cannot be expected to ask for anything less. We have to give Him the first place or else we cannot serve Him. "Not worthy of me." These four words, repeated twice in verse 37, are most precious. Even if I leave father, mother and children, I am still not worthy of Him. And why? Because He is the glorious Lord. Yet Jesus takes a step backward here and seemingly says that if we lay aside our father, mother and children we are worthy of Him. This One is the Lord whom we serve. No other ever dares to make such a demand, for I know how much He has given me. O Lord, it is right that I love You more than all. There is no question about it.

There is a third "not worthy of me" in verse 38. The three musts of a Christian are: (1) to diminish the position of father, mother and children, (2) to love the Lord, and (3) to take up one's cross. The Christian is a person who takes up his cross and walks. If we do not take up our cross we are not worthy of Him. How is it that we have no wounds? How is it possible that we can travel the way of ease? Today the Lord is calling us just as He called the disciples of His day on the earth. O Lord, for the sake of being worthy of You I am willing to bear any cross.

"He that findeth his life shall lose it; and he that loseth his life for my sake shall find it" (v.39). Here the matter of reward is mentioned. Here, the word for "life" in Greek is the natural life—that is, the soul life. "Find" and "lose" are shown to be in contrast. What is the meaning of "find"? Father and mother are loving, and in loving them there is joy. This is to "find." It means to follow one's own natural desire, it thus making one's self happy. To "lose" signifies the opposite of "find" and means to not follow one's own desire. If today for the sake of the Lord we deny the demands of the natural life, in the future—in the kingdom to come—we will find full and complete satisfaction.

"He that receiveth you receiveth me, and he that receiveth

me receiveth him that sent me" (v.40)—here the Lord speaks of himself and the disciples jointly. How very intimate this is. Then, the Lord's words recorded in verses 41 and 42 may have reference to the time after He would die and return to heaven. He will not forget one of these little ones. (Evidently, at the moment the Lord was speaking, there were children present. And so it would appear that He pointed out one of them.) Even giving a cup of cold water to one of these little ones will not fail to be rewarded. How manifold are the opportunities for reward! Reward has only one significance, which is, that what we do is pleasing to the Lord. Future reward represents today's pleasure.

Chapter 11 verse 1 must be joined to this fifth division, for only at verse 2 does the scene change.

6 | Division Six 11.2-30

Except for verse 1, all of chapter 11 forms the sixth division. 11.2-30 shows how the Lord was rejected by His contemporaries. It also shows (near the end of the chapter) how He calls all those who would desire after Him.

11.2-6 Verse 3 tells how John asked, "Art thou he . . . ?" Verse 2 shows that John the Baptist was already in prison. And in chapter 14 we learn of his murder. "Now when John heard in the prison the works of the Christ" (v.2). He had already been in prison for quite some time. It may come as a surprise that John should have asked such a question when we compare verses 2 and 3 here with the first and second chapters of John's Gospel. John the Baptist should not have asked. Nevertheless, when a person is placed in a difficult situation, the clearest of believers may become doubtful.

Verse 6 — Here the Lord points out John's trouble. John the Baptist had sent his disciples to ask this question, yet not because his disciples had disbelief, nor because he himself had fallen away, but because he was offended. The word "offend" in Greek carries the idea of blaming or being unhappy with. So this verse 6 may be phrased in this way: "Blessed is he whosoever shall not blame me or be unhappy with me." John had become somewhat unhappy with what the Lord had been doing. Sometimes we too are not happy with the way of the Lord because of our lack of fellowship with Him. Actually, the nature of the question asked as recorded in verse 3 was an exceedingly serious matter, it intimating that John may have had another person in mind as the Messiah. He fell to such a low degree that he blamed the Lord and was unhappy with Him.

We know how the Lord is greatly resisted by sinners. Yet many a time He also experiences resistance from His very own servants, of whom the Baptist was one. Even so, when He heard this word from John's disciples, He did not display any hurt feeling. On the contrary, He answered, "Go and tell John the things which ye hear and see: the blind receive their sight, and the lame walk, the lepers are cleansed, and the deaf hear, and the dead are raised up, and the poor have good tidings preached to them" (vv.4-5). The last clause is literally, "poor men are evangelized." The reply of the Lord probably conveyed to John something like the following: It is true that you are in prison, John, but there are blind who need to receive sight . . . I must preach the gospel to the poor. Though you are imprisoned, I still have My work to do. Whoever does not blame Me, whoever is not unhappy with Me, whoever is not offended in Me because of his own plight but rather praises God for the grace which has come upon him, that man is blessed.

John had most likely felt that his need was the greatest, his plight was the deepest, his situation the severest. God was therefore not right in refraining from solving his problem first. How many want the *Lord* to be their servant. How many servants of the Lord want the Latter to serve them instead of their serving Him. This is not apostasy; this is being unhappy with the Lord. But those who know God will always accept the circumstances which God has allowed. Rebellion causes you to lose joy so that you may not be a blessing before men. Subjection is therefore the first condition. "Blessed is he whosoever shall find no occasion of stumbling in me." If you do not blame the Lord, your sorrowful tears will eventually turn into tears of joy. For a servant of the Lord, the way of joy lies in not being offended in the Lord. Submit, therefore, to His way.

11.7-19 Despite John's being offended with Him, we see from verse 7 that the Lord graciously began to speak on the Baptist's behalf; otherwise, people would have had serious doubts about John. "But wherefore went ye out? to see a prophet? Yea, I say unto you, and much more than a prophet" (v.9). Why more than a prophet? Because he is My forerunner (see v.10): he is closer to Me in ministry than was any other prophet of the past. Let us see that John's greatness lay in his special closeness to Christ, for he had prepared the very way and coming of the Lord and had had a significant part in the Lord's work. This is why John was great.

"Verily I say unto you, Among them that are born of women there hath not arisen a greater than John the Baptist: yet he that is but little in the kingdom of heaven is greater than he" (v.11). This word is truly hard to explain. Wherein is John greater than all that are born of women? For many others would seem to have been more spiritual than John. Even in the matter of prophesying, Jeremiah and some other prophets were unquestionably greater than he. Yet this greatness of John's derived from the fact of his having been close to the Lord. If one understands the "greater" in the first clause, he will know the "greater" in the second. It is not a matter of a person being spiritually greater or positionally greater. No, John is only greater than the prophets because he is closer to the Lord. And by the same token, believers of today who are in the kingdom are greater than John because they are closer to the Lord than even he was; for although John was indeed very close to the kingdom, he was nonetheless still outside it at that time while those of today are in it now.

Matthew 5-7 gives the contents of the kingdom of the heavens. Matthew 13 discloses the outward appearance of the kingdom of the heavens. Those who are in the kingdom of the heavens are closer to the Lord than John, hence they are greater. The kingdom of the heavens here refers to the present age. It is true that the kingdom of the heavens includes the millennium, but it is not altogether absent today nor has it been postponed till the millennial period has actually arrived. We know that the kingdom of the heavens in the millennium shall include Abraham, Isaac and Jacob (see Matt. 8.11), but John, according to the Lord here, is even greater than these, thus proving that John, too, is to be included in the kingdom of the heavens. However, "from the days of John the Baptist until now" (11.12), more people have entered the kingdom of the heavens. First there are the Jews, and later on will be the Gentiles. Both John and the Lord proclaim: "the kingdom of heaven is at hand." In that age, all who come into the kingdom of the heavens are neither born of women nor of the flesh, but are born of God. They are also those who obey God. It is not that the kingdom has been postponed but that the men who enter it have changed. John had once declared that the kingdom was at hand, but there are now those today who are in the kingdom. Hence they are greater than John. Today these ones are not only the men of the kingdom of the heavens, these ones are also—as part of the body of Christ—members of the King. And hence, the smallest finger of our Lord is greater than John!

There is yet another difficulty in verse 12: "from the days of John the Baptist until now the kingdom of heaven suffereth violence." In a literal translation of the Greek in this passage it should read: "the kingdom of the heavens is forcibly treated"—which means that the kingdom of the heavens must be treated violently: "and men of violence take it by force." The taking is active. From the viewpoint of the kingdom, it must be forcibly treated. From the viewpoint of the men who gain the kingdom they shall have forced themselves into it. The "men" spoken of by Jesus here refer especially to those who follow the Lord. When Jesus was on earth the kingdom of the heavens had begun. And hence that is why it is not possible for the kingdom to be entirely postponed to the future, although, as was said earlier, it shall be most fully manifested during the millennial period.

A few more words need to be added here regarding verse 12. This passage does not apply to the matter of initial salvation. It refers exclusively to the kingdom. Salvation does not depend on our effort, since the more we try, the farther we are from it. We are saved by faith, not by effort nor by works of righteousness. But the kingdom of the heavens is a different matter, for it is to be entered forcibly by those who, having become disciples of the King, do violence to their self-life that they may qualify to enter the kingdom of the heavens.

"For all the prophets and the law prophesied until John" (v.13). This clearly distinguishes the dispensation. God's revelation in the Old Testament ends with John. Both the contents and the outward appearance of the kingdom of the heavens had their commencement while the Lord was on earth. Of course, these were to become even more manifested after the coming of the Holy Spirit on the day of Pentecost. Yet we must remember that all the works which our Lord did on earth were done on the ground of Pentecost. It was for this reason that He needed to be baptized.

"And if ye are willing to receive it, this is Elijah, that is to come" (v.14). The work of Elijah is with the children of Israel. And if the Israelites are willing to receive it, John can, and will be, Elijah for them. But the Jews would not receive it, so he could not be Elijah. It has to wait until the time of the Great Tribulation before Elijah will come. Then shall the children of Israel receive it, and the Lord will come. That will be the time when the kingdom of the heavens shall *fully* appear on earth. Today it has not yet appeared in that fashion, but we cannot say there is no kingdom of the heavens present. For not only is there to be a final manifestation of the kingdom, there are also the contents and the outward appearance of it today.

Indeed, John was in many ways like Elijah of old. When he was zealous, he was red hot; and when he was offended, he could really complain.

"He that hath ears to hear, let him hear" (v.15). This word refers to what has been said above.

"But whereunto shall I liken this generation?" (v.16) Today the Jews are like children: "We piped unto you, and ye did not dance; we wailed, and ye did not mourn" (v.17). They are like children who care for nothing and reject whatever is suggested.

"For John came neither eating nor drinking" (v.18a). This eating and drinking refer to one's conduct at feasts; which is to say, that John cared little about good food and fine drink. In his heart and spirit John beheld the wrath of God. He had such a heavy burden in him that he had lost his appetite for eating and drinking. Accordingly, John's critics "say, He hath a demon" (v.18b)—that is to say, they accused him of not being social enough!

"The Son of man came eating and drinking" (v.19a). Jesus is here saying, as it were: I come to bring in grace and love. Not only is there the absence of the wrath of God at this time, there is also salvation available. Because I represent the love of the merciful Father, I maintain contact with people. I cannot fast, I can only rejoice. I must eat and drink with publicans and sinners, I must be their Friend.

"And they say, Behold, a gluttonous man and a winebibber" (v.19b). In response, the Jews say the Son of man is wrong. From the viewpoint of the Jews, it is wrong to refrain from eating and drinking and also wrong to eat and to drink. When people have their mind set against anyone, then no matter *what* that person does, to them it is wrong. John, who has seen the wrath of God, neither eats nor drinks, but those who do not see that wrath reckon him as mad and unsocial. On the other hand, the Lord Jesus, who has seen the mercy and grace of God, can only rejoice. And the Jews, who have failed to see God's mercy and grace, consider Jesus to be gluttonous and a winebibber. Thus the Jews, having neither seen God's severity nor His love, refuse to fear God or draw near to Him. There are these two aspects of God— severity and mercy, judgment and salvation. But the Jews saw neither of these. Consequently, they would not receive the ministry of either John *or* Jesus. This chapter began with the complaint of John, but now it is the complacency of sinners that is brought into view. There is no hope for such sinners.

"And wisdom is justified by her works [or, children]" (v.19c). In Proverbs 8 the name of the Lord is Wisdom. So the children of Wisdom are those who are the Lord's. They always accept God's orderings. They accept the judgment as well as the love of the cross. They acknowledge that whatever God has done is full of wisdom and fully justified. In short, whatever their Lord does is right.

11.20-27 From verse 20 we come to the second part of this chapter 11. What we have seen earlier is the attitude of the Jews at that time towards the Lord. They have their subjective prejudice. They cannot be moved by anybody. "They repented not" (v.20b). Because of their subjectivity they will not accept or repent. Whether men believe or not is not determined by how many problems they have. It is governed by subjectivity and hardness of heart.

Commencing from verse 21 we read what the Lord says concerning the kind of people who shall incur woe. For He came not only to be Savior, He came also to be Judge. Whoever refuses to accept the salvation of God will remain under judgment. This is the first time He pronounces a "woe" upon men. The more the privilege, the greater the responsibility. This is as true with sinners as it is with believers. Tyre and Sidon are seaports, centers of gross worldliness. Chorazin and Bethsaida are inland cities. The Lord tells us that the latter have more opportunities, and yet they do not repent. Therefore, woe to them.

"But I say unto you, it shall be more tolerable for Tyre and Sidon in the day of judgment, than for you" (v.22). This indicates that the future judgments are not all the same. Among the unbelievers, some will receive lighter judgment while some will receive heavier judgment. The punishments vary in degree. Let us look at verses 21 and 22 together. The latter speaks of judgment; the former shows how to avoid judgment: repent in sackcloth and ashes. Repent, and you will not fall into judgment. Repentance means a change of mind. Now you look at yourself differently from the former time. Without repentance there is no way to escape the judgment of God.

"And thou, Capernaum, shalt thou be exalted unto heaven? thou shalt go down unto Hades" (v.23a). Capernaum is lifted up to heaven because the Lord has made it the center of His work on earth. Though it is thus graced so abundantly now, it later shall certainly fall into Hades. (Hades is under the earth, where the dead go. It is different from Hell, which is the place of punishment. According to Revelation 20.14, Hades, along with Death, will one day be cast into Hell.) This means it shall be made totally desolate as though a place for the dead. This word has even now been fulfilled: Capernaum is today no more: travelers are not able to accurately find even its definitive location. The Lord performed many miracles in Capernaum, but the people as a whole there would not believe. This proves that unbelief is not due to fewer miracles.

"But I say unto you that it shall be more tolerable for the land of Sodom in the day of judgment, than for thee Capernaum" (v.24). The Lord once again tells us that there will be different degrees of judgment and of punishment because the wrath of God is not the same towards all.

In verses 20–24 we learn that the Lord twice pronounces "Woe unto thee." Beware lest we try to understand the life and nature of the Lord with our old life and nature. Being so full of the flesh we cannot utter weighty words. Even if we say them, there is no power. We voice them only when we get angry. This is what our old life and nature is. How different it is with the Lord! When He says these weighty words, He is not angry at all. If young brothers use such strong words, it will most likely be because they have lost their temper. But after many years of discipline, we ought to be able to utter heavy words without losing our self-control. Whenever young brothers get angry they most often sin. But those who have learned much before the Lord should be able to be angry and not sin (see Eph. 4.26). Let us therefore not measure the Lord according to our limited capacity. Though our Lord speaks forth such strong words, He is nonetheless full of love.

How do we know this? Let us note the ensuing verses. "At that season Jesus answered and said, I thank thee, O Father, Lord of heaven and earth . . ." (v.25a). In verse 20 we have the word "then"; here, we have the phrase, "at that season" or "on that occasion" or "at that time." He could still pray. Thus it proves that when voicing such strong words, His heart was still full of the love of God. His fellowship with the Father had not been interrupted, and His heart continued to be filled with thanksgiving.

What is the intent of this story? It tells us of the rejection of the Lord. Here our Lord encountered the same situation as John had encountered earlier in this chapter. Both are being rejected. But how did John express his feeling? His words implied dissatisfaction. The Lord, on the other hand, thanked the Father at the zenith of His own rejection. In Him there was no fret, no dissatisfaction, but only fullness of unshakable peace. Why was He thankful? "Thou didst hide these things from the wise and understanding, and didst reveal them unto babes" (v.25b). Why did Chorazin and Bethsaida not believe? Why did Capernaum not repent? Because they were the wise and understanding. Yet these did not become a cause for dissatisfaction in Him; on the contrary, they created the reason for His thanking the Father.

Let us learn a great lesson here: these things were allowed by God, yet the Lord cheerfully accepted them from the Father. Moreover, He held no personal animosity towards these people: "O Father . . . thou didst." Let us accept every single thing from the hand of God. The whole earth is in His hand, so we can only accept that which is in His hand: we can only obey. Let us learn to submit to the circumstances which God has permitted, for such—and such only—is the way of Christian rest. All our happenings and circumstances are ordered or arranged or permitted according to God's will. Our Lord not only accepts, He even gives thanks! When God's arrangement and our opinion differ, that is the time when the cross works best. If we submit and say, "O Father, I thank You," this proves that the cross has truly done its work in us.

"Thou didst hide these things from the wise and understanding." These things are hidden to them because of their *own* wisdom and understanding. They are quite knowledgeable in earthly matters, but they are strangers to spiritual matters. Human wisdom and understanding are useful in any branch of learning except in spiritual matters. "And didst reveal them unto babes." People who are child-like are teachable, they are those who are eager to learn, who acknowledge that they know nothing, and who must depend on others. Babes are like pieces of white paper on which nothing is written. When people are in that condition God will reveal himself to them. Why is it that you receive no revelation? Perhaps you are too wise; you may know the world too much. Yet should you be more simple and learn to trust, you may receive many revelations. From the wise and understanding God hides these things. But if, by your child-like attitude, you are able to find out what God has hidden, you will be honored.

"Yea, Father, for so it was well-pleasing in thy sight" (v.26). It will be most helpful to us if we can truly learn to say to God, "Yea, Father." If we love God, we will just naturally pay attention to the things that are pleasing in His sight. The Lord not only harbored no dissatisfaction on account of His rejection, He even made this circumstance the cause of praise: "Yea, Father, for so it was well-pleasing in thy sight." Once there was a brother who was blind, deaf and dumb. In being asked by another brother why he *was* blind, deaf and dumb, he gave as his answer: "Yea, Father, for so it was well-pleasing in Your sight."

"All things have been delivered unto me of my Father: and no one knoweth the Son, save the Father" (v.27a). The Son of God is a mystery. If the Father reveals Him to us, then we know Him. If God does not reveal Him to us we will not know Him.

Not all can easily know Him. If you have no trouble in knowing Him it is because the Father has revealed Him to you. Before you are shown, however, the Lord is a mystery to you. He is not only a foreigner but also a stranger to you: "no one knoweth the Son, save the Father." If you read this from an objective stand-point, you will see the Lord as the Son of God, and you will worship Him. Otherwise, subjectively-speaking, you will consider Him to be mad, for who can say such words?

"Neither doth any know the Father, save the Son, and he to whomsoever the Son willeth to reveal him" (v.27b). This is also a tremendous statement. Who is this Man? If you were to read this word in the position of an unbeliever, you could only say that Jesus of Nazareth is the Son of God. In the words of this verse the Lord is pointing people to know the Father. Hence He must be the Son. If He were not God the Son He would not be able to lead us to know the Father. Now the Father knows Him, and He leads us to know the Father. Since the Father has delivered all things into His hand (v.27a), salvation, too, is in His hand. The Gentiles as well as the Jews are all in His hand. All men, in fact, are in His hand. For this reason He is able to utter the word that is found in the next verse.

11.28-30 "Come unto me, all ye that labor and are heavy laden, and I will give you rest" (v.28). Since all things have been delivered to Him, He can invite men to come to Him. "All ye that labor and are heavy laden"— this includes the Gentiles as well as the children of Israel. It also includes the Samaritans. Thus we gradually notice the change in dispensation. In studying the Scriptures we need to watch for the progress in revelation. How does it turn to be "all" here? Chapter 10 gives us the principle; chapter 11 gives us the outworking.

At the outset of chapter 11 the Lord bears witness for John the Baptist. This is a great turning. Formerly, John had borne witness for Christ, but then he became somewhat offended. So now it requires the Lord to testify for him. How does all this come about? "From the days of John the Baptist until now the kingdom of heaven suffereth violence, and men of violence take it by force" (11.12). The Lord had also said: "if ye are willing to receive it, this is Elijah, that is to come" (11.14). While the Lord was on earth He labored among the Jews, yet He also worked among the Gentiles. Due to His rejection by the Jews, His work among them ceased; but His work for the Gentiles now commenced. If, said Jesus in so many words, you Jews had had faith, this one (John the Baptist) would be the Elijah who is to come. But since you did not accept, you must wait until Elijah comes at a future date. Your faith could have advanced the coming of Elijah, but your unbelief has now postponed his coming. Elijah must indeed come, and if you had been willing to accept it, the coming of Elijah would have been advanced in time.

In a similar vein, it ought to be pointed out that although according to God's plan the kingdom is to come after the Church age, nevertheless, because of our faith as believing Gentiles, we may have a foretaste *now* of the kingdom powers to come (see Heb. 6.5). As a result of faith, the Lord's work on earth towards the Gentiles has never ceased, for it has enjoyed wide acceptance (by comparison with the Jews). And thus "the powers of the age to come" are in some measure even with us now. But the Lord's work towards the Jews suffered tremendous opposition; only a small number of the Jewish people ever received Him while He was on earth. So that by the time of chapter 11, that work of His towards the Jews had nearly come to an end. Hence, the Lord declared "all" (v.28). Thank the Lord, His work is no longer restricted to the Jews. It includes the Gentiles as well as the Jews: it includes *all* who labor and are heavy laden.

As described here by the Lord, man is marked by two situations: (1) to "labor" is to be positive and active. To labor is to take action to obtain an objective. But (2) to be "heavy laden" is something negative and passive; things are pressed down upon us: family problems, sins, worries, all kinds of sufferings—all these are burdens beyond human forbearance. Yet such people

can come to the Lord, who will give them rest. The world is truly
a wearying place. True rest can only come from the Lord. Thus
His work on earth is to invite all the needy ones — whether Gentile or Jew — to come to Him for rest. Besides John 3.16, Matthew 11.28 has saved many people.

"Take my yoke upon you, and learn of me; for I am meek
and lowly in heart: and ye shall find rest unto your souls" (v.29).
The Lord himself is a man of rest. When Jesus was rejected and
suffered greatly, He praised the Father, for He accepted the
discipline, ordering and pleasure of God. He is meek, having
no resistance. He is lowly, not expecting better treatment. His
heart is truly meek and lowly. Consequently, He was able to praise
the Father even though He encountered so much difficulty.

"Take my yoke upon you." The red heifer mentioned in
Numbers 19 is a type of Christ. No yoke had ever come upon
it (19.2b). (A yoke represents the will of the master, which differs from the will of the ox or cow. The master uses the yoke
to control the will of the ox.) Our Lord has no need to be yoked,
for His will is always one with the Father's will. He is, in fact,
the only One who *is* of one will with God. We, therefore, will
conflict with God's will unless we are under the Lord's yoke. "Take
my yoke upon you." Given the inward nature and character of
our Lord on earth, He bears no yoke. Yet according to outward
appearance, He seems to *be* under a yoke; for He continually
submits himself under the hand of God. Upon ordinary men
of the earth this yoke is *disciplinary* in nature. Upon our Lord,
though, it is *unitive* in character, for He does not need the control of the yoke. We, on the other hand, need such control. We
should be yoked together with the Lord. This means we need
to be so united with Him that we, too, touch His spirit. On the
one hand, to be yoked together is truly for the purpose of service, but on the other hand it is to adjust us to the Lord's footsteps.
In following the Lord we may have the same footsteps. This is
what He requires of us.

The second word is, "learn of me." In difficulty, there is still praise. The Lord wants us to learn of Him, that we may find rest. The "rest" in view in verse 28 is the kind we are given in coming to Christ. It is an eternal rest. But besides this rest of forgiveness by God, there is another kind which we find in times of shattered hopes and blocked pathways. This rest pertains to our emotion: it is the rest of the soul. The first rest comes through faith; this second rest comes by obedience. Here, I learn to walk in the Lord's path. I obey by obeying with Him as I am yoked together with Him. For whatever falls on me also falls upon Him. Our Lord is One who bore His yoke singly. He bore the yoke alone in order to save us. Our being yoked together with Him differs from His individual yoke. Nonetheless, the moment we obey, we enter into rest and turn to praise. Christians should not only have the eternal rest, they should also be filled in their souls with this second rest while living in the world of today. The rest of the soul today is obtained through obedience. Each time, the tears which flow out of obedience are more joyful than all the happinesses in the world.

"For my yoke is easy, and my burden is light" (v.30). Is it hard? No, not hard. For the Lord himself says it is easy. His demand is never too hard. Yes, the Lord says to us: "I have yet a yoke to give you, but My yoke is easy." When is the cross the heaviest? On the way of bearing it. When is it no longer heavy? When you are hung on it. When the cross itself bears you, you will not feel heaviness anymore, for you have died, so you feel no pain. If you have truly died to self you will feel no yoke at all. This yokeless yoke is easy. This burdenless burden is light.

7 | Division Seven 12.1-50

Chapter 12 is another division. It deals with the matter of the sabbath.

12.1-8 "At that season Jesus went on the sabbath day through the grainfields; and his disciples were hungry and began to pluck ears and to eat" (v.1). This plucking of ears in grainfields was allowed in the Old Testament period (see Deut. 23.25). But on this particular day a problem arises, for as the disciples were conducting themselves this way, along came the Pharisees. I think if the disciples were hungry that day, our Lord must have been even hungrier. Yet He did not eat. He would not even do the things that were permitted.

"But the Pharisees, when they saw it, said unto him, Behold, thy disciples do that which it is not lawful to do upon the sabbath" (v.2). Was it true that there could be no eating on the sabbath? There was no rule among the Pharisees against eating on the sabbath; there was not even any sanction by the Pharisees against plucking the grain ears, which might have been considered by some people to be work on the sabbath day. No, what the Pharisees objected to was the *rubbing* of the grain ears together on the sabbath — for *this* they viewed as *work*! So that the Pharisees had established a regulation against such activity being done on the sabbath day in order to preserve the sanctity of the day. Yet no such restriction had been part of the law of God as delivered to the Israelites through Moses. It had been "tacked on" by the tradition of the Jewish Fathers and upheld by these Pharisees of a later day. And hence these Pharisees spoke to the Lord according to their own decision on this point.

"But he said unto them . . ." (vv.3–8). In answering, the Lord did not point out to them that these were their traditions and not those commanded by God. Instead, He used other ways to answer them. He actually responded to the attack of the Pharisees with four points.

What is the sabbath? God gave the sabbath to the children of Israel as a sign of His covenant with them (see Ez. 20.12,20; Ex. 20.8, 34.21). The Ten Commandments were the covenant God made with the children of Israel, and the sabbath was the sign of that covenant. Hence this article from the Decalogue is different from its other nine articles. The other nine of the Ten Commandments are moral in nature; this one commandment— the Fourth—is an order. Sin is intrinsic to the nine commandments, but not to this one. According to this Fourth of the Ten Commandments, work is forbidden on the sabbath. If the sabbath is violated, it is not because sin is intrinsically involved, but because it is the effect of forbiddance. Consequently, there are two kinds of command inherent within the Ten Commandments. One is forbidden for the sake of God, which is the sabbath. The other is the kind where sin is intrinsically involved—as it was surely involved in these other commandments of the Ten. The sabbath spoken of in the Fourth Commandment represents the government of God, the other nine represent the nature or character of God himself. When God covenanted with Israel He took the sabbath as a sign or pledge. In annulling His covenant with the children of Israel He could only remove one commandment out of the Ten, that which touches upon His government. If He should remove any of the other nine commandments He would touch upon His own nature and also man's morality. Only in the case of the commandment concerning the sabbath would such removal *not* affect His own nature or man's moral responsibility. Hence, the change or removal of this one commandment proves the setting aside of Israel. God could not set aside any of the other nine commandments; but He could do so with respect to this one. For this Fourth Commandment was governmental in nature. It had nothing to do with intrinsic sin.

"Have ye not read what David did . . .?" (v.3) The Lord cited the instance of David entering the house of God and eating the showbread. This also happened on the sabbath day, for the showbread which David had been given to eat by the priest had just then on the sabbath day been removed from before the Lord in order to put hot bread in its place when the old showbread was taken away (see 1 Sam. 21.6). This event in David's life had to have taken place on the sabbath, for according to Leviticus: "Every sabbath day he shall set it [the showbread] in order before Jehovah continually" (24.8). How thoroughly acquainted was our Lord with the Scriptures. It was God's decision that the showbread was given to the priests to eat. David was not a priest, yet he ate it, and ate it on the sabbath day. Why could he eat it? Because David had already been anointed king. He is a type of the Christ ("Anointed One" of God) whom God has established. In ordinary times, David had no need to eat showbread. Due to persecution, however, he became hungry, and his followers were also hungry. So they ate the showbread on the sabbath. Likewise, our Lord was also rejected, and his followers were hungry. Their plucking the ears and eating them was no different from David's eating the showbread. According to Darby's version, there is in 1 Samuel 21.5 this clause: "and the bread is in a manner common." Since David was not on the throne, all bread was common. Therefore, he and his followers could eat. This bread could not be judged by the covenant which God had originally made with the children of Israel. This was an extraordinary time. For at that very moment the ark was not in the house of God. The priests served in an empty house, and David was not on the throne. When David became king, there was a great change in dispensation. When the Lord shall come, there will be an even more thorough and drastic change.

Read Numbers 27.21 and 1 Samuel 2.35–37. "He shall stand before Eleazar the priest, who shall inquire for him by the judgment of the Urim before Jehovah: at his word shall they go out, and at his word they shall come in, both he, and all the children of Israel with him, even all the congregation" (Num. 27.21). The "him" and "he" all refer to Joshua. Joshua represented government as political leader. Eleazar was the priest. From Moses onward, the authority of the priest had stood higher than the authority of the political person. "And I will raise me up a faithful priest, that shall do according to that which is in my heart and in my mind: and I will build him a sure house; and he shall walk before mine anointed for ever" (1 Sam. 2.35). Here was a fundamental difference. The anointed was to be David, and the priest was to be Samuel. This was a complete turnabout. Here, the priest must now hearken to the word of the political leader or king. This indicated a change of dispensation. From Moses to David, the priest was head and the leader was subordinate. But from David onward, the political leader who by this time was a king became head, and the priest became subordinate.

In the incident before us from Matthew 12 we find the Lord telling the Pharisees that the priest was no longer the head, that the King of all kings was now head. The history of the Jews was to undergo another and even more radical change—this time with respect to the sabbath. The rejection of the Lord by the Jews was the cause for the change of position with regard to the sabbath day. This change did not affect the other nine commandments, but it greatly influenced the commandment concerning the sabbath.*

*Unfortunately, as explained elsewhere, the notes end here.—*Translator*

PART TWO

THE EARLIEST STUDY ON MATTHEW*

*The notes of this earliest study on Matthew by the author cover only chapters 1 and 2. They were prepared by Watchman Nee and appeared in the *Morning Star* magazine published by the Morning Star Publishers, Chefoo, China. Inasmuch as the notes were written shortly before and during the time he himself had started the publication of *The Christian* magazine in 1925 at Lo-hsing Pagoda, Foochow, China, these notes must have been written in the mid-1920s, from roughly 1924 to 1926.—*Translator*

Introduction: the Word of Christ

Many today deem the word of Christ recorded in the Gospels to have been spoken only to the Jews and not to present-day Christians as well. They feel that so far as the latter are concerned, His words were either to serve as an exemplary body of principles or as a medium for communicating moral values. Let us search the Scriptures, however, to find out whether His word must be absolutely obeyed or His word has only an indirect influence on us who are His followers.

"If any man love me," the Lord declared, "he will keep my word: and my Father will love him, and we will come unto him, and make our abode with him. He that loveth me not keepeth not my words: and the word which ye hear is not mine, but the Father's who sent me" (John 14.23-24).

Our Lord also tells us of the work of the Holy Spirit. We all acknowledge that this present age is the age of the Holy Spirit. Let us see what the work of the Holy Spirit is, according to the words of Christ: "the Holy Spirit ... shall teach you all things, and bring to your remembrance all that I said unto you" (John 14.26); and, "If ye abide in me, and my words abide in you, ask whatsoever ye will, and it shall be done unto you. ... If ye keep my commmandments, ye shall abide in my love; even as I have kept my Father's commandments, and abide in his love" (John 15.7,10).

Without the need of any special explanation, it is quite clear that these Scripture verses teach us plainly that we who are

disciples of Christ should keep His word, that is, His commandments; otherwise, we cannot say we love Him.

Just before His ascension, Christ gave His last great com-
mission: "Go ye therefore, and make disciples of all the nations,
baptizing them into the name of the Father and of the Son and
of the Holy Spirit: teaching them to observe all things whatsoever
I commanded you: and lo, I am with you always, even unto the
end of the world" (Matt. 28.19-20). Now just as believers must
obey the Lord's command to disciple all the nations, so they must
also not forsake His word of command to observe all things which
He has taught. Whatever He commanded His disciples on that
day we must follow today.

"Let the word of Christ dwell in you richly; in all wisdom"
(Col. 3.16).

"If any man teacheth a different doctrine, and consenteth not
to sound words, even the words of our Lord Jesus Christ, and
to the doctrine which is according to godliness; he is puffed up,
knowing nothing, but doting about questionings and disputes
of words, whereof cometh envy, strife, railings, evil surmisings"
(1 Tim. 6.3-4). Not consenting to the words of Jesus Christ will
produce countless sins.

"God, having of old time spoken unto the fathers in the
prophets by diverse portions and in diverse manners, hath at the
end of these days spoken to us [New Testament people] in his
Son . . . Therefore we ought to give the more earnest heed to
the things that were heard, lest haply we drift away from them"
(Heb. 1.1, 2.1).

Upon reading these Bible verses which are to be found in
the letters sent to the Church by the apostles, how can we say
that we need not obey the words of Christ as recorded in the
Gospels?

"Hereby we know that we know him," the apostle John
declared, "if we keep his commandments. He that saith, I know
him, and keepeth not his commandments, is a liar, and the truth
is not in him" (1 John 2.3-4). He who keeps the words of the

Lord Jesus, he alone has truth in his heart; he who does not keep His commandments does not know Him, for he is a liar. Are not the words and commandments of Christ recorded in the four Gospels? If so, then how can we say we obey Him if we do not observe those direct commandments of His found in the Gospels?

Our forefather sinned through disobedience (see Rom. 5.19). All the people in the world are "sons of disobedience" (Eph. 2.2). But God not only has saved us from future punishment but has also saved us unto holiness and obedience. Obedience is of utmost importance. Please read Romans 15.18, 16.26; 1 Corinthians 7.19; 1 Thessalonians 4.1-2; 2 Peter 3.2; and Hebrews 5.9.

"Never man so spake," the people had said of Christ (John 7.46). His words are words of grace. We ought to hear Him and obey Him.

1 | The Ancestry of Jesus 1.1-17

A. Notes

(1) Verse 17 divides the genealogy into three periods of fourteen generations each. In counting the generations from Abraham onward, one finds there are actually only forty-one generations, one generation short. But by carefully reading verse 17 in conjunction with the Old Testament record, we note that the first period begins with Abraham and ends with David, the second period starts with David and finishes with Josiah, and the third commences with Jechoniah and concludes with Christ.

Hence David becomes both the end of the first period and the beginning of the next; but Jechoniah does not conclude the second period (still the kingdom) for he has already been rejected by God; Jechoniah only commences the third period — that of the Jews being carried away into captivity (see Jer. 22.24-30).

The third period covers the time from the carrying away of the Jews to Babylon all the way down to Christ. Jechoniah seems to have been born at the time of the carrying away of the Jews (see v.11 of Matt. 1); so that the second period ended with his father Josiah (v.10), while Jechoniah himself began the third period.

(2) Matthew presents the Lord Jesus as King, therefore a genealogy is given, for a king must have a pedigree. Mark, however, presents the Lord Jesus as Servant, and hence there

is no need for a genealogy to be given. Luke presents the Lord Jesus as the Son of man, so a genealogy is once again given: even an ordinary man will have his progenitor. John, on the other hand, presents the Lord Jesus as God, and hence no genealogy *can* be given, since deity has neither beginning nor end.

(3) Since Matthew presents the Lord Jesus as King whose grace overflows to the Gentiles, his book of the generations originates with David and Abraham. He cannot be King and Savior if He is not the progeny of both David and Abraham.

(4) "Christ" (v.1) is a Greek word which denotes "the Anointed One." It is the same as the Hebrew word "Messiah." In the olden days, kings and priests and prophets were all anointed at the time of receiving office. They were then hallowed (separated for a special purpose) from the multitude. Please read Leviticus 4.3, 6.20; Exodus 28.41; 1 Samuel 9.16; 2 Samuel 23.1; 1 Kings 19.16.

"Jesus, who is called Christ" (v.16). This is to indicate that He is especially hallowed to God to be our perfect Prophet, Priest and King. To be "anointed" has another sense, in which is conveyed the idea of being full of the Holy Spirit and knowledge. The Bible records the fact that God does not give the Holy Spirit to Him by measure (see John 3.34). So that His name is truly fitting: "God's Anointed."

"Jesus Christ" (v.1) indicates that the lowly One has been exalted on high. This is the first name in the New Testament.

(5) "The book of the generations" (cf. v.1 with v.17a) is a phrase that appears in the original Biblical languages only once more — this time in Genesis 5.1. In Genesis, the phrase is used to indicate the book of the generations of the first Adam; here in Matthew it is the book of the generations of the "Last Adam." These two books of the generations stand opposite to each other. The Jews pay great attention to genealogy, for the latter reveals the origin of a person. Whether or not Jesus is truly King depends

on the demonstration of His direct lineage from David. Hence this Book of Matthew serves to prove His Kingship by presenting at the very beginning a trustworthy genealogy.

(6) "The son of David, the son of Abraham" (v.1). As the Holy Spirit breathes out this particular Scripture passage, He only mentions these two names. This is because His intention is to use these two men as the focal point in the establishment of the great promise regarding the Messiah. And that is why the Lord Jesus is not called the Son of the other persons in the genealogy, but only the Son of David, the Son of Abraham. Here, the phrase "the son of David" is put before that of "the son of Abraham." Yet those without revelation would have surely placed the phrase "the son of Abraham" first in keeping with a logical chronology. But this Gospel intends to show that the Lord Jesus is, *first of all*, the King of the Jews before He gives grace to the Gentiles. Consequently, it first mentions "the son of David" to indicate that He is the legal heir to the throne, and only then does it mention "the son of Abraham" to signify how God will show grace to the whole world through Him.

The word "son" has many meanings among the Jewish people. It may denote a son, a grandson, a progeny, an adopted son, a disciple, or a beloved. Here, it means the Lord Jesus is the progeny of these two men. His genealogy must be traced to David because the promise of Messiah is directly confirmed to David (see 2 Sam. 7.12,16). Hence Christ must come from this family. In proving Him to be the Messiah, the evidence must be presented that He comes from David. Please read Psalm 132.10–11; Isaiah 11.1; Jeremiah 23.5; compare also with John 7.42; Acts 13.22–23; Romans 1.3. If David is not Jesus' ancestor, He can have no share in the throne of David (see Luke 1.32). In Matthew, the name "son of David" is used of the Lord Jesus nine times (see 1.1, 9.27, 12.23, 15.22, 20.30, 21.9,15 and 22.42).

Apart from the name "Christ" itself, the first name as well as the last in the New Testament is David (see Rev. 22.16).

"The son of Abraham." The promise of the birth of Christ is also given to Abraham. For God at the beginning promised Abraham to have a seed (see Gen. 12.3, 21.12). After Isaac was born, Abraham, in obedience to God, offered his son. God saw the sincerity of Abraham's heart and said to him: "in thy seed shall all the nations of the earth be blessed" (see Gen. 22.15–18). The Letter to the Galatians explains that the seed promised to Abraham was not many, but one: "to thy seed, which is Christ" (Gal. 3.16). From this viewpoint, therefore, God had indeed promised Christ to Abraham. The Lord Jesus is called "the son of Abraham" here because God had personally promised Abraham (see Luke 1.73), and Abraham had also joyfully received it (see John 8.56). Since Jesus is the Christ, He must come forth in the lineage of Abraham.

"The son of David, the son of Abraham." Christ as the Son of David inherits the throne; but as the Son of Abraham, He inherits the land (see Gen. 15.18). At His first coming, He becomes the Son of Abraham; at his second coming, He shall be the Son of David. As the Son of Abraham, He was crucified, buried, and resurrected. He is preached to the nations that all might be blessed. All who believe in Him become the children of Abraham (note: the offering up of Isaac serves as a type of the death, burial and resurrection of Christ; and according to Hebrews 11.17–19, Abraham received the promise after he had offered Isaac). As the Son of David, He will wear the crown of glory and exercise dominion over the world, thus bringing peace to the earth. We who suffer with Him shall reign with Him for a thousand years. As the Son of Abraham, He is kind and suffers shame; as the Son of David, He is righteous and receives glory. Though our Lord was born to a humble family, his ancestry traced itself back to the Jewish royal house. From the viewpoint of fleshly man, people see Him as having been born in a manger and reared in a carpenter's home. Who therefore knows that He is the Son of David, the Son of Abraham? No wonder the carnal liberal theologians of today see only His humanity and forget His divinity.

(7) "Abraham begat Isaac; and Isaac begat Jacob; and Jacob begat Judah and his brethren" (v.2). Isaac had an elder brother, Ishmael, and Jacob had an elder brother, Esau, and Judah had eleven brothers. But this verse merely says Judah and his brethren, without mentioning Isaac's brother and Jacob's brother. For God's promised blessings through the Messiah were given to the sons of Jacob — that is to say, to the whole house of Israel; they did not include the brothers of Isaac and Jacob. Furthermore, Ishmael was born "by the handmaid [Hagar] after the flesh," whereas Isaac was born "by the freewoman [Sarah, Abraham's wife] . . . through promise." So the inheritance passed out of Ishmael into Isaac (see Gal. 4.22-31). God is faithful to His promise. Whatever He promises, He performs. His promise is promised to "the freewoman." Therefore, all who are not born of the "freewoman" are not forcibly drawn into His promise. This is the way of God's promise.

The reason why Jacob's brother is not named is because it is written in the Scriptures, "Jacob I loved, Esau I hated" (Rom. 9.13). This is the marvelous way of God's election. "I will have mercy on whom I have mercy, and I will have compassion on whom I have compassion" (Rom. 9.15), thus showing that the purpose of God according to election "is not of him that willeth, nor of him that runneth, but of God that hath mercy" (Rom. 9.16). Notwithstanding this sovereign way of God's election, it is not done casually but rather according to His "foreknowledge." For God knows beforehand who will be willing to accept grace and so be blessed: "the elect . . . according to the foreknowledge of God the Father" (1 Peter 1.1,2). First, foreknowledge; then, election. Due to God's love for Jacob, his sons became the twelve tribes of Israel.

"Judah and his brethren." According to the flesh, Reuben was the firstborn; therefore it should have read: "Reuben and his brethren." According to inheritance, Joseph was the greatest among the twelve sons (see Gen. 49.24,26); so here it should have read: "Joseph and his brethren." Because the Holy Spirit gives revelation, however, it is written as "Judah and his brethren." This is due to the fact that Judah was the *political* head of the whole house of Israel, and the Messiah (also called Shiloh) would therefore necessarily come out of him (see Gen. 49.10). This Book of Matthew deals with things concerning Shiloh (the Prince of Peace or Peace-Giver), Judah's seed or progeny; hence, Judah is here being exalted.

(8) "And Judah begat Perez and Zerah of Tamar . . ." (vv.3–6). For the history of Tamar, please read Genesis 38.11–30. Perez and Zerah were twins. They were named together here, probably with the intention of recalling the way they were born.

Tamar is the first of four famous women named in this book of the generations. The other three are Rahab (v.5), Ruth (v.5), and the wife of Uriah (v.6). These four women are all Gentiles: Tamar probably was a Canaanitish woman; Rahab might also have been a Canaanitish woman; Ruth was a Moabitess; and the wife of Uriah was most likely a Hittite woman.

Hezron (see 1 Chron. 2.4–5, Ruth 4.18–19, and 1 Chron. 2.9); Ram (see Ruth 4.19, 1 Chron. 2.9–10); Amminadab (see Ruth 4.19–20, 1 Chron. 2.10); Nahshon (see Ruth 4.20, Ex. 6.23).

Rahab here must certainly be Rahab the harlot (see Joshua 2.1, 6.25). She was married to Salmon, the son of Nahshon. There is no discrepancy in time if this is Rahab the harlot. If this were not Rahab the harlot, there would surely have been more detailed description given. Hence this Rahab must have been as well known a person as the other two women (Tamar and Ruth); and consequently, the Scriptures here do not especially introduce her, for aside from Rahab the harlot, there is no other Rahab as well known as this one.

Boaz (see Ruth 4.21, 1 Chron. 2.11–12); Obed (see Ruth 4.21– 22, 1 Chron. 2.12); Jesse (see Ruth 4.22, 1 Chron. 2.12–13,15).

"David the king." David was not the only king cited in this book of the generations, yet the Holy Spirit affixed the title of king to David alone. From this detail we can know that God was paying special attention here to the throne of David. Matthew speaks of Jesus as the successor to the kingly throne of David, and hence the title is especially mentioned here to disclose the purpose of this Gospel.

The wife of Uriah was Bathsheba (see 2 Sam. 11.3).

(9) "And Solomon begat Rehoboam . . ." (vv.7–11). Solomon (see 2 Sam. 12.24); Rehoboam (see 1 Kings 11.43); Abijah, also called Abijam (see 1 Kings 14.31, 2 Chron. 12.16); Asa (see 1 Kings 15.8, 2 Chron. 14.1); Jehoshaphat (see 2 Chron. 17.1); Joram (or Jehoram) of Judah (see 2 Kings 8.16, 2 Chron. 21.1); Uzziah (see 2 Chron. 26.1, 2 Kings 14.21); Jotham (see 2 Kings 15.7, 2 Chron. 26.23); Ahaz (see 2 Kings 15.38, 2 Chron. 27.9); Hezekiah (see 2 Kings 16.20, 2 Chron. 28.27); Manasseh (see 2 Kings 20.21, 2 Chron. 32.33); Amon (see 2 Kings 21.18, 2 Chron. 33.20); Josiah (see 2 Kings 21.24, 2 Chron. 33.25).

"The carrying away to Babylon" began with Jehoiakim (see 2 Chron. 36.5–6), continued with Jehoiachin (vv.8–10), and concluded with Zedekiah (vv.10b–20).

(10) "And after the carrying away to Babylon, Jechoniah begat Shealtiel . . ." (vv.12–16).

Jechoniah was the same as Jehoiachin (cf. 2 Chron. 36.9 and 2 Kings 24.8 with 1 Chron. 3.16 and Jer. 24.1). He was also called Coniah (see Jer. 22.24–28).

"Jechoniah begat Shealtiel," thus showing that Jechoniah was not without child. Yet Jeremiah prophesied, "As I live, saith Jehovah, though Coniah the son of Jehoiakim king of Judah were the signet upon my right hand, yet would I pluck thee thence . . . O earth, earth, earth, hear the word of Jehovah. Thus saith Jehovah, Write ye this man childless, a man that shall not prosper in his days; for no more shall a man of his seed prosper, sitting upon the throne of David, and ruling in Judah" (Jer. 22.24,29–30). In reading the phrase, "write ye this man childless," it may seem to us that he was childless. Where, then, came Shealtiel?

Let us understand that the word "childless" appearing here did not mean literally childless; it only meant that no seed of his would ever sit upon the throne of David to rule in Judah. Judging from these few words of Jeremiah, therefore, Jesus Christ must necessarily be born of the virgin Mary. Why? Because on the one hand God had said of Jechoniah that his seed would not ascend to the throne of David and on the other hand the same God had promised to give Christ that very throne (see Luke 1.32–33). Now Joseph was a descendant of Jechoniah; but if Jesus were to come from Joseph according to flesh, He too would be a seed of Jechoniah—and thus He could not ascend to David's throne nor would God give that throne to Him. Consequently, since God has given Christ the throne of David, is that not proof that Jesus could not be a progeny of Jechoniah biologically born of Joseph?

Shealtiel (see 1 Chron. 3.17); Zerubbabel (see 1 Chron. 3.19).

"Mary, of whom was born Jesus, who is called Christ" (v.16). There is a sudden grammatical change here in this entire book of the generations of Matthew. All which precedes reads that so-and-so begat so-and-so; also, all is paternal in succession. Yet here it fails to say, "Jacob begat Joseph, and Joseph begat Jesus who is called Christ"; it instead says, "Mary, of whom was born Jesus, who is called Christ." This is maternal in succession. What is indicated here is that Jesus had no relationship with Joseph according to the flesh. His relationship with Joseph only came from Mary. How carefully does the Holy Spirit write the Scriptures. There is not a single word misused. The record clearly testifies that our Lord was born of the virgin Mary. He was not an illegitimate child of Joseph as modern man thinks. His being born of Mary solves all skepticism. The Greek word for "beget" is *gennao*, It is primarily used of men, wherein it denotes the thought of begetting or causing to be born; it is far less frequently used of women, and in that context it conveys the idea of bringing forth or delivering into the world.

(11) "So all the generations from Abraham unto David are fourteen generations . . ." (v.17). "So" follows what goes before. From Abraham to David are fourteen generations; from David to the carrying away to Babylon are also fourteen generations; and from the carrying away to Babylon to Christ, another fourteen generations. "So" does not denote "it therefore is"; rather, it denotes "if thus computed."

Though the "fourteen generations" phrase is mentioned three times, they nonetheless are not added together to be forty-two generations. 14 is 7 (a perfect number) multiplied by 2 (the number of witness or testimony). 14 is thrice mentioned, and 3 is the number of manifestation. Thus the total of the generations cited in this book of genealogy testifies to the fact that there must be one Jesus (Jehovah Savior).

(12) "And Nahshon begat Salmon; and Salmon begat Boaz of Rahab" (vv.4–5). The house of Rahab the harlot was attached to the wall of Jericho, and Rahab therefore lived on the city wall (see Joshua 2.15). The Lord had said to Joshua that when the wall of the city should fall down flat, "the people shall go up every man straight before him" (6.5). Later, when the wall did fall down flat, "the people went up into the city, every man straight before him, and they took the city" (6.20). The word "straight" is most important. Yet please note that when the wall fell down flat, Rahab's house still stood (see v.22). Since the people compassed the city so that the vanguard and the rearguard touched each other, they naturally could each go straight up except those who happened to be standing before the particular part of the wall where the house of Rahab was situated. These men could not go straight up: they had to make at least a slight detour around Rahab's house in order to enter the city. Nevertheless, the Bible

clearly says, "every man [went] straight before him." If some had
to follow a detour into the city, would this not contradict the clear
statement of the word of God? There must be an explanation.

Let us recall that at that time the priests who bore the ark
did not participate in storming into the city, since this was not
their duty. Most likely these priests who bore the ark stood right
up at the particular segment of the city wall where Rahab's house
was. They did not enter the city to seize it, and the house of
Rahab happened to be there blocking their way. The others—
the warriors—went straight up into the city, inasmuch as there
was no house of Rahab blocking them. How trustworthy is the
word of God.

Furthermore, the tribe of Judah was right behind the ark,
since this tribe always led the way. And Nahshon the son of Amminadab was over the host of the tribe of Judah (see Num. 10.14).
This is the same Nahshon cited in Matthew 1.4 (cf. with Num.
10.14). So that when the wall of Jericho fell, Nahshon must have
been following the ark, which—as already indicated—was close
to Rahab's house. Moreover, his son should be with him. They
therefore went straight up into the city by the side of Rahab's
house. In reading verse 22 of Joshua 6, one cannot escape the
assumption that the two spies (who had promised Rahab her life)
were at the very side of Joshua. (And would not the most appropriate place for Joshua to be situated be somewhere in close
proximity to the ark?) From reading verse 23 ("the young men
the spies went in, and brought out Rahab . . ."), one might also
deduce that these two spies must have been of the tribe of Judah,
since they were right at the door of Rahab's house when they,
in obedience to the Lord's command, went straight up into the
city.

Spies were usually from among the princes of the people (see
Num. 13.2). Nahshon, being a prince, was probably one of the
two spies. The Scriptures, however, refer to the two spies as "two
young men" (Joshua 6.23)—it therefore being reasonable to sup-
pose that the other spy was Salmon, the son of Nahshon. Thus

Rahab had earlier saved the life of both Nahshon and Salmon (see Joshua 2.1ff.), and now Salmon saved Rahab's life. These two fell in love. At the time when the book of Joshua was written, Rahab was still living (see Joshua 6.25). Yet she was placed "without the camp of Israel" (v.23). How, then, did it develop that she eventually "dwelt in the midst of Israel" (v.25)? Doubtless, she must have changed her faith and become married to an Israelite. Apart from the "Salmon [who] begat Boaz of Rahab" (Matt. 1.4), who else could that Israelite be? Consequently, the Rahab in Matthew 1 must be Rahab the harlot mentioned in the Book of Joshua. As we read the generations given in Ruth 4.18-22, we cannot but think of Rahab the harlot. For the Nahshon in verse 20 of that passage is the same Nahshon found in Numbers 10.14, the father of Salmon. Now Boaz was born in the time of the Judges, and between Nahshon and Boaz was the generation of Salmon. Since the Book of Joshua concerns itself with the period between the time of Numbers and that of the Book of Judges, the contents of Joshua must therefore be contemporaneous with the years of Salmon. And inasmuch as Rahab lived during the time of Joshua, she was obviously a contemporary of Salmon. Matthew recorded the fact that a Salmon married a Rahab. Who could this Rahab have been except the harlot Rahab spoken of in the Book of Joshua? The reason why her son Boaz cared so tenderly for Ruth and later married her was probably due to his father's example of having saved Rahab's life and then marrying her.

B. *Typology*

(1) "Abraham" (v.2) is the Father of Faith. He is a type of all believers who are justified by faith (see Rom. 4.22-24). He considered his own body as good as dead, yet he looked to God and His promise. And as he believed in God, he was justified by Him. This is indeed an excellent type of believer's justification by faith.

(2) "Isaac" (v.2) is: (a) a type of the Lord Jesus Christ. He was the only begotten son of promise (cf. Gen. 17.19 and 22.2 with John 3.16). He was obedient unto death (cf. Gen 22.9–12 with Phil. 2.8). He was laid on the altar (cf. Gen. 22.9 with 1 John 2.2 and 1 Peter 2.24). He rose up from the altar (cf. Gen. 22.12–13 with Matt. 28.6–7). He took a Gentile woman as wife (cf. Gen. 24.6–7 with 2 Cor. 11.2). He went half way to meet his bride (cf. Gen. 24.61–65 with 1 Thess. 4.16–17).

(b) a type of New Testament believers (read Gal. 4.21–31).

(3) "David the king" (v.6) is: (a) a type of the Lord Jesus in relation to the Jews at His first coming. David was "the anointed one" who experienced rejection and was subject to wanderings, homelessness and dangers. At His first coming, the Lord Jesus was likewise treated by the Jews: He was a King who was rejected by men.

(b) a type of the second coming of Christ who shall destroy the Antichrist and judge the nations. David was a warrior king. He spent his whole life on the battlefield after he had killed Goliath (a type of Antichrist). At the appearing of His coming, the Lord Jesus will destroy the Antichrist (see 2 Thess. 2) and fight against the nations (see Rev. 19.11–21). This will be the last world war, called the war of Armageddon. The latter gets its name from the place name of "Har-Magedon" mentioned in Rev. 16.16 and generally known as the Mountain ("Har") of Magedon or Megiddo, the same as the ancient Israelite hill-city of Jezreel cited in the Old Testament and that overlooked the plain or valley of Jezreel.

(4) "Solomon" (v.6) succeeded his father as a king of peace. He manifested great wisdom, judged the people with righteousness, and had peace and prosperity in the kingdom. This typifies the state of the millennial kingdom which the Lord Jesus will establish after the judgment of the nations. In the future, the

Lord Jesus as the warrior King is typified by David; and as the King of peace, by Solomon.

C. Spiritual Teachings

(1) "David," "Abraham" (v.1). This verse shows forth the two most important covenants in the Old Testament: both God's covenant of promise with Abraham and His covenant of kingship with David are fulfilled in Christ. It was about two thousand years before Christ that God had covenanted with Abraham, and about one thousand years before Christ that He had covenanted with David. By this we see that God is faithful and righteous. Once He promises, He will never forget even after one thousand or two thousand years. Even at times when His promise may seem unfulfilled, nevertheless, when the time comes for its fulfillment, it is always fulfilled. God is always faithful. Although neither Abraham nor David saw the promised Messiah in their own lifetime, when the fullness of time came, God sent forth His Son, born of a woman. Therefore, let us who are believers not become impatient, imagining that the Lord has failed. God the Father has His timing. Let us rather trust and obey Him.

(2) The promise given by God concerning the *first* coming of the Lord Jesus Christ was fulfilled two thousand years later. We must not ask, "Where is the promise of his coming?" (2 Peter 3.4)—even though this promise concerning His *second* coming was given almost two thousand years ago. "Forget not this one thing, beloved, that one day is with the Lord as a thousand years, and a thousand years as one day. The Lord is not slack concerning his promise, as some count slackness; but is long-suffering to you-ward, not wishing that any should perish, but that all should come to repentance" (2 Peter 3.8–9). Let us not be disappointed, because at the appropriate time He "that cometh shall come, and shall not tarry" (Heb. 10.37 paraphrasing Hab. 2.3).

(3) Our Lord not only came from a carpenter's family, He also came from a royal house. He is King. May our soul magnify the Lord. May we see His regal quality, His greatness, glory and honor, that we might praise Him.

The Lord Jesus is not only "the son of David," He is the "son of Abraham" as well. He is Isaac, the Son of Abraham. Isaac means, appropriately, laughter—"I bring you good tidings of great joy which shall be to all the people" (Luke 2.10). Thank God, the Lord Jesus is related to us inasmuch as He is given to the Gentiles.

(4) "The book of the generations" (cf. v.17 with v.1). (a) There are only names to be found in the book of the generations. What spiritual teaching can possibly be gleaned from them? Yet our Father God is most economical; He will never use vain words. Each and every name in the genealogy tells its story and teaches its lesson. But it requires careful searching out to find these lessons.

(b) Our Lord was with God in the beginning. Though He was on an equality with God (see Phil. 2.6), He nonetheless had a human genealogy. He possessed an ancestry on earth. This is humility. How marvelous that our Lord is willing to humble himself and assume an ancestry such as we sinners have!

(5) "Isaac" (v.2) is born through promise and is free. God desires us to be free, to be born through promise that we might be children of God (see Gal. 4.21-31). We ought to rid ourselves of the slavish heart and fleshly mind. Since at the beginning of our Christian walk we come in through the Holy Spirit, how dare we complete it in the flesh?

(6) "Jacob" (v.2). We believers are chosen not because we are any different from the rest of the people, nor because of our righteousness and good works. God has chosen us because of His sovereign mercy. We are chosen just as Jacob had been (see

Rom. 9.12–16). Jacob was not any better than Esau, and yet God chose him. Thank the Lord for giving us His grace freely. The very remembrance of this can keep us from boasting. The more we understand grace, the more we will praise the Lord.

(7) "Judah" (v.2): (a) "it is evident that our Lord hath sprung out of Judah: as to which tribe Moses spoke nothing concerning priests" (Heb. 7.14). Thank the Lord, we who had no relationship with Christ, alienated from the commonwealth of Israel and strangers to the covenants of promise (Eph. 2.12), have now a place in Christ.

(b) Judah was the fourth son of Jacob, but in Matthew's genealogy only Judah's name appears. For God does not dispense grace according to the high or low position in the flesh, "but God [chooses] the foolish things of the world . . . the weak things of the world . . . the base things of the world, and the things that are despised, . . . yea and the things that are not" (1 Cor. 1.27–28). His ways are higher than our ways. Let us adore and worship His greatness.

(8) "Tamar," "Rahab," "Ruth," and "the wife of Uriah" (vv.3–6). All these women except Ruth are morally unclean, and even Ruth belongs to the abominable tribe of Moab. In themselves, they could have no part with Christ. Yet, through the great mercy of the Lord, they have a place in Him. All this shows us how humble is the Lord Jesus that He would join himself with sinners. He is a friend of sinners. He receives sinners. He comes to save the lost.

All four women were Gentiles. They serve as a type of all the Gentiles of this age who will have received grace in Christ. Formerly they were alienated from the commonwealth of Israel and strangers to the covenants of the promise, but then through grace they were married to God's elect people, thus forming an inseparable bond. The Gentiles were not at all related to Christ, yet now they are called of God to leave their old state and by faith be joined to Christ so that a marriage relationship could be established. The fact that these women are used to serve as a type of the Gentiles is illustrative of a consistent feature to be found in the Book of Matthew of including episodes in the life and ministry of Jesus that relate to the Gentiles (see, e.g., 15.21–28).

We Gentiles are comforted by seeing how these four women received grace. Great sinners such as they were, were received by the Lord. Would not He therefore receive us in spite of our many sins? As we come before the Lord, we must not consider our sins as too great to invite His grace. He will not cast us out. We may rejoice and be glad, for the Lord Jesus is our Savior.

These women were all remarried. Because of their particular remarriages, they were entered into the book of the generations of Christ. We as sinners have also lost our virginity through sin, but if we will forsake sins and hate sin as we do death, and then turn to Christ, we will be received by Him. This is what we ought to do.

The Lord Jesus Christ was born. Though He was the Son of God and the holy and glorious Lord, He was nonetheless unashamed to join His name with the name of sinners to be found in the book of the generations. He thus acknowledged by this that sinners were related to Him. How, then, could we ever be ashamed to confess His honorable name in the world? May we glory in praising and spreading His name.

The fact that Matthew was moved by the Holy Spirit to record women's names in the genealogy is enough to surprise us. But we are further surprised to discover that he failed to record all the women's names; he actually left out the names of some famous women such as Sarah and Rebekah and purposely put in the names instead of a harlot, an adulteress, and a foreign woman. The Holy Spirit uses them intentionally as examples of sinners, causing us to know that the Lord does not despise publicans and harlots.

"The wife of Uriah." Her name was Bathsheba (2 Sam. 11.3).

The Holy Spirit does not call her "Bathsheba" here, He instead calls her "the wife of Uriah." All the other women mentioned in the book of the generations were called by their own names, but she was referred to by the name of her former husband. How sharp is the warning penned by the Holy Spirit here! Although David had confessed and repented of his sins, and was also forgiven by God, nevertheless, a black spot was left in history. For God hates sin and He will not lightly despise it.

"Begat Solomon." The first child born out of the illicit union of David with Bathsheba died. Solomon was born of Bathsheba after David's repentance. We stand amazed at the boundless grace of God.

Now the Lord Jesus later was reckoned a descendant of Solomon, he who had been sired by David with Bathsheba. What a strange affinity Christ has had with fallen man! How true is the adage, "Jesus is willing to receive sinners."

(9) "And Solomon begat Rehoboam . . ." (vv.7–8). A good father, Solomon, begat a bad son, Rehoboam. A bad father, Rehoboam, begat a bad son, Abijah. A bad father, Abijah, begat a good son, Asa. A good father, Asa, begat a good son Jehoshaphat. A good father, Jehoshaphat, begat a bad son, Joram. All this proves that the good or bad character of one's ancestry has little relationship to the good or bad character of the progeny themselves.

(10) "Manasseh" (v.10). A man so wicked as Manasseh had his name listed with the holy Lord Jesus Christ. Indeed, however, "where sin abounded, grace did abound more exceedingly" (Rom. 5.20).

(11) Verses 12–16 — Of these many names, all except two or three of them were relatively unknown persons, and yet our Lord was related to them. He was "as a root out of a dry ground" (Is. 53.2). He chooses the base things of the world, the things that

are despised, and the things that are not (see 1 Cor. 1.27–28). He is the Savior of the common people. By looking at His genealogy we can know how He humbled himself. How can we therefore dare to exalt ourselves before Him?

(12) Verse 17 — As a consequence of all that happened during these three periods, the fall of mankind could be labeled as total. In each period of fourteen generations all of mankind is presented as sinners. Had there been one perfect man during the entire four thousand years of human history, God would have had no need to make the Sinless One as sin. Yet the people in these three periods were all born of blood, of the will of the flesh, and of the will of man (even Isaac, as good a person as he was, was no exception). And the four women involved could easily represent their origins, too. But our Lord was born of the virgin Mary and the Holy Spirit. Such a birth is totally and forever impossible to the people of the world. Yet this enables Him to be Savior.

"Fourteen"—This number, which is repeated three times here, is arrived at by taking 2 (the number of testimony) and multiplying it by 7 (the number of perfection). It testifies to the complete failure of mankind and the perfect victory of Christ. Incidentally, the number 14 in Greek is calculated like the Chinese fourteen, which is 10 plus 4. 10 (total responsibility) plus 4 (God's creation or man) means human responsibility. In these very numbers themselves, God has concealed great wisdom.

D. Comparison

(1) Compare the four Gospels. Of the four, only Matthew and Luke record the genealogy of the Lord Jesus. Matthew presents especially Jesus as King, and therefore a genealogy is necessary; because as far as the throne is concerned, it is required to prove that Jesus is the legal heir. Luke particularly presents the Lord as Man, so he also presents a genealogy. This is because,

so far as human relationship is concerned, it is necessary to describe His lineage. Mark specifically presents Jesus as the Servant, and hence he gives no genealogy; for according to the rule regulating slaves, there is no need to have any genealogical record. John uniquely presents the Lord Jesus as God, wherein no genealogy is given, since in the Godhead there is not even the possibility of a genealogy.

(2) Compare Matthew with 1 Chronicles: (a) In Matthew 1.8-9—Jehoshaphat, Joram, Uzziah, Jotham are mentioned. In 1 Chronicles 3.10-12—Jehoshaphat, Joram, Ahaziah, Joash, Amaziah, Azariah (Uzziah), Jotham are listed. By comparing these two records we discover that in the genealogy of Matthew the three generations of Ahaziah, Joash and Amaziah are missing. Why did the Holy Spirit omit these three generations in writing this portion of the Scriptures? Several reasons can be given: (i) These three were the descendants of Athaliah the daughter of the wicked king Ahab and wicked queen Jezebel. Athaliah tried to destroy all the royal seed of the house of David. So that God remembered her sin and forgot her sons to the third or fourth generation (cf. Ex. 20.5). (ii) By omitting these three, the entire book of the generations could be evenly divided into three periods of fourteen generations each. (iii) Under the divine government of God—that is to say, under the theocracy—these could not be considered as legal successors. (iv) What follows after Matthew 1.1 is but an extended explanation; so that what is given is adequate in serving this purpose.

(b) In Matthew 1.11-12—Josiah, Jechoniah, Shealtiel, Zerubbabel are cited. In 1 Chronicles 3.15-19—Josiah, Jehoiakim, Jechoniah, Shealtiel, Zerubbabel are named, among others. By comparing these two passages we realize that in the genealogy given by Matthew the generation of Jehoiakim was left out and Zerubbabel the son of Pedaiah was given as Shealtiel's son.

There were several reasons why the name of Jehoiakim was deleted: (i) he was set up by Pharaoh; (ii) he exacted heavy taxes from the Jewish people for Pharaoh (see 2 Kings 23.35); and (iii) he did not turn to Jehovah but was evil in God's sight at a time of national disaster.

Though Zerubbabel was not born of Shealtiel, he was still reckoned as his son. This was probably done in conformity to the words of Deuteronomy 25.5–6 which declares: "If brethren dwell together, and one of them die, and have no son, the wife of the dead shall not be married without unto a stranger: her husband's brother shall go in unto her, and take her to him to wife, and perform the duty of a husband's brother unto her. And it shall be, that the first-born that she beareth shall succeed in the name of his brother that is dead, that his name be not blotted out of Israel."

(3) Compare Matthew and Luke. Both Matthew and Luke (3.23–38) recorded the genealogy of the Lord Jesus, but they differ in many points. The genealogy in Matthew follows the lineage of Solomon; while that of Luke, the lineage of Nathan. Matthew records forty-odd generations; but Luke, seventy-odd ones. Matthew begins with Abraham, Luke ends with Adam and God. Matthew outlines his genealogy forward in time, Luke traced backward. Matthew calls the Lord by the name of Jesus Christ; Luke simply calls Him Jesus.

Upon comparing these two books of the generations, we find a most puzzling point: Matthew 1.16 states that "Jacob begat Joseph"; but Luke 3.23 reads: "Joseph, the son of Heli." By reading the verses preceding that of Matthew 1.16 and the verses succeeding that of Luke 3.23, we come to know that Jacob and Heli were two different persons, not one person with two names. If that be the case, will not this give Joseph (nominal father of the Lord Jesus) two fathers? Yet it is impossible for one person to have two biological fathers. How, then, can this seeming discrepancy be reconciled? We know that after David the lines of succession given in Matthew and Luke differ: Luke records forty-two names while Matthew records only twenty-seven.

Unbelieving commentators would naturally conclude that one of the two must be wrong. They deem error to be inevitable here because of the extensive number of years covered by the genealogy plus the same names shared by people. But is this really an error? If so, the enemies of faith in the early centuries would have certainly noticed it. These critics were mostly people of great learning, and skillful in critique. Yet they did not find these records to be erroneous, neither did they even cast any doubt on them. We can assume, then, that the records given by both Matthew and Luke must be highly accurate. The Jews, too, can be cited as a witness, for they would have doubtless voiced their own objections had there been any discrepancy between these two records. Since they offered no criticism of these two genealogies, this fact sufficiently proves that they accounted them to be truthful. (What we see here is the fact that contemporary people could have much more easily detected any error in these genealogical records than can today's critics, yet the contemporaries said nothing against these records.)

Here, then, are two different explanations which can be offered to resolve the problem: (a) Some regard Joseph as the *actual* son of Jacob, but he was also the son of Heli according to law, that is, as an heir. According to the custom of the Jewish people, if one died without having a son, his brother would marry the widow, and the first son born would succeed in the name of the deceased. According to this explanation, therefore, it can be assumed that Heli died without a son, so his brother Jacob married the widow and begat Joseph. With the result that Joseph was a son born of Jacob's flesh but was also the legal son of Heli. So that this is why the Scripture says in Matthew, "Jacob begat Joseph," and in Luke, "Joseph, the son of Heli." Even so, we cannot prove the brother relationship between Jacob and Heli.

(b) The second explanation, therefore, is seen to be more satisfactory. Some believe that Matthew in his Gospel gave the genealogy of Joseph, while Luke in his Gospel gave that of Mary. Since, according to this explanation, Joseph was a half son to

Heli, he was deemed to be the son of Heli. We know without any doubt that the Lord Jesus was not really the biological son of Joseph, and thus He could not possibly be the Son of David unless there was clear evidence that Mary herself was a descendant of David. Otherwise, the Lord Jesus would not be related to David in the flesh. Who can deny that the Holy Spirit moved Luke to demonstrate that Mary came from David? Accordingly, He having come from Mary, the Lord Jesus was related in the flesh to David indeed. And hence, Jesus was called the Son of David and the heir of God's promise to David.

2 | The Birth of Jesus 1.18-25

(1) The first section just discussed has shown forth for us the royalty of our Lord; the section now before us reveals His other feature which is not disclosed in the book of the generations.

Joseph occupies a significantly large place here. We see how he pondered and had his puzzle solved after an angel appeared to him. We also see how he took Mary as his wife and accepted the Lord Jesus as his nominal son. The relationship of Joseph with Mary was most intimate and deep. No one could have been more concerned about the pure virginity of Mary than he, since the future blessing of his family revolved around this very matter. So that in His word, God especially discloses to us the fact that Joseph fully believed in the virginity of his wife, thus enabling the divine record to shut the mouths of many unbelievers; for if Joseph, who was so close and intimate a person to Mary, entertained no doubt, then there could be no possibility for bystanders to gossip.

There were many reasons why God foreordained an *engaged* virgin to be the mother of the Lord Jesus: (a) she would not be stoned to death because she had a concerned and caring fiancé; (b) she would receive help and comfort when they fled to Egypt; and (c) God wished by this means to conceal this mystery. The Jews were witnesses to many miracles performed by the Lord, yet they did not believe. They took Him to be only the son of a carpenter. Now had they heard that Jesus was born of a virgin, they would have rejected Him even before they had had an opportunity to see these miracles. For this reason, the apostles always preached the death and resurrection of the Lord Jesus first, because those who would consequently believe and be saved would have no problem believing His virgin birth. Such is the wisdom of God.

The prophecy of "the seed of the woman" (see Gen. 3.15) was already four thousand years old. But here and now, God caused it to be fulfilled. Since He was not the son of Joseph, He could without any question be reckoned as "the seed of the woman." The prophecy of Isaiah concerning the virgin that "shall be with child, and shall bring forth a son" (Matt 1.23 quoting from Is. 7.14) was often quoted among the Jews and expressed the expectation of many hearts. Although God's ordained way for propagating human life is through the union of man and woman, nevertheless, for the Son of God to be "the seed of the woman," He must be born through the female sex alone in order to show forth His supernatural birth.

"Immanuel" (v.23b). This is an amazing fact. The Lord Jesus being God automatically eliminates the possibility of there ever being the biological fatherhood of Joseph with respect to Jesus. He is Immanuel, the heir to the throne (Is. 9.6–7). Hence Matthew alone recorded this. Jesus is King; therefore He represents His people. He is "the Almighty God," "Father of eternity" (Hebrew original); hence, He has great strength. He is man, as well as God, and so, He is Immanuel. God and man, man and God. The Highest became the lowest: God became man: the King became as it were a "criminal." Only the Highest could condescend to be the lowest.

Before our Lord was conceived in the womb of a virgin, God had already provided a Joseph to protect His infant body. Before a rich man had been buried in his own tomb, God had prepared another Joseph to preserve the Lord's dead body (see Matt. 27.57–60, Luke 23.50–53, John 19.38–41). The first Joseph took care of His birth; the latter Joseph took care of His burial and resurrection. Thus, two Josephs commenced and concluded the earthly life of the Lord Jesus. The Holy Spirit termed each of these Josephs a "righteous man" (Matt. 1.19, Luke 23.50). The most important element of earthly life is the parents; accordingly, the New Testament begins with the narrative of Jesus' parents. This would seem to be a hint to us that the God whom the Lord would later preach is the Father of those who believe.

(2) "Now the birth of Jesus Christ was on this wise: When his mother Mary had been betrothed to Joseph, before they came together she was found with child of the Holy Spirit" (v.18).

Of the birth of the various kings listed in the book of the generations, one or two words were quite sufficient; concerning our Lord Jesus Christ, however, a more detailed description was felt necessary to be given. He should have the preeminence in all things. In the earlier section of Matthew 1, His birth was mentioned. But the genealogy given could not fully show Him forth. Consequently, the Holy Spirit approached Jesus' birth from another angle so as to proclaim this wonderful Savior in another way.

Since the birth of our Lord was so different from the births of these earlier kings, the Holy Spirit opened up the description of Him with these words: "Now the birth of Jesus Christ was on this wise"— thus separating this Man's birth from all who were born of the flesh. This is a mysterious, marvelous subject. Let us approach it with godly faith, not a curious mind. In the womb of the virgin the Holy Spirit formed the physical body of our Lord. Both the angel and Matthew told the *fact*, but they did not tell us *how* this fact was accomplished. We do not know how the Almighty and the Infinite could dwell in a womb. He in whom are all things was borne by a virgin. We need not be concerned to pry too deeply into this divine mystery. We are thankful that it pleased God to at least reveal *this* fact to us, since this was the only way Jesus the Son of God could have been born. Had He been born of a human father, then how could He have possibly been without a sinful nature? Yet He was born of a woman by the instrumentality of the Holy Spirit, and not by that of man; therefore, Jesus was without sin. Here we witness the fact that the Holy Spirit also labored in the redeeming work of God.

According to the law, the Lord Jesus should be the son of Joseph, for Joseph was in the direct line of royalty. But the prophet made Him out to be the Son of a virgin instead of the son of Joseph. In the eyes of the law, Joseph was an important person; even so, the Messiah could not be a real son of Joseph. All the wisdom of the world could not foretell this, nor could all the powers of the world have prearranged the environment. Yet in God's eternal plan, He caused Joseph and Mary to be engaged, thus uniting the two lines of Solomon and Nathan. Through this uniting, the Lord Jesus became the Son of Joseph according to law, but the Son of Mary in actuality. What man needs is the condescension of God; and what God desires is the exaltation of man. How could this be done? Only Jesus Christ could provide the answer.

(3) "And Joseph her husband, being a righteous man, and not willing to make her a public example, was minded to put her away privily" (v.19).

If Mary was not already disgraced, she at least must have been under a cloud of suspicion. God respected her and dispensed great grace to her, though she was temporarily under a dark cloud. Those who have received immense grace from God are usually misunderstood. Mary was dangerously close to being publicly humiliated or worse by her fiancé. Had she been engaged to a cruel and impatient person, she would most likely have died an ignominious death by stoning. But God had already arranged to have her engaged to a gentle and loving man. And at the right moment, Joseph was given understanding of the real situation and took her to be his wife. Let us learn to trust God more. Let us always keep a conscience free of offense. God will take care of our name. Though we may be threatened and misunderstood, at the appropriate time God will declare our true character and deliver us: "Commit thy way unto Jehovah; trust also in him, and he will bring it to pass. And he will make thy righteousness to go forth as the light, and thy justice as the noonday" (Ps. 37.5-6).

Righteousness is to give one his due. It is the opposite of mercy. Joseph was a righteous man who singularly observed the law of God. But he was not just righteous, he was also most merciful. His mercy, however, carried within it righteousness. As a matter of fact, the very word "righteousness" includes in its original the sense of goodness. When Joseph discovered his fiancée was pregnant, naturally he was most unhappy. An ordinary man would have angrily accused and publicly disgraced her. Joseph, however, had a royal heart in keeping with the fact that he was of the royal house. Due to his merciful heart, he did not want to make her a public example in spite of the apparent sin of his betrothed. Fornication was a mortal sin; the adulterous woman must be stoned to death (see Deut. 22.22-24). Nevertheless, Joseph would endure and secretly put her away. According to law, a husband could divorce his wife (see Deut. 24.1). On the one hand, he was not willing to put Mary to death; on the other hand he was not willing to marry her because of his righteousness. And hence, he decided on giving Mary a customary letter of divorce and on the two of them parting in secret to avoid public condemnation. Joseph was truly a chosen one of the Lord. In dealing with a serious matter, we should adopt the most merciful way possible.

(4) "But when he thought on these things, behold, an angel of the Lord appeared unto him in a dream, saying, Joseph, thou son of David, fear not to take unto thee Mary thy wife: for that which is conceived in her is of the Holy Spirit" (v.20).

Joseph did nothing hastily. "Thought" means "considered." The angel said to him "fear not"—which word reveals the agony of his heart. Thank God, for "the meek will he guide in justice;

and the meek will he teach his way" (Ps. 25.9). We ought to be circumspect in all things. In a serious matter such as the one that confronted Joseph, there needs to be a waiting upon God and a seeking to know His will. And at the appropriate time God will direct.

In the New Testament there are six dreams recorded: it happened to Joseph four times (see Matt. 1.20, 2.13,19,22); to the wise men once (see Matt. 2.12); and to Pilate's wife once (see Matt. 27.19). Here the angel of the Lord is described as appearing to Joseph in dreams; in Luke's Gospel, on the other hand, the angel is described as appearing directly to Zacharias and Mary. This is not because of a personal reason on the part of the angel, but it was because the unbelief of Zacharias went so much deeper than did that of Joseph. It was probably due to the failure of the house of David (especially the failure of Jechoniah). Joseph was the representative of that house, so that the blessing to him could not be open, but was covered with a veil. Mary was not a descendant of Jechoniah, and the relationship of Joseph with the Lord Jesus was only established through his being wedded to Mary. Nevertheless, God was gracious to him and caused him to know His will.

The angel reminded Joseph that he was a "son of David" so as to prepare his heart to accept the following message that the Messiah would become flesh through his wife. He could confidently be wedded to Mary because that within her womb had been caused by the creative power of God. That Body in her womb is holy and perfect, uncontaminated by sin, thus fit to be offered as the Sin Offering for mankind. Joseph could therefore accept Mary with confidence.

Why had not Mary told the truth to Joseph? As it turned out, her chastity had been preserved without her speaking a word, for she believed that the God who had caused her to conceive was well able to vindicate her name. She entrusted her future and everything else into the hand of God, knowing that His arrangement was the best. Faith sustained her; indeed, she had great faith. Each time a person receives great grace from God, he will be greatly tested for his faith. Thank the Lord, He will not allow those who trust in Him to be put to shame but will defend their purity. Let us not avenge ourselves, for vengeance belongs to the Lord (see Rom. 12.19). If the Lord is truly born anew in our hearts, we too will encounter difficulty; yet He shall lead us through the dark valley.

(5) "And she shall bring forth a son; and thou shalt call his name Jesus; for it is he that shall save his people from their sins" (v.21).

How vastly different here in Matthew are the words "she shall bring forth a son" from those in Luke 1.13 which say that "thy wife Elisabeth shall bear thee a son." Zacharias was the biological father of John the Baptist, and so we read the words, "shall bear thee a son." But our Lord Jesus was not the biological son of Joseph, since Jesus was born of the Holy Spirit. And hence God had said to Joseph that Mary "shall bring forth a son" and not "shall bear thee a son." How full of wisdom is our God!

The meaning of "Jesus" is "God the Savior" or "Jehovah Savior." The equivalent term in the Old Testament is Joshua. By carefully comparing the life of Joshua with that of the Lord Jesus, we can readily see how the former is a marvelous type of the Latter. But Joshua is a man not free from blemish, whereas our Lord is God, the perfect One. From Abraham and David downward, no name could be compared with this Name—Jehovah Savior, the lowly Jesus. The Son of God in obedience to God's command was born to become the Son of man, and He was called Jesus. His name, in fact, is His life. But so, too, His name is His work as well. What His name is is precisely how He lives and what He does: "shall save his people." May our Father God be merciful to us who are called Christians that we may be true to our name and be like the holy Son. How often we are not the least bit like what we are called. May the Lord have mercy on us.

He shall save His people from their sins. This was totally op-

posite to the expectation of the Jews at that time, since they longed
for a Messiah who would save the nation — a Christ who would
cause the Jews to be strong and rich, a Savior who would destroy
the yoke of the Romans. Yet the Lord Jesus came, not to set up
an earthly kingdom, nor to deliver them from their national foe,
but to save them from their sins, which in reality constituted their
greatest enemy. The term "his people" originally pointed to the
children of Israel; after "the middle wall of partition" was broken
down (see Eph. 2.14), it came to include all the saved ones from
"every tribe, and tongue, and people, and nation" (Rev. 5.9)

The word "he" here is emphatic; so that in the original there
would have been added to it the word "himself." It thus means
that "He himself" shall save His people from their sins. This was
not done by others, because no one could do it except the Lord:
He alone could accomplish it because He alone is "Jesus." Truly,
Jesus is the One "who his own self bare our sins in his body upon
the tree, that we, having died unto sins, might live unto righteousness" (1 Peter 2.24). Jesus first has saved us from the *penalty*
of sin, so that we shall not perish. Yet He now saves us from the
power of sin, so that we may not fall. And He shall in the future
save us from the *presence* of sin, so that we shall be wholly spiritual.
What a Savior He is. How much He has truly done for those
who believe in Him. His very being is to save people, for that
is His name: Jesus — Savior. How tremendous is the testimony
of that Name towards the world. Today we still call Him Jesus,
because He continues saving people. Blessed are the sinners who
have heard that Name. Yet how much greater is the need to know
that blessed Name by those among the chosen people who look
for the Messiah.

The salvation of our Lord is perfect. He is not a half Savior,
because He not only saves those *in* sins but also those *out* of sins.
He delivers them from the power of sin so that they no longer
are bondslaves to sin. All who believe in the Lord Jesus as Savior
ought to experience the deliverance from sin. His name is Jesus.
He will save us from sinning as well as from hell. His salvation

is not like a life belt that saves people in water. His salvation is like a lifeboat that saves people out of water. He is able to save to the uttermost. If we have not received the salvation from the power of sin, we have received only half a Jesus: He has not manifested himself fully in us. What a pity that many of God's children are still ignorant of this glorious fact. They are quite content with but escaping eternal death. May He cause us to know His *full* salvation so that the world will see more of the Lord Jesus in us and know more of the power of that Name.

(6) "Now all this is come to pass, that it might be fulfilled which was spoken by the Lord through the prophet, saying, Behold, the virgin shall be with child, and shall bring forth a son, and they shall call his name Immanuel; which is, being interpreted, God with us" (vv.22–23).

The Holy Spirit tells us that all this is come to pass that it might fulfill the word of God. How would we ever know that all this is about the Lord Jesus unless the Holy Spirit had pointed it out to us? This is true with all the words in the Scriptures. For without the leading of the Holy Spirit we are not able to enter into all the truth. "Fulfill" in the Greek original implies final, complete accomplishment. It means that notwithstanding the fact that many things which happened in the past appeared to be fairly close to fulfilling this prophecy, they were merely preparing the way to this *final* accomplishment. Now, though, the total consummation of this prophecy has at last arrived; for Christ is the finality of all prophecies. He is over all and in all. The Holy Spirit is extremely precise in the use of words. He does not say here that "the prophet himself so spoke" but says instead that it "was spoken by the Lord through the prophet." Such is God's plan. He first decides to do something, then he gives prophecy about it. Prophecy is given to man. The fulfillment of prophecy, which is, that God causes a certain thing to happen as prophesied, is to enable us to believe that Jesus is the Christ.

Through Matthew, the Holy Spirit proves that Christ is the

Messiah to come, that Jesus of Nazareth is the Holy One of Israel about whom the prophets prophesied, as follows:

(a) His mother (1.23)—she would be a virgin.
(b) His birthplace (2.6)—it would be Bethlehem.
(c) His sojourn in Egypt (2.15).
(d) His home (2.23)—it would be at Nazareth.
(e) His forerunner (3.3)—it would be John the Baptist.
(f) His preaching circuit (4.13-17).

There is a definite article "the" before the word "virgin." It intimates that this virgin is the one—the only one—whom God has specially prepared. The word which God spoke to Ahaz the king through Isaiah (7.14) was now fulfilled.

It is most interesting to look at the Name given in verse 21 and the Name given in verse 23 together. Our Lord is Immanuel as well as Jesus. These two Names belong to one Person. Though in the Old Testament God had revealed the name "Immanuel," He had not disclosed His Son's other name, which is Jesus. God so loved that Name that He temporarily hid it from the children of Israel. In Matthew, however, He announced His Son to be Jesus before He declared Him to be also Immanuel, inasmuch as saving people from their sins must precede the blessing of God being with us. The issue of sin must first be resolved before there can be the possibility of God's holy presence.

In this Gospel we see the Lord Jesus as Immanuel. This was to serve as a reminder to the Jews, for they had already forgotten this prophecy. Their expectation was for a heroic, strong king who was nonetheless only a man. They were looking for a God-man to be their Messiah. They had no idea of a suffering Christ, since they only wanted a glorious Christ. Even this limited conception of theirs was rather murky, because they did not know that this Christ would come with the dual nature of God and man. Had they read Isaiah 7 carefully, they would have seen that the coming Messiah is to be God as well as man. Verse 14 says He is God; verses 15 and 16 tell of His human conditions. Yet they had a veil upon their hearts; therefore, they were unable to see the glory of Christ. Despite the fact that the Jews considered their Messiah to be only a man, the word of God had made it clear that He was to be more than man, He would also be God. So that in Matthew's Gospel God had to explain to these pitiful Jews the hard-to-understand passage from the Old Testament prophetic book. If they rejected this Messiah, they would· bring upon themselves perdition; for the Lord Jesus is not only the Son of Abraham and the Son of David, He is also Immanuel. Such is the testimony God had given concerning His Son. How could they have believed in the words of Isaiah but rejected the record of Matthew? Truly, they neither knew the Scriptures nor the power of God.

"Without controversy great is the mystery of godliness; he who was manifested in the flesh" (1 Tim. 3.16). Immanuel is the greatest mystery in the world. None can ever truly analyze it in its fullness. Formerly men had fallen away from God and dared not draw nigh to Him. There seemed to be a great rift which separated men from God and God from men—a rift, such, that neither could cross over. Although in the Old Testament period many persons were used by the Spirit of God, God could nonetheless not dwell among men nor join men to himself. Today, though, it is altogether different. Christ has been born. God has come to earth, uniting humanity with divinity. The Godhead had originally existed alone, and man had only belonged as it were to "another" species. Human life was so far inferior to God's life, in fact, that there was no possibility of union.

This impossibility ended, however, with the birth of the Lord Jesus. For sure, He is God; but He also possesses the spirit, soul and body of man. So that He is perfect God and perfect man. Jesus is the God-Man, with divinity and humanity joined in one in Him. He is the bridge that has spanned the great rift between man and God. His birth joins man to God and God to man. The Lord Jesus is God, but He also has human nature. Though He is God, He nonetheless has human experience; thus divinity draws close towards humanity. Jesus is man, yet He also possesses divine nature. As this God-Man, the Lord Jesus dwells among men and manifests the reality of God to men, thus enabling humanity to be drawn close to divinity. In human relationships, that of husband and wife is the most intimate, inasmuch as they become one flesh. Yet the affinity of the husband and wife is far inferior to that of God and man. For God and man are joined in one in the Lord Jesus Christ.

The Lord Jesus being Immanuel is not simply a doctrine for us to propagate, abstractly teaching that He has in Him both divinity and humanity. We must take note of what He has accomplished. The purpose of His having this dual nature is to bring man to God and God to man in himself. His being Immanuel is for the purpose of demonstrating how man could become so close to God and God to man. Formerly God was regarded as being so high up in heaven, beyond the reach and touch of man. Was there not an insurmountable distance between the created and the Creator? How could the Infinite and the finite touch each other? Now, though, because the Lord Jesus is God and man, man and God, therefore, in Him, God and man are joined in one. Jesus is himself Immanuel, so that man through His manhood draws nigh to His "God," and God through Jesus' Godhood draws near to His "man." This is truly an amazing union which introduces the gospel that is to be preached. After the work of the cross is done, these things are all fulfilled. We ought to lift up our voice to give all the glory to God. How wonderful is His plan!

A dear saint once commented as follows: The end of Matthew chapter 1 serves to sum up the place which the Gospels occupy in the progressive record of God's way in dealing with man. In the Old Testament, God is presented as being *for* His people. In the Gospels, He is presented as being *with* His people. And in the Epistles, He is presented as being *in* His people. These three steps — God for us, God with us, and God in us — disclose the way and the end of God's dealing with man. Holiness abides eternally in heaven, becomes flesh in this world, and dwells in the saints.

The angel of the Lord caused Joseph to remember this passage in the Scriptures so as to enable him to resolve his doubt and take Mary in peace. Whenever we are overshadowed by the dark cloud of doubt, a word from God — even one Bible verse — can restore our soul: for the word of God is powerful: it refreshes man's heart. Living as we do in this last age, with so many things pressing in upon us, we shall easily offend God if we do not store His word in our hearts more faithfully. May God the Father use His word to revive and reinforce us. May He cause us to recall His word as Joseph did and treasure the Bible at times of reading or even while dreaming. The Lord Jesus himself, of course, is more intimate and loving. Yet the written word is still very precious because it bears witness to the living Word, even to Jesus. How blessed was Joseph, in that He was familiar with the Lord's Scriptures and was instructed in His word by means of a dream.

(7) "And Joseph arose from his sleep, and did as the angel of the Lord commanded him, and took unto him his wife" (v.24).

Joseph was not disobedient to the heavenly vision (cf. Acts 26.19). He immediately obeyed God. As soon as he arose, he did what the angel of the Lord had commanded him to do. He raised no question such as Zacharias (the priestly father of John the Baptist) had done (see Luke 1.18ff.). To him, the word of the prophet and the vision of the angel were sufficient. He did not delay in his obedience to God. Later on, he several times received even more directions from God. The first reward of obedience is more power to obey. Each time God directs, He expects His people to obey. To one who deliberately rebels, God will not guide his way. Obedience is not an utterance, it is an act: "took unto him his wife." What Joseph formerly would not do, now he gladly did because he had the revelation of God. God is able to change man's mind; but He refuses to change the mind of one whose heart is set against doing His will.

Now when Joseph took to himself his wife, how happy he must have been; for what he had earlier suspected now proved to be false. But then, too, how much more thankful to God must Mary have been, because the unbearable burden of her chastity was now lifted. Previously, special honor had become for her a special disgrace; yet the God who could give honor was well able also to dismiss the disgrace which had issued from the honor given. There is nothing impossible with God.

(8) "And knew her not till she had brought forth a son: and he called his name Jesus" (v.25).

In this one Scripture verse, the entire misconception of Mary having maintained a lifelong virginity is smashed. Joseph did not know her till after she had brought forth the Lord Jesus. The Roman Church worships the holy mother and teaches the false doctrine of Mary's continual virginity. They dogmatically state that after she gave birth to the Lord Jesus, she did not bear any other children. They maintain that the brethren of the Lord mentioned in the Scriptures were born by a former wife of Joseph. All these assumptions are created by the Roman Church; they cannot at all be found nor substantiated in the Scriptures. We cannot gather one single shred of evidence from either the Scriptures or history to prove such a fantasy.

Anyone reading the Scriptures without prejudice would naturally accept these mentioned brethren of the Lord as having been born of *Mary* later on. Psalm 69 is a Messianic psalm, as made clear by the fact that the Holy Spirit applies its verse 9 to our Lord Jesus Christ (see John 2.17). Now let us look at the preceding verse: "I am become a stranger unto my brethren, and an alien unto my mother's children." Who, then, would dare to say that Mary never gave birth to other children? According to the Scriptures, she at least brought forth four sons and two daughters. There is absolutely no evidence in the Scriptures or in history that Joseph had a former wife by whom these other children might have been born. Furthermore, after the time of the birth of the Lord Jesus, the Scriptures do not call her a virgin anymore.

To elevate Mary the way the Roman Church has done is to ignore the fact that she was of like nature with us all; and that, moreover, she needed the atoning blood of the Lord Jesus just as we all do. Is it not strange that on the one hand the Roman Church elevates the virgin above her proper place while on the other hand the modernists (the unbelieving party among the Protestants) debase the virgin below her original state! May God have mercy on them both.

Joseph "called his name Jesus." This was the duty of the nominal father. In Joseph having taken Mary as his wife, the Son of Mary became the seed of Joseph, the seed of David. Hence He was also the King of the Jews. Through His mother, our Lord became the Son of David. According to law, this was through his nominal father.

Notwithstanding that this chapter 1 was written especially for the Jews, we, too, as believing Gentiles, may find many blessings for ourselves. Whenever the Lord Jesus is lifted up and God's grace is poured out, it humbles and blesses man. The Son of God condescended to be the Son of man, that we, the children of men, might be called the children of God. God became man in order to participate in flesh and blood with us. The closer He draws near to us, the more we ought humbly to praise Him. In the succeeding chapters we shall see how the Jews rejected the Lord and how the Gentiles received blessing. Let us extol His name, for we who were afar off are now brought near (see Eph. 2.13).

(1) "Now when Jesus was born in Bethlehem of Judaea in the days of Herod the king, behold, Wise-men from the east came to Jerusalem, saying, Where is he that is born King of the Jews? for we saw his star in the east, and are come to worship him" (2.1-2).

Herod was an Idumaean. His being king indicated that the scepter had already departed from Judah (see Gen. 49.10a). But the "Shiloh" (the Prince of Peace or Peace-Giver) was coming (see Gen. 49.10b). Many historians tell us that the people of the world at that time were all looking for a king to be raised up in Judah. And now the King of glory had come to the world. In Bethlehem (which in Hebrew means the "house of bread" or the "place of food"), the Bread of Life for the world had been born. What a pity that not many accept this Bread of Life. The kings of the earth are mostly antagonistic towards Him. Whereas on the one hand the Lord Jesus is born, there is on the other hand a Herod ruling by usurpation. The King is now born and ought to be adored; yet He is persecuted. This was true at that time, and it is still true today. At the first coming of the Lord, an Idumaean was sitting on the throne to resist Him. And at His second coming, there will be the Antichrist as king in Jerusalem who will likewise oppose Him.

What surprises us about these wise men from the East is that they knew about the birth of the Messiah earlier than the people in Jerusalem. These wise men, according to the original word, were probably the astronomers, prophets or dream-interpreters of those days. Though they embraced many superstitions in their lives, their learning was nonetheless not to be despised. Here we see how God met them on their way in order to deliver them out of darkness into light. The word "east" probably has reference to Arabia or Persia. We cannot pinpoint it any more exactly than that. Yet it is certain that the "east" was an area quite far from Jerusalem. They braved the discomforts and perils of a long journey to the holy capital of the Jews in order to worship the Lord Jesus. This truly amazes us. We do not often witness the intellectual doctors of the world willingly prostrating themselves at the feet of the Lord Jesus. Yet these were willing to come from afar and worship the Lord, for they were *true* doctors of wisdom.

For several centuries the Jews had been expecting the King to come. Even so, when He was eventually born among them He was not acclaimed by them. He received the worship of wise men from the East, but He was rejected by His very own people. These wise men from the East knew that He was the "King of the Jews"; nevertheless, the Jews were later to cry out: "We have no king but Caesar" (John 19.15). The Gentiles—not all, but at least a part of them—worship Him. Henceforth, God is also to be the God of the Gentiles, for His work commences in the hearts of those who accept the Lord Jesus. How perfect is the picture here. Jesus came to His own people, the Jews, yet His own people would not accept Him. However, a part of the Gentiles came to worship Him. This is a type of the present Gentile age.

One fact we should recognize, which is, that at the time the wise men arrived in Jerusalem, the Lord Jesus had already been born for over a year. For upon their first seeing the star, they had had to make many preparations for the long journey, which doubtless took them many days due to the inconvenience of travel in those days. Furthermore, even after they had arrived in the land of Judea, they had to wait for the answer of the scribes before they could move ahead farther, and this took additional time. From reading the Scriptures carefully we can discern the fact that these wise men did not see the Christ Child at the time of His birth. The situation surrounding His birth is recorded in Luke's Gospel. The shepherds saw the "babe" (2.16). The wise men, however, beheld a "young child" (Matt. 2.11). The shepherds saw the manger, but the wise men entered into a house. Moreover, Herod "slew all the male children that were in Bethlehem, and in all the borders thereof, from two years old and under, accord- ing to the time which he had exactly learned of the Wise-men" (Matt. 2.16). This is another proof that the Lord Jesus whom the wise men saw was no longer a newborn babe.

It was probably in Nazareth and not at Bethlehem where the wise men first beheld the Lord Jesus. For by that time He was already over one year old. This even probably occurred during the period between the time of Luke 2.39 and that of 2.40. When we read Matthew, we notice that this Evangelist only recorded where the Lord Jesus was born and not also where He stayed. Although Herod had sent the wise men to Bethlehem, Matthew did not say that they actually went there; his account only stated that they came to "where the young child was" (v.9). For had they indeed gone to Bethlehem, why should God have guided them any longer by means of the star, since Herod and his scribes had already instructed them where the child would be born? Not knowing the exact time of the birth of the Messiah, these wise men had been shown the star in the East. Now, though, being wrongly instructed by men as to where the child could *at this time* be found, they had to be further guided by God, by means of the star, to the right place. Yet would not this imply that the wise men had traveled to Jerusalem in vain? Not so, for we can see that God had His wisdom here. He wished to prove to the world that His Son had indeed been born at Bethlehem as the fulfillment of prophecy.

How would the wise men, by noticing and observing this star, have come to know that the Messiah had been born? This, too, may be traced. Daniel's prophecy of the seventy sevens (Dan. 9.24–27) had been given while the prophet had been dwelling in the East. These wise men had probably computed the time and therefore knew it. In addition, they no doubt were aware of the life and prophecy of the last Gentile prophet, Balaam, who had lived many centuries earlier. Though he had been a wicked man, he was nonetheless used by God to pronounce the future glory of Israel. He had prophesied: "There shall come forth a star out of Jacob" (Num. 24.17). Perhaps, then, these wise men of the East obtained their knowledge of the star and its significance from Balaam's prophecy. As to how this singular star could have appeared, we need not attempt to explain or rationalize. We should have no difficulty with this phenomenon if we believe that this was a miracle. The unbelieving world always requires a rational explanation. But cannot God do whatever He wants to do? God's servants need not struggle for an explanation to satisfy the mind of men. If they believe, let them believe. If they do not believe, we will not lower our dignity. Here we see how God is the Sovereign of all things. He is willing to guide all those who seek His Son with an honest heart. Our prayer is that God would enable us to see the Lord in all things. May we be led to Him. If we are open, even the star will guide us.

"Came to Jerusalem." They did not know where Christ should be born, for their knowledge was limited. They naturally assumed that Christ the King should be born in Jerusalem, the capital, not realizing that He was to be born in little obscure Bethlehem. Jerusalem of the world was indeed not to be the birthplace of Christ; therefore, those who follow Him should walk with Him in places unnoticed and unknown by the world. How very opposite is this from human thought. How difficult for the flesh to accept this. The wise men reckoned that they could find Christ in Jerusalem, not knowing that Herod the Idumaean was on the throne. Since Jerusalem already had her Herod, there was no place left there for the King from heaven to occupy. Instead, the

King from heaven was to be merely a sojourner who would lie in a manger at Bethlehem.

How strong was the faith of these wise men. How eager was their expectation. And how deep was their love. They beheld His star in the East, but this alone could not satisfy them. They must *see* the King. And having seen Him, they worshipped Him. May our hearts be like theirs. Unless we see His face and prostrate ourselves at His feet, we will never truly be satisfied. Thank the Lord, our present longing in the spirit shall soon be reality. Through the deed of these Easterners, God reproved the unbelief of the Jews. The Jews had the prophecies of the prophets as well as the types of the law, yet they dwelt in total darkness. Hence God used these Easterners to remind them. Perhaps many so-called believers today need to be reminded in many things by those who truly believe.

(2) "And when Herod the king heard it, he was troubled, and all Jerusalem with him" (2.3).

Herod was troubled because he thought he would lose his throne with the coming of the Christ. It is also possible that there was some uneasiness in his evil conscience. In truth, many are like Herod. They are afraid they will lose glory and position if Christ should gain their heart. With the coming of the Lord Jesus into their lives, they would have to give up the pleasures of the world. Without exception the flesh shrinks back at the presence of Christ and His demands. Only those who love the Lord welcome Him.

It is no surprise that Herod should be troubled. What is surprising, however, is to learn that "all Jerusalem [was troubled] with him." God had brought these Gentiles to the Jewish holy city to unveil the thoughts of the Jews. Under this divine probing, their hidden thoughts were being exposed; for the birth of the Promised One had not only not filled their hearts with joy but it had even caused their hearts to be troubled. Their former ideal and declaration had been for the coming of the Messiah to deliver them. So that God now tested them with the coming of His Christ. Surely this would be the opportunity for them to express their hearts if they truly meant it. But, alas, they were deeply troubled instead. All their previously expressed anticipations had proved to be false. Now this was what happened at the *first* coming of the Lord. Yet this might easily happen again at His *second* coming. Today many profess to look for the coming again of the Lord. But probably when the Lord shall actually come, they will be as the people of Jerusalem had been at His first coming.

Let us see that what really matters is not our current ideal and word, but the actual condition of our heart and spirit. If today we are not intimately close to the coming Lord, if our hearts have hidden sins or other loves, or if we lack within us a spirit of ascension (rapture) and have no intimate fellowship with Him, then I am afraid we too will be troubled at His coming.

(3) "And gathering together all the chief priests and scribes of the people, he inquired of them where the Christ should be born. And they said unto him, In Bethlehem of Judaea: for thus it is written through the prophet, And thou Bethlehem, land of Judah, art in no wise least among the princes of Judah: for out of thee shall come forth a governor, who shall be shepherd of my people Israel" (vv.4–6).

The Herod in the midst of the chief priests and the scribes was still the same Herod. It is not to the benefit of the Church if the world's kings become intimate with it. Many unregenerated remain the same when even among the believers. How much more would Herod remain Herod while in the midst of these unregenerated Jewish religionists.

How familiar the chief priests and the scribes were with the Old Testament Scriptures. They did not need to spend time searching, since they could recite from memory. They even knew the meaning of the Scriptures they recited. They knew, for example, that the word of Micah (5.2) referred to Christ. The wise men from the East had thought that Christ must surely be in Jerusalem, but the Jewish religionists immediately and confidently pointed out that Christ was to be born in Bethlehem. The research and judgment of these scribes was altogether correct. Even so, we do not see any appropriate action taken by them. They could send forth others, but they themselves would not go to see their newborn King. They did not go to seek out Christ, because they had no heart for Him.

How sad that with such understanding of the Scriptures they had no love for the One to whom the entire Scriptures bore witness. They knew the prophecy and they knew geography, yet they did not know that they had in their hands the very key into the spiritual realm of God. And as a result, they would not themselves enter in. May the Lord keep us from knowing many doctrines, prophecies and geography of the Bible if at the same time we miss the Lord of glory whom these things declare. May we not be like these chief priests and scribes who knew how to teach others with God's word and yet failed to teach themselves those very things. They were too familiar with the Scriptures. Studying God's word for other people can frequently lead to the peril of losing one's own love towards the Lord. We ought to search the written word under the influence of the living Word.

Although Bethlehem was a small town, it now became great because the Lord Jesus had been born there. In fact, anything touched by the Lord Jesus carries with it honor and glory. How great must be the glory to the insignificant person who has ever touched the Lord. Here, Jesus was referred to as King. This is in perfect accord with the purpose of this Book of Matthew. In this Gospel we learn that Christ came to save the Jews first. That is indeed the order in the Scriptures. But due to the Jews' rejection of the Lord, we Gentiles receive grace. The very prophecy of Micah already mentioned conveyed such a thought, too, because after the birthplace of Christ was mentioned, Micah continued on by saying, "now shall he be great unto the ends of the earth" (5.4).

(4) "Then Herod privily called the Wise-men, and learned
of them exactly what time the star appeared. And he sent them
to Bethlehem, and said, Go and search out exactly concerning
the young child; and when ye have found him, bring me word,
that I also may come and worship him" (vv.7–8).

The hearing of the word did not profit Herod spiritually at
all. In effect, the seed of the gospel had fallen by the wayside
(cf. Matt. 13.4,19). Having thus been alerted as to the birthplace
of Christ, he refused to lay his crown at Jesus' feet; instead, he
sought to kill Him. What he had learned actually hurt, offended
and angered him. Are there not many who are just like Herod?
Now having learned of the place, he then inquired about the time.
Yet he carefully inquired only in order to destroy. He calculated
that Christ must have been born at the time the star had first
appeared, and thus this bit of information instantly enabled him
to set in motion his wicked work of annihilation. As a matter
of fact, Herod's inquiry of the wise men privately was altogether
for an evil purpose. Such surreptitious action disclosed a devious
intention on his part. Yet all his diligent inquiries proved ulti-
mately to be in vain. Truth is never afraid of light. Whenever
people inquire about our Lord, let us have the perfect answer
ready.

The scribes instructed the wise men, and Herod sent them
forth. Yet besides these Gentiles from the East, who else among
the Jews themselves worshipped the Lord at this time? None.
"He came unto his own, and they that were his own received
him not" (John 1.11). We see how the king, the priests, the scribes
and the people rejected the Lord; none of them went to search
out Christ with the wise men. Yet this absence of the Jewish
reverence for Jesus at that time only served to highlight the fact
of how the Jews were to reject Christ later on. Still, God must
have His witness; so that if the Jews did not want Him, the Gentiles would come in. This is the extended grace of God. What
a shame to the Jews that the Gentiles, whom they had despised
as dogs, would now be the ones to accept the very first lesson

on prophecy given by the Jews, while the latter themselves refused to receive Christ. When Christ came, He was welcomed by all the ends of the earth, yet rejected by His own countrymen!

The Lord wanted the Jews to realize their fault. The very fact that the Gentiles knew the birth of the Messiah first ought to have reminded them and stirred up their zeal, yet they treated God's warning with the utmost complacency. Their difficulty was in knowing Christ. It was relatively easy for them to know and acknowledge from the Scriptures that Christ was to be born in Bethlehem, for this did not test their conscience nor expose their thoughts. But it was hard for them to acknowledge the "descendant" of the humble Joseph, the Son of Mary, to be the Messiah. If the Christ had indeed been born, then they ought to have honored and obeyed Him in the beauty of holiness. But their flesh could not bear all this.

The sin of Herod was truly great. He was not content with simply rejecting Christ, he also wanted to kill Him. Outwardly he spoke quite righteously, yet inwardly murder lurked in his heart. He used lie and pretence to cover up his wicked intention. This sly sinner knew not that this Christ was Immanuel. How foolish he therefore was. Nowadays there are many who use the false name of worship to execute their destructive purposes. How numberless those of the Herodian party still are even today!

(5) "And they, having heard the king, went their way; and lo, the star, which they saw in the east, went before them, till it came and stood over where the young child was. And when they saw the star, they rejoiced with exceeding great joy" (vv.9-10).

They had not verbally promised Herod to return and bring him word. They had not even acknowledged it with silence. We, too, must be careful about our promises lest we be compelled to repent later. After they had heard the king's word the wise men went their way. What about the chief priests and the scribes—what did they do? They remained in Jerusalem. They were content with just knowing where Christ should be born. Or was it that they dared not to do anything for fear of Herod's wrath? If so, how weak must be their faith towards God! Even so, how could these scribes excuse themselves, since these Gentile wise men had traveled such a long distance to worship the King?

They "went their way." It was a good thing for them to have left Herod. Their hearts would never be satisfied unless they saw and worshipped Christ. The star they had earlier seen in the East now reappeared. This bit of information is proof that the star had not guided them all the way without exception: it had *not* led them to Jerusalem. Now after they had left Herod, the scribes and Jerusalem, they saw God's guiding star. In our own experience we find that God prepares for us in the same way. If we truly obey Him, He without fail shall supply all our needs. He will often let those who know little but are faithful to him know what they should do, just as He did with these wise men. What is abominable to Him, however, is our pretending to know many things yet not knowing His Son.

This star was probably a slow-burning meteor, since it continually "went before them" (v.9). God was pleased to use this miracle to lead them. Let us be careful here lest we ask God for a star to lead us in this present age, for the former time and situation involving these wise men was something quite special. We Christians now have the Holy Spirit indwelling us, and we also have the Bible that has been inspired of God. These two witnesses are sufficient for guiding us into doing the Lord's will. Many saints are deceived by the Enemy masquerading as an angel of light (see 2 Cor. 11.14) because they seek for supernatural guidance. Let us clearly recognize the fact that this star went before the wise men till it led them to Christ; it did not lead them to itself but to "where the young child was." God's starlight always leads people to Christ. Today we are the starlight of the world (cf. Matt. 5.14a,16). Let us be careful that we lead people not to ourselves but straight to Christ that they may worship Him.

We are not to stop till we lead them to Him.

"Till it came and stood over . . ." The star would not rest till it came to where the Lord Jesus was. Our heart will find no rest till it rests in the Lord. How beautiful it is to know that the Lord is where I stand.

"And when they saw the star, they rejoiced with exceeding great joy." They knew that God had led them, and their faith was reinforced. They realized that their long journey had not been in vain, and so they rejoiced with exceedingly great joy. All who seek the Lord find such joy, which richly repays them for all their former toils.

(6) "And they came into the house and saw the young child with Mary his mother; and they fell down and worshipped him; and opening their treasures they offered unto him gifts, gold and frankincense and myrrh" (v.11).

"They came into the house," not to "the manger"— therefore, the place was not Bethlehem. Moreover, the One whom they now saw was "the young child," not "the babe"— so, the Lord Jesus was not newly born. It was "the young child with Mary his mother" and not "Mary with her son." The Child was mentioned first, and *then* the mother. This was to show that the Lord Jesus must have the preeminence in all things. This young Child was far greater than the mother. Furthermore, Joseph was not even mentioned, though he might have been there. "And they fell down and worshipped him." They worshipped the Child, not Mary. "And opening their treasures they offered unto him gifts." They did not offer to Mary: the Lord Jesus alone is worthy to receive worship and gifts from men. Mary was but a human being who ought not to have any of this glory. The Roman Church is to be blamed for such an unbiblical practice, for in their sin of idol worship they venerate Mary and lift her higher than the Lord Jesus Christ. Let us ever be mindful that Christ is alone worthy to be worshipped: we ourselves must never share His glory nor allow others to share His glory. May He have the first place in all things.

"Saw . . . worshipped . . . offered"—All who look for the Lord shall see Him: all who really see Him worship Him: and all who truly worship Him offer to Him. Before they had seen the Lord Jesus, their treasures were closed. But upon seeing the Lord, their treasures were opened. May we keep all things for Him, telling nothing and showing nothing to men; let us, instead, offer them all to Him. How beautiful it is to pour out our heart to the Lord—how joyful to present all at His feet. Our heart desire should always be to keep our love and labor exclusively for the Lord. Let us allow Him to see all, but let us never expose them to the world. Lord, I have kept many things for You. Apart from You, I will not let anyone see them.

The house that the wise men entered was most likely a poor lodging; yet it was there that these true hearts poured forth their worship. Before their knees were bent, their hearts were already bowed. Before the gifts were offered, love was first offered. I cannot begin to imagine the heavenly joy that must have filled their hearts. "Gold and frankincense and myrrh" were noble, costly things. How liberal were their offerings. Yet these were merely expressions of their hearts. How sad that saints who come before the Lord to worship, mostly keep their gold, frankincense and myrrh at home. They deem the fact that they have come, to be itself quite an accomplishment! How, then, they say to themselves, can anyone now expect them to offer gold and so forth? Yet what the Lord Jesus wants of us is our hearts, not our things. But although this is quite true, who is the one who can offer his heart to Jesus without ever offering things? The world is yet to find the person who, laying up his treasures on earth, can have his heart in heaven (cf. Matt. 6.19–21). That is simply impossible!

These precious gifts, especially the gold, were very helpful to the holy Son in His flight to Egypt. Joseph, being poor, probably could not have afforded such a trip without this offering. But God had already made provision for him. God called these wise men from afar to supply the need of the Son. The Almighty God has His emissaries everywhere. This ought to encourage us to do God's will with assurance. For where He sends, He also supplies. Had these wise men from the East known how useful their offerings were to become, their joy would have truly been without measure. If believers nowadays would only realize how their offerings can meet the expenditure of a trip to Egypt by the Son of God, they would not offer so little. Indeed, every penny offered for the gospel's sake becomes the traveling expenses for sending the Son of God into the hearts of men. Be sure, though, that what you offer is really used for the Lord.

What a contrast is provided between the knowledge of the scribes and the action of the wise men. Here we see the difference between knowing prophecy and knowing Christ. One is but knowing the letter of the Bible with brainpower; the other is coming to Christ through the drawing power of God the Father. The Scripture knowledge of these Gentile wise men could not in any way compare with that of the Jewish chief priests and the scribes. To put it in modern terms, these chief priests and scribes could recall chapter and verse, whereas the wise men were altogether ignorant. But had the Scripture knowledge of these Jewish religionists done them any good? Actually, without their realizing it, they had become Herod's assistants in doing harm to God's King. Too many are those who know the Scriptures only in their mind and are being used by Satan.

The scribes recited the Scriptures about Christ with their head; the wise men sought Christ himself with their heart. It is far happier to be a simple person who worships Christ at His feet than to be a learned scribe whose heart is cold and far away from the lovely Lord Jesus. Better is it to have a heart full of the compassionate love of Christ than to have a head filled with the mental knowledge of the letters of Scripture. How much more preferable is a heart that remembers the Lord to a mouth that only verbalizes the words of Scripture.

In this regard, the situation today is not any different from those earlier days of Herod. There are many who can quote Scripture like the chief priests and scribes of old, but few are there who will open their treasures and gladly offer all to the King of kings as did the wise men. What we lack is zealous love, not external knowledge. This is not to suggest that Biblical knowledge is useless; it is only said to indicate that mere knowledge of the Lord Jesus as presented in the Bible without there also being a heart desire towards Him accomplishes very little. If Christ is not taken as the center, even the most exact knowledge of the Scriptures is altogether useless. Not only is it useless, but such knowledge can easily become an instrument of Satan for resisting Christ. May God draw us and cause us to see our Savior on every page of Holy Writ that we might turn to Him in our hearts.

One thing is important to be remembered here: just as was the situation at the *first* coming of the Lord, so shall it be at His *second* coming. How very pitiful that many who know the Lord's coming, and even study prophecy about it, are not waiting expectantly for His return. They still live for themselves and mind the things of the earth. I am afraid there are legions of such people in the earth today. They talk and talk about the Lord's coming, yet they shall be those who shall remain on earth at His coming. How deplorable and dreadful this is. It is a heartbreaking thing for someone to preach to others and yet his own self be rejected. What I fear is that many study and even preach the second coming of the Lord, but few there will be of them who shall be raptured at His coming. May the Lord instruct our foolish hearts and teach us how to distinguish between having a loving affection for the Lord and having a mere mental knowledge of theology. It would, of course, be best if we could have both the love of the wise men and the knowledge of the scribes. If this is not possible, however, then let us rather be the wise men and not the scribes. For as the Scriptures declare: "If any man loveth not the Lord, let him be anathema. Maranatha" (1 Cor. 16.22).

The saints of God agree that these three gifts carry deeper implication than merely the outward. Gold stands for kingliness or divinity. Frankincense represents the fragrance of the life of the Lord Jesus—as to how it always diffuses a sweet savor and arises as a sacrifice acceptable to God (see Eph. 5.2; cf. also 2 Cor. 2.15 and Phil. 4.18). It also suggests the intercessory work of Christ. Myrrh was used in those days to embalm the body. After His death, the Lord Jesus was also embalmed with myrrh. So that it signifies the death of the Lord, how He died on the cross to atone for the sins of the world.

We today can easily find such applications in God's word for these things, and so we believe. But it took some time for the disciples of the Lord to understand. Although the wise men might not have known such implications in meaning surrounding their gifts, we nonetheless know that their worshipping hearts were sincere and true. And hence, God was pleased to use their gifts to show forth the life of His Son. The offerings here were a partial fulfillment of the prophecy to be found in Isaiah 60.6. There, only gold and frankincense were mentioned, myrrh having been left unmentioned. This is because the prophecy in Isaiah 60.6 awaits its total fulfillment at the second coming of the Lord Jesus, when at that time there will be no more death and hence no need to mention myrrh, which, as was learned above, signifies death.

The offerings of the wise men were without doubt most valuable. We ought to offer our best and our all to the Lord who so loved us and gave himself for us.

(7) "And being warned of God in a dream that they should not return to Herod, they departed into their own country another way" (v.12).

Even these Gentile wise men received intimate direction from God. May all the intellectual and academic doctors of the world take this to heart. They had already decided on returning home by the same route, but they nonetheless obeyed God by changing their route after they had been so instructed. It is better for us not to make up our mind before we know the will of the Lord. If, inadvertently, we have already decided, let our decision be held in a flexible state. Then, should God instruct us differently, we shall be in a position to obey immediately. As soon as we know that our plan is not according to God's will, we should instantly change our course. We must not be stubborn or rebel against God. The best way, of course, is to wait till we know the Lord's will before we take any action. We should not have any pre-conceived idea. These Gentile wise men at that time did not have the gift of the indwelling Holy Spirit as do we today who know the Lord; consequently, it was difficult for them to seek God's will. The Lord, however, knew how to deal with His feeble people of that day.

Let us understand that in the olden days, God often used dreams by which to enlighten people, for the Holy Spirit had not yet descended. Today, though, we must not depend solely on dreams as our guidance. In doing things we should have the witness of the Holy Spirit in our hearts. Especially in this last age, it is very risky to rely on a dream alone. Human psychology now rampant in the world, and the evil spirits, may easily manufacture all kinds of dreams.

"Should not return to Herod." Having seen Christ, there was no need to see Herod again. With the Lord filling our hearts, why should we turn back to see the kings and other political leaders of the earth? Those who do not have the Lord Jesus have to seek the world and the good pleasure of its kings and politicians. We, however, have no such need.

"They departed into their own country another way." They were not disobedient to the heavenly vision (cf. Acts. 26.19). They would rather obey God than have the praise of Herod. All who obey the Lord care nothing for the praise of the world. "Another way"—Indeed, all who have gained Christ should go another way. There ought to be a difference between the way before and the way after our knowing the Lord. The former way can no longer be traveled. It is true, of course, that all who have Christ should go back to witness for Him; even so, they must go "another way." The world will fail to see the salvation of the Lord through us if we believers do not show forth a different walk. May the children of God manifest their newness of life.

4 | The Escape of Jesus 2.13-23

(1) "Now when they were departed, behold, an angel of the Lord appeareth to Joseph in a dream, saying, Arise and take the young child and his mother, and flee into Egypt, and be thou there until I tell thee: for Herod will seek the young child to destroy him" (2.13).

As indicated a moment ago, the Holy Spirit had not come down yet, so God frequently used dreams and angels to guide people. Today we generally do not need these supernatural methods of guidance because we have the words of the Scriptures and the inward witness of the Holy Spirit. Here, also, we do not see that God delivered Immanuel by means of any miracle. As any other human being might do in similar straits, the incarnated Lord had to flee for His life. The young Child and his mother must go to Egypt. God did not interpose His almighty power to save his Son from this journey. By reading the story of the Lord's early years, we come to see how He experienced life, as it were, of an ordinary man. He did not occupy any special position among men. Commencing with His birth at Bethlehem, our Lord lived daily under the shadow of Calvary. For He had been born to fulfill that very task of death on the cross. Although He was far above the fallen race, the Lord Jesus nevertheless accepted the limitations of man. Only God knows how to humble himself from on high in such fashion.

The way Joseph was addressed here by the angel in a dream

reveals the fact that aside from his being the guardian of the Lord Jesus, he had no other relationship to Him. Mary was the mother of Jesus, but Joseph was not His biological father. Nevertheless, Joseph was given a great work and position, for it pleased God to allow him to serve the Son of God. For the sake of Christ, Joseph left his country. If we wish to serve the Lord, we, too, should not expect comfortable days. Whatever the responsibility God places upon us, we must obey and depart from our native place to go to the place which He will show us. Nor do we dare to return according to our own thought. Without His speaking, we should not take any step: "be thou there until I tell thee" is what the believer must learn. Stay wherever God has designated for us to be. Follow closely the will of God, and do not turn from it. The servants of the Lord do not move without the Lord's order. The guidance of the Lord comes one step at a time: He will not tell us all our future. Here it was time for Joseph to rise up and go to Egypt; but as to the farther future, he had to wait for further instruction. So let us follow the Lord step by step.

How peaceful are those who are not anxious for tomorrow. Have faith and trust to give over the future into His hands. It is man's natural tendency to wish to plan ahead for a hundred years, but God wants us to follow Him patiently. We may not see the future, but we have faith to trust in God's faithfulness. It is hard to wait; yet it is harder still to wait in a place like Egypt. Even so, the security and prosperity ahead of us depend upon our current obedience. Before the Lord gives an order to move, let us stay where we are.

"For Herod will seek the young child to destroy him." This was Herod's intention. What he had earlier said were all lies. When the time came, all the hidden thoughts in his heart were exposed: he was filled with the lying and murderous thoughts of Satan himself. Indeed, Herod was like Satan, who has been a liar from the very beginning and who later on became a murderer (see John 8.44). But God knew all things. And He knows how to protect His own. Let us therefore realize that all things are in His hand.

(2) "And he arose and took the young child and his mother by night, and departed into Egypt" (v.14).

What obedience and faith! He believed in what God had said though he had neither felt any wind of trouble nor seen any hint of peril. "By night" probably indicates the very night he had dreamed. This was consequently an instantaneous obedience. Oftentimes we fall into danger or become entangled with problems because we neither believe nor obey. It does seem that those who have intimately gained Christ frequently walk in the night, whereas the world appears to walk in broad daylight. The Son of God had to go down to Egypt and stay there with His family until further notice. Accordingly, let us not be surprised if we too have to flee in haste—even fleeing in the night—and have to remain in Egypt awhile.

"Egypt" at that time was also a Roman province, but it was not under Herod's jurisdiction. Many Jewish people resided there. God ordered the family to flee there to seek refuge from Herod. This was most appropriate. Egypt was formerly the place where the children of Israel had suffered persecution; now it became a refuge for the King of the Jews. God is able to change all things in order to benefit those who love Him.

(3) "And was there until the death of Herod: that it might be fulfilled which was spoken by the Lord through the prophet, saying, Out of Egypt did I call my son" (v.15).

This verse fulfills the word of Hosea 11.1. But upon reading this chapter of Hosea, there would seem to be some problems associated with the fulfillment of this prophecy. First of all, the passage in Hosea does not seem to be prophesying. And second, the passage does not seem to be referring to Christ. Yet let us remember that the Holy Spirit who gave revelation to Hosea gave revelation also to Matthew. The Holy Spirit certainly knows what

He speaks, for how can men know the thought of the Holy Spirit more than the Holy Spirit himself (cf. 1 Cor. 2.11ff.)?

If we were to read casually, we would quite naturally miss the thought of the Holy Spirit. But if we search carefully with faith, we shall discover the mystery within. On the surface, it would appear as though God through Hosea were reproving the children of Israel. For they had forgotten the grace of God in His delivering them out of Egypt and had turned away to worship Baal. This was indeed a reproof by the prophet pointed at the nation of Israel. Even so, for Matthew to say in his Gospel that the first verse of Hosea 11 has prophetic reference to Christ could not have been stated without there having been some careful consideration on his part. Matthew somehow reckoned that the going down by the Lord Jesus to Egypt was especially for the sake of fulfilling what he termed were words of prophecy in Hosea 11.1. Accordingly, there must be some deeper meaning here.

Israel, in the Old Testament Scriptures, was often called the son of God — for example: "Thus saith Jehovah, Israel is my son, my first-born" (Ex. 4.22). What, then, is the relationship between God's calling of Israel out of Egypt in those earlier days of the Jewish Exodus and the departure from Egypt of His Son now?

Let us use Isaiah 49 as a point of reference. There, the prophet is found combining the Lord Jesus and Israel as one: "Jehovah hath called me from the womb; from the bowels of my mother hath he made mention of my name: . . . and he said unto me, Thou art my servant; Israel . . ." (vv.1,3). Who was this Israel? Was it the nation of Israel? "And now saith Jehovah that formed me from the womb to be his servant, to bring Jacob again to him, and that Israel be gathered unto him" (v.5). Here was another Israel. By reading these verses together, we learn that the servant in question was called Israel, and that he was sent by the Lord to gather Israel. Thus, there were two Israels. "Yea, he saith, It is too light a thing that thou shouldest be my servant to raise up the tribes of Jacob, and to restore the preserved of Israel [the same Israel as in verse 5]: I will also give thee for a light to the Gentiles, that thou mayest be my salvation unto the end of the earth" (v.6). Who was this servant? All Christians would answer that this was clearly the Lord Jesus. And hence, here in this passage of Isaiah we find that Christ, who, as the Servant, was himself called Israel, was the One who was to save Israel, the people. On the one hand, the prophet Isaiah saw Christ and Israel as the same, but on the other hand he at the same time saw Christ and Israel as different entities. Seeing them to be the *same*, the prophet in his record of Jehovah's words called Christ the Servant as Israel. Seeing them to be *different*, the prophet in his record of Jehovah's words noted that the Servant was to save Israel.

It is most meaningful to read Hosea and Matthew together. From the Old Testament record we know how the children of Israel had failed. So Hosea spoke unflinchingly of their sins. From the New Testament record, beginning with Matthew, we know that Christ finally came. Yet the children of Israel not only did not receive Him, they even planned to kill Him as well. Their failure was therefore total. But God in His grace called His Son out of Egypt, and He joined Israel to His Son. The coming of His Son out from Egypt was the coming out again of Israel itself from Egypt. According to the requirements of the law, the children of Israel had failed beyond remedy; but the God of mercy called Israel out of Egypt again in His Son so that He might deal with them afresh as a new beginning of their history. (The coming out of Egypt told of in Exodus had been the commencement of the history of the nation of Israel.) The grace of God now restored their position in Christ; otherwise, they would have been cut off forever. For this reason, the Holy Spirit said through Matthew that the coming out from Egypt of the Lord Jesus was done to fulfill the word of the Lord through Hosea. There in Hosea 11.1, the prophet had mentioned Israel as coming out of Egypt, for he had incorporated Israel as it were into the Lord Jesus. In sum, then, it may be said that the children of Israel had failed under law, but God restored them in grace. This was the wisdom of the Holy Spirit. If natural man had been writing this story, he would not have known or recognized that this event in the Christ Child's life was actually fulfilling the word of Hosea. Only "the Spirit searcheth all things, yea, the deep things of God" (1 Cor. 2.10).

Even so, we must be careful to note that the prophet had also viewed Christ and Israel as being different. In this respect, then, the words in Hosea 11 were not all pointing to Christ. The Holy Spirit in Matthew said specifically that only the word "called my son out of Egypt" referred to Christ. The other words in that chapter of Hosea did not apply to Christ.

Although Christ's going down and coming out of Egypt was to fulfill Israel's own experience of Egypt, the two goings and comings were quite different in character. In the case of Israel, Egypt for them had been a fiery furnace. Due to their many impurities, they needed to be purified. By contrast, in the case of Christ, Egypt for Him was not to be a place of slavery; rather, it served as a temporary address for Him. Egypt could neither tempt Christ nor take Him captive, as had happened in the case of Israel. In a narrow sense, it can be said that Christ's coming out of Egypt caused the children of Israel, who were in Him, to be restored afresh to God. On the other hand, in a much broader sense, it can be said that His coming out of Egypt creates in Him a new history for a world that had terribly fallen since the days of Adam. In Biblical typology, of course, Egypt signifies our bondage to sin. Except for God "calling" us, we are not able to come out. The condition of the Lord Jesus, however, was totally different. He could not be bound by sin. The calling He received was to come to the world to accomplish the work of redemption. Willingly, He suffered the opposition of men and the forsaking by God that He might finish the work of restoration. And after He was resurrected, He really came "out of Egypt." We, too, are now anticipating a future coming out of Egypt.

How marvelous is the salvation of God. Regardless the situation of His people—whether they were in distress or in joy, Christ joined himself to them in every respect except in the matter of sin. He was tempted in all respects, yet without sin. He experienced all the blessings in human life. He lived together with His people. What a comfort this knowledge of His life can be to us. He will not let His people suffer any affliction without His being with them and being afflicted with them. Observe how attentive God was to His Son's footsteps — even to the matter of His flight to Egypt. To men, there does not seem to be any significance that can be attached to Christ's going down and then coming out of Egypt. But God had already prophesied about it. The Lord Jesus knew from experience what going down into Egypt must mean for His people, for His sufferings in our "Egypt" went far beyond the sufferings of the children of Israel. Let us therefore see from all this how much He truly loves us!

(4) "Then Herod, when he saw that he was mocked of the Wise-men, was exceeding wroth, and sent forth, and slew all the male children that were in Bethlehem, and in all the borders thereof, from two years old and under, according to the time which he had exactly learned of the Wise-men" (v.16).

In spite of his wiles, Herod was defeated. The wise men had not mocked him at all, yet *he* thought they had done so. The proud one always suspects his being despised by others. He became exceedingly angry and slew all the male children within their first two years of age; for, he thought, if the Christ Child did not die, then he would not be able to keep his throne. Hence, in order to preserve his throne, he cared not at all about murdering many innocent children. He selfishly thought that by such means he could kill off the new King and keep his crown forever. How people will always try their utmost to destroy the Lord Jesus! Of course, had Christ actually been eliminated, His grace could not come upon the many who are perishing. Yet, can man successfully wrestle with God? Can Christ ever be destroyed? How sad that the world is not lacking in people who perpetuate Herod's folly.

Let us turn to another matter. Unbelievers often raise the question as to why Christ fled from Israel and allowed those many innocent children to suffer and die. They consider the gospel of Jesus Christ to be the cause for innocent blood to flow. The fact of the matter is that *Christ* was not the cause of their murder; they were eliminated by the cruelty of Herod. Through no fault of His own, Christ had become the innocent cause of the killing of these innocent children. How can we blame the Lord Jesus for what Herod under the instigation of Satan did? It is not the gospel itself, but the *opposition* to the gospel, that draws blood. This is but a partial reply, for the full answer can only be given by the Lord of all things. In any case, he who gave the order to have these innocent children murdered died a tragic death himself not long afterwards (see the writings of the highly respected Jewish historian, Josephus). And he must answer to God in the future for what he did.

(5) "Then was fulfilled that which was spoken through Jeremiah the prophet, saying, A voice was heard in Ramah, weeping and great mourning, Rachel weeping for her children; and she would not be comforted, because they are not" (vv.17–18).

In Matthew chapter 1 the Holy Spirit through the Gospel writer had pointed out to the children of Israel how blessed it was to have Christ (as Immanuel) joined with them. But due to their rejecting Christ (as shown in the first half of chapter 2), they must suffer great affliction. They had brought the woe upon themselves. It also indicated the greater affliction they would endure in the future. Whoever rejects grace invites judgment.

Let us notice the ways the word "fulfilled" has been used. There were three different ways in which Old Testament prophecies were fulfilled: (a) "that it might be fulfilled which was spoken by the Lord through the prophet" (Matt. 1.22 and 2.15); (b) "that it might be fulfilled which was spoken through the prophets" (Matt. 2.23); and (c) "was fulfilled that which was spoken through ... the prophet" (Matt. 2.17). The first phrase above ("might be fulfilled") means that its fulfillment was the purpose of the Old Testament prophecy which now was fulfilled. Matthew 1.22–23 is an example. The second phrase (again, "might be fulfilled") means that this fulfillment was included in the words of the prophets, but it was not the whole thought of the Holy Spirit. Matthew 2.23 is an example (in the original, the word "might" is not there). The third phrase ("was fulfilled") means that this fulfillment agreed with what the prophet had said. The fulfillment concurred in spiritual thought, but it was not the true motive of the prophecy. Matthew 2.17–18 is such an example.

Therefore, what happened here coincided with that which Jeremiah had spoken. When Bethlehem was mourning for her sons, it sounded like Rachel weeping in her neighboring tomb (she had been buried at or near Bethlehem—see Gen. 48.7). Here, Rachel was taken to represent the nation of Israel. They wept in those days; they weep today; and they will weep again during the Great Tribulation. The quotation here was found in Jeremiah 31.15. Rachel (as Israel), however, ought to be comforted, for in spite of the death of her children, their Savior had escaped. Wherever Christ is not, there is bound to be great mourning.

(6) "But when Herod was dead, behold, an angel of the Lord appeareth in a dream to Joseph in Egypt, saying, Arise and take the young child and his mother, and go into the land of Israel: for they are dead that sought the young child's life. And he arose and took the young child and his mother, and came into the land of Israel" (vv.19–21).

The days of this Idumaean king were over. Herod had gone to his own place. Not only was he unable to slay the Lord Jesus, but also, he himself had died. All who wish to kill our King will not live long. The angel of the Lord did not even mention the name of Herod but only referred to him as one of those "that [had] sought the young child's life." The holy angel even disliked uttering his name, because he was such a terrible murderer. O

my soul, let it meditate on the end of those who are at enmity
with the Lord.

Joseph of old had cared for the children of Israel in Egypt,
but so did this later Joseph now take care of Israel, the Son of
God. Please note again that the Scriptures always mention the
Child first, and then the mother. This is God's thought about
His Son. "And he [Joseph] arose." He arose and brought the whole
family back to the land of Israel. His obedience is worth imitating.
God had promised him that He would tell him again. Now the
time had come for receiving further instruction. And as God
ordered, so Joseph obeyed. He truly demonstrated a life of faith,
for without faith none can obey. Those who know and trust God
can alone hearken to Him.

Let us note here that "the land of Israel" was mentioned, not
Judea or Galilee. This is full of meaning, for it brings in the idea
of the New Covenant. God, in this one expression, indicates that
it was not a land under the control of the nations but was a land
inhabited by the Jews. Yet the world of that day did not look
upon this territory as "the land of Israel"; even so, God was mindful of the relationship of the glory of His Son to His own people.
Since Immanuel was now born of the virgin, why not indeed
call this area "the land of Israel"? God did not want the nations
to tread upon this land. But would the Jews welcome the Lord
Jesus as King? The time had not yet come because after one
Herod died, another Herod was born.

(7) "But when he heard that Archelaus was reigning over
Judaea in the room of his father Herod, he was afraid to go
thither; and being warned of God in a dream, he withdrew into
the parts of Galilee" (v.22).

Joseph had already obeyed the Lord, for he "took the young
child and his mother, and came into the land of Israel" (v.21).
Yet after he arrived in his own country, he could not help but
fear, because the cruelty of Archelaus was not in any way behind
that of his father, the Great Herod (note that after the Great

Herod had died, the kingdom was divided among his three sons). Though Joseph had his human weakness and fear, the Lord was still mindful of him and made provision for him: "God is faithful, who will not suffer you to be tempted above that ye are able" (1 Cor. 10.13). So that God told Joseph in a dream to go to Galilee. Probably we, too, have had such an experience. Sometimes we are weak and of little faith, unable to measure up to the Lord's standard. Yet God deals with us in mercy and is mindful of us, knowing that we are but dust. He will open a living way out ("the way of escape" —1 Cor. 10.13) for us. How tender is our Lord.

Galilee was despised, for there the Gentiles and the Jews dwelt together. The Bible has even called it "Galilee of the nations" (Is. 9.1) and "Galilee of the Gentiles" (Matt. 4.14) because the people of the Gentile nations had settled there and were by this time in the majority. Galilee means "the circle." Although the children of Israel have rejected the Lord, their future shall be glorious, for they will come full circle and regain their lost blessings. Here in Galilee, in an obscure and simple place, our Lord spent His early years. He belonged to the common people; He did not have the air of an urbanite. And hence, all you who are poor may come to Him. Just as He had blessed the people in the past, He will bless you now. Oh, may He come to our "Galilee" and dwell with us! Our Lord lived in Galilee. How simple He was. May all the children of God learn to be Galileans, unaffected by the fashion of this age. Especially those believers who live in big cities need to exhibit a Galilean lifestyle. For how unlike our Lord we still are.

The inhabitants of Galilee were despised by the Jews since these Galileans had little communication with Jerusalem and Judea. Most of the Jews living there were those who had come back from the Babylonian Captivity. Although they spoke the same language as other Jews, there was nonetheless a cleavage between them. And yet Christ came to that very place. Here we see the desolation of men, but we also see here the manifestation of grace. Such a place was truly most appropriate for grace to be manifested. Our King always befriends the sinners and the despised ones. He is truly a condescending One.

(8) "And came and dwelt in a city called Nazareth; that it might [the word "might" is not in the original] be fulfilled which was spoken through the prophets, that he should be called a Nazarene" (v.23).

Joseph brought the family "into the parts of Galilee" and settled down in Nazareth. They had lived there before (see Luke 1.26, 2.4,39), so it was quite natural for them to return to that particular town. However, even this move was not by his own choice; he had been instructed by God. This town was most insignificant. We recall the words of Nathanael: "Can any good thing come out of Nazareth?" (John 1.46)—which observation reveals how this place was indeed despised by men. But our Lord buried himself in lowliness till the time came for His manifestation at age 30. What a lesson for us! If there was ever a place in Palestine which perfectly corresponded to the rejected Christ, that place was Nazareth. The real King was repudiated by His own people. The rejected King dwelt in a forsaken town. At that time Nazareth was not only despised by the people who lived in Judea, even the Galileans themselves disdained it (for let us recall that Nathanael was himself a Galilean). This reveals how truly base that city was considered to be.

Though the Gentile wise men had come to worship Christ, His very own nation and people rejected Him. This was the ultimate result despite God's many years of care over them. The Lord Jesus did not employ His power of the miraculous for self-protection; instead, He went down to Egypt with His people. There, He suffered afflictions with them. But when He came back from Egypt, the children of Israel would still not have Him. He could not go to Jerusalem nor return to Bethlehem. He must go to the despised and forsaken town of Nazareth, a community without fame. In the eyes of the Pharisees, Nazareth had nothing good to recommend itself. It had neither history nor memorial.

It had not produced any great man. Yet Christ must take this lowest of places. Although the cross was to be the end of His earthly walk, His entire life was but one long extended crucifixion. Such was His portion.

We should take note of the more accurate way to quote the words of Matthew 2.23 that make reference back to the prophets concerning Jesus and Nazareth: "So that was fulfilled the [thing] spoken through the prophets" (Greek original). Yet the thing had not been spoken by just one particular prophet; it had been "spoken through [several of] the prophets." And even though these prophets had not plainly referred to Him as a Nazarene, they had nonetheless implied in their prophecies the idea of His being a Nazarene. (Let us not misconstrue this as His being a Nazarite—see Num. 6; our Lord was not a Nazarite like John the Baptist was—see Matt. 11.18-19, Luke 7.33-34).

What, then, was the meaning of the Lord being a Nazarene? This word of verse 23 ("that he should be called a Nazarene") summed up many past prophetic utterances which were later confirmed by the conduct of the Jews in Jesus' day. For when many of Jesus' contemporaries became aware that He had been born, and had then spent most of His life in Nazareth, they assigned this name to Him as a token of mockery. Everyone in those days just naturally knew that this particular characterization of Him meant His being despised. To call Him a Nazarene was to deride Him. Many were the prophets who prophesied this very aspect of His life: for example, (a) "He was despised, and rejected of men; a man of sorrows, and acquainted with grief: and as one from whom men hide their face he was despised; and we esteemed him not" (Is. 53.3); (b) "I am a worm, and no man; a reproach of men, and despised of the people. All they that see me laugh me to scorn: they shoot out the lip, they shake the head" (Ps. 22.6-7); and (c) "they shall smite the judge of Israel with a rod upon the cheek" (Micah 5.1). There can be found many passages like these in the Old Testament prophecies wherein Christ is shown to be despised as a Nazarene.

The word "Nazareth" appears to be the feminine form of "*Netzer*"—conveying the idea of a "sprout" or a "shoot." A shoot is obviously something small. This image, too, agrees with the thought of being despised. Christ was a Nazarene—that is to say, He was nothing but a small shoot! Many prophets had prophesied concerning this little shoot as well; for example: "there shall come forth a shoot out of the stock of Jesse, and a branch out of his roots shall bear fruit" (Is. 11.1). Here, Christ is not referred to as a shoot out of the stock of David; for if this were so, He would be cut down without having the outward glory of a king that would have befitted someone out of David. It would therefore be more fitting for Him to be a shoot out of Jesse—who was a commoner. The name "Jesse" means "Jehovah exists." Jehovah is the God of resurrection. So that though this Shoot was lowly, it nonetheless had life. Though it be cut down by men, its future glory would still be great. Jeremiah 23.5 and 33.15 are Scripture passages that call Him "a righteous Branch" or "a Branch of righteousness." So does Zechariah 6.12: "Behold, the man whose name is the Branch: and he shall grow up out of his place; and he shall build the temple of Jehovah."

His lowliness was expressed by His love and service. He humbled himself even to death. Yet His work was resurrection. Such humility is worthy of our contemplation. When the Jews of those days used this name of "the Nazarene," it was employed to express their scorn and derision of Jesus.

But, Thou Nazarene, Thou hast nonetheless conquered! Jesus the Nazarene is the greatest name in the world. While the world may mock the Lord, let us who are His own praise Him. It is regrettable that the love of the saints towards the Lord is often weaker than the hate of the world towards Him. The world had called those who followed the Lord Jesus "the sect of the Nazarenes" (Acts 24.5). But how many of those who claim to follow Him really have the life of the Nazarene? Is it not a pity that many have forgotten that they follow Jesus *the Nazarene*? He is not only the Savior of Israel, He is also the Savior of the world.

The children of Israel who had long been tested by God and eventually failed are but the representation of the world. Our Redeemer is the kingly Savior. Although He has now ascended back to heaven and has been glorified, the world treats Him today just as Israel of old had done. On the lips of those who oppose Him today, the name "Jesus the Nazarene" has but one meaning (that of opprobrium); yet in the mouths of the godly, it has a different meaning; for here, honor and shame join hands together. The cross is a shame, but it is also the glory of the Lord. Those whose eyes have been opened to this secret see far more clearly than does the world.

This brief discussion has shown what the Son of God received when He first came to this world. In spite of the fact that He was Immanuel as well as the Son of David, generally speaking, from the days at Bethlehem to the time of His coming out of Egypt, no one, from the king down to the populace, welcomed Him.

Matthew is a marvelous Gospel. The author reveals the plot of the entire book from its very commencement so that we may know the future end. Here we are shown in the Gospel's opening two chapters how Messiah came to the midst of Israel for the sake of saving them from their sins. The Jews, however, were so deeply sunk in sins that they had no heart for Him. They were full of rituals and traditions, and boasted of their special privileges. And because of this spiritual and moral poverty, the Lord Jesus was rejected by them even at the commencement of His days. Thank God, though, that a few Gentiles came to worship Him.*

---

*As explained elsewhere, these notes were concluded at the end of Matthew chapter 2.—*Translator*

TITLES YOU
WILL WANT TO HAVE

by Watchman Nee

Basic Lesson Series
Volume 1—A Living Sacrifice
Volume 2—The Good Confession
Volume 3—Assembling Together
Volume 4—Not I, But Christ
Volume 5—Do All to the Glory of God
Volume 6—Love One Another

The Church and the Work
Volume 1—Assembly Life
Volume 2—Rethinking the Work
Volume 3—Church Affairs

Interpreting Matthew
Back to the Cross
The Character of God's Workman
Gleanings in the Fields of Boaz
The Spirit of the Gospel
The Life That Wins
From Glory to Glory
The Spirit of Judgment
From Faith to Faith
The Lord My Portion
Aids to "Revelation"
Grace for Grace
The Better Covenant
A Balanced Christian Life
The Mystery of Creation
The Messenger of the Cross
Full of Grace and Truth—Volume 1
Full of Grace and Truth—Volume 2
The Spirit of Wisdom and Revelation
Whom Shall I Send?
The Testimony of God
The Salvation of the Soul
The King and the Kingdom of Heaven
The Body of Christ: A Reality
Let Us Pray
God's Plan and the Overcomers
The Glory of His Life
"Come, Lord Jesus"
Practical Issues of This Life
Gospel Dialogue
God's Work
Ye Search the Scriptures
The Prayer Ministry of the Church
Christ the Sum of All Spiritual Things
Spiritual Knowledge
The Latent Power of the Soul
Spiritual Authority
The Ministry of God's Word
Spiritual Reality or Obsession
The Spiritual Man

by Stephen Kaung

Discipled to Christ
The Splendor of His Ways
Seeing the Lord's End in Job
The Songs of Degrees
Meditations on Fifteen Psalms

ORDER FROM:
Christian Fellowship Publishers, Inc.
11515 Allecingie Parkway
Richmond, Virginia 23235